William J Fay 5.65
78-8

Augsburg Commentary on the New Testament

ROMANS

Roy A. Harrisville

Augsburg Publishing House

Minneapolis, Minnesota

Augsburg Commentary on the New Testament
ROMANS

Copyright © 1980 Augsburg Publishing House

Library of Congress Catalog Card No. 80-65550

International Standard Book No. 0-8066-8864-5

MANUFACTURED IN THE UNITED STATES OF AMERICA

CONTENTS

ABBREVIATIONS

KJV   King James Version

JBL   *Journal of Biblical Literature*

NTS   *New Testament Studies*

RSV   Revised Standard Version

WA   M. Luther, Kritische Gesamtausgabe (Weimar, 1883-). WATR refers to the table talks in the Weimar edition.

ZTK   *Zeitschrift für Theologie und Kirche*

FOREWORD

The AUGSBURG COMMENTARY ON THE NEW TES-
TAMENT is written for laypeople, students, and pastors. Laypeople will use it as a resource for Bible study at home and
at church. Students and instructors will read it to probe the
basic message of the books of the New Testament. And pastors will find it to be a valuable aid for sermon and lesson
preparation.

The plan of each Commentary is designed to enhance its
usefulness. The Table of Contents presents a topical over-
view of the biblical book to be discussed. The Introduction
provides information on the historical circumstances in which
the biblical book was written. It may also contain a summary
of the biblical writer's thought. In the body of the Commentary, the interpreter sets forth in brief compass the meaning
of the biblical text. The procedure is to explain the text section by section. Care has also been taken to avoid scholarly
jargon and the heavy use of technical terms. Because the readers of the Commentary will have their Bibles at hand, the biblical text itself has not been printed out. In general, the editors
recommend the use of the Revised Standard Version of the
Bible.

The authors of this Commentary Series are professors at
seminaries and universities and are themselves ordained clergy-
persons. They have been selected both because of their exper-
tise and because they worship in the same congregations as

the people for whom they are writing. In elucidating the text of Scripture, therefore, they attest to their belief that central to the faith and life of the church of God is the word of God.

The Editorial Committee

Roy A. Harrisville
Luther-Northwestern Seminaries
St. Paul, Minnesota

Jack Dean Kingsbury
Union Theological Seminary
Richmond, Virginia

Gerhard A. Krodel
Lutheran Theological Seminary
Gettysburg, Pennsylvania

INTRODUCTION

Twelve years after his baptism, the greatest thinker in an entire millennium of western Christianity told how his struggle to give himself to God was at last resolved:

> I heard the voice of a boy or a girl . . . chanting over and over again, "Pick it up, read it; pick it up, read it". . . . I quickly returned to the bench . . . for there I had put down the apostle's book. . . . I snatched it up, opened it, and in silence read the paragraph on which my eyes first fell: "Not in rioting and drunkenness, not in chambering and wantonness, not in strife and envying, but put on the Lord Jesus Christ, and make no provision for the flesh to fulfill the lusts thereof." I wanted to read no further, nor did I need to. For instantly, as the sentence ended, there was infused in my heart something like the light of full certainty and all the gloom of doubt vanished away.

The man was Augustine, the "apostle's book" Romans, and the paragraph Romans 13 (*The Confessions,* Book Eight, *The Library of Christian Classics,* trans. Albert C. Outler, Philadelphia: Westminster, 1955, pp. 175-176).

Shortly before his death, the greatest Reformer of them all described the decisive change that had occurred in him:

> It is true; I had been seized by an uncommon desire to understand Paul in the Epistle to the Romans. And thus far it was not cold blood around the heart that hindered me, but one single word . . . "in it the righteousness of God is revealed."

9

For I hated that word "righteousness of God" which . . . I was taught to construe philosophically as a formal or active righteousness (as they call it), by which God is just and punishes sinners and the unjust. . . . So I raged furiously and with a confused conscience. Still, I hammered persistently away at that passage in Paul, afire with eagerness to know what he means. Then, thanks to God's mercy and meditating on it day and night, I paid attention to the context. . . . I began to understand God's righteousness as something by which the righteous lives as by God's gift, that is, by faith, and that this is the sense—through the gospel God's righteousness is revealed, that is, a passive righteousness by which the merciful God justifies us through faith, as it is written: "The just lives by faith." Right then I sensed I had been wholly reborn, and had entered by open doors to very paradise.

That man was Luther, and the passage Romans 1:17 (WA 54, 185, 14 - 186, 9, author's transl.).

Two hundred years later, at Aldersgate, John Wesley, scholar of Christ Church and Lincoln College, Oxford, found his heart "strangely warmed" at a reading of Luther's preface to the epistle, and later gathered up his experience in a translation of the Moravian hymn:

Jesus, Thy blood and righteousness
My beauty are, my glorious dress;
Midst flaming worlds, in these arrayed,
With joy shall I lift up my head.

After the carnage of the First World War, a young Swiss pastor at Safenwil, driven by the preacher's distress and task, and disillusioned with the prevailing method, concluded that God Himself must be the starting point of all theology, and Romans the place to begin. In his exposition of the book, the nineteen hundred years separating author and interpreter became transparent, and twentieth century scripture interpretation was born. Karl Barth's *Römerbrief* bubbled and boiled like a volcano. He hurled his ideas and sentences like an expressionist his paints:

Introduction

God, the pure and absolute boundary and beginning of all that we are and have and do; God, who is distinguished qualitatively from men and from everything human, and must never be identified with anything which we name, or experience, or conceive, or worship, as God; God, who confronts all human disturbance with an unconditional command, "Halt," and all human rest with an equally unconditional command "Advance"; God, the "Yes" in our "No" and the "No" in our "Yes," the First and the Last, and, consequently, the Unknown, who is never a known thing in the midst of other known things; God, the Lord, the Creator, the Redeemer:—this is the Living God (*The Epistle to the Romans,* trans. Edwyn C. Hoskyns, London: Oxford, 1950, pp. 330-331).

At every significant juncture in the life of the Christian community this letter has stood, and for every giant of faith ever raised up to effect some change in that community, it has furnished the fire. And, for all the souls who have carried the embers which some great event or person has later fanned into flame, this last will and testament of Paul of Tarsus has spelled warmth and light. On an Ash Wednesday, with minutes left to live, my father called to his nurse and made her read these words:

Who shall separate us from the love of Christ? Shall tribulation, or distress, or persecution, or famine, or nakedness, or peril, or sword? As it is written, "For thy sake we are being killed all the day long; we are regarded as sheep to be slaughtered." No, in all these things we are more than conquerors through him who loved us. For I am sure that neither death, nor life, nor angels, nor principalities, nor things present, nor things to come, nor powers, nor height, nor depth, nor anything else in all creation, will be able to separate us from the love of God in Christ Jesus our Lord (Rom. 8:35-39).

For years, "Lutheran" interpretation of Romans has been suspect, since it is alleged such interpretation roots in the assumption that the experiences of Paul and Luther were similar, if not identical; that the one could thus be read in light of the other. The impropriety of a psycho-religious interpretation of Paul, according to which his resolution of the religious question followed an intense spiritual struggle, has been amply demonstrated. The encounter on the Damascus road did not involve a man vainly seeking relief from an anguished conscience, but a robust Pharisee. Those passages in which Paul explicitly refers to his existence prior to faith (Gal. 1:13-14 and Phil. 3:5-6) reveal nothing of an inner preparation for his conversion. To reverse an old cliché, Paul's religion is his theology; his "historical significance lies nowhere else than in the fact that he was a theologian." It is unfortunate that all such criticism has allowed the psychologistic interpretation of Luther to stand.

At any rate, the assumption of this volume is that Romans is not to be read against the background of Paul's unspeakable suffering from the Law, or on the premise that setting aside the Torah was the great need of his soul. On the contrary, the Torah was upheld, made to stand by the revelation of God's righteousness (Rom. 3:21). For this reason, Paul does not use his Bible as a proof-text, but most often appeals to the Old Testament after an already concluded train of proof. This volume will attempt to make clear the context and meaning of the scores of Old Testament references in Romans, a note perhaps infrequently struck.

For many more years, it was asserted that Paul's teaching concerning justification did not lie at the core of his thought, but was a polemical tool developed for battle with his opponents—a time-conditioned, provisional thing, a "smaller crater," as Albert Schweitzer once dubbed it, "within the larger crater of his concept of Being in Christ." This view is still tenaciously held to by some, though the majority no longer shares it. Now, the debate rages over the question whether or not Paul's idea of justification is to be understood against the background of apocalyptic, that late and peculiar child of prophecy which dreamed in surrealist fashion of God's final control of history.

In other words, interpreters of Paul are divided on the issues of God's righteousness as future, as God's "might which establishes salvation," or as present gift, and thus disagree as to whether or not Paul's concept has its true home in Jewish apocalyptic thought, or is unique to him. Neither side of the debate does justice to the term. For if the hallmark of apocalyptic thought is demonstrability—God's visible manifestation of himself at the "end of days"—in Paul that thought suffered a "fracture," a drastic revision in light of the event which for him was the content of the gospel par excellence: The death of Jesus. For Paul, Christ's cross made totally unobservable and incapable of historical verification any qualitative change in history or human affairs. God's victory had occurred "under the sign of its opposite"—defeat, tragedy and death—a victory clear only to those willing to fly in face of the empirical evidence: "The righteousness of God is revealed through faith for faith" (Rom. 1:17). Paul was not a pietist. The difference between his gospel and the seer's drama lay in the collapse, the fracture of apocalyptic as a coherent scheme.

On the other hand, to conclude from the non-demonstrability of the change that Paul construed justification as an event in the "heavenly forum," an action by which God merely declares the sinner righteous, while the structures of existence remain the same, unaltered, is thoroughly to misunderstand the apostle. If Paul was not a pietist, neither was he "orthodox." For him, justification and union with Christ were not merely two facets of the same prism, but one and the same event. For this reason, he saw a material connection between the believers' justification and their baptism. And for this reason, he could call his readers to a specific, concrete, and palpable activity which comported with their new existence, though the origin, character, and goal of that activity could

13

not be demonstrated or perceived. In Romans, it is God who gives *himself* in his salvation-creating power.

The Law upheld, though not as a way to righteousness; justification at the heart of Paul's gospel, though not against the background of an apocalyptic unrevised; the new existence as hidden, in Christ, though not without concreteness—these are assumptions which the reader will encounter throughout. For the rest, I am committed to the proposition that use of the scientific methods of scripture exposition must be wedded to "theological interpretation," believing that scripture truly discloses itself only to those who are willing to hear its claim, and who are conscious of the effects of the Christian tradition, to which belong those experiences of faith reflected in the church's confession. Without such commitment to the gospel as "theological interpretation" demands, I have nothing at all to say—certainly nothing of my own.

For information regarding the manner in which the gospel was carried to Rome, the composition of the congregation in that great city, the occasion and purpose of the epistle, its authenticity and style, and the troublesome questions relating to Chapter 16, the reader will find ample reference throughout the commentary. A few words may be added here respecting the date and place of the epistle's composition.

There is only one datum in all the New Testament by which to fix the chronology of Paul's life and letters. It is a reference to Paul's having spent a year and a half in the city of Corinth before his encounter with Gallio, proconsul of the Roman province of Achaia (its citizens once celebrated in Homer's *Iliad*) of which Corinth was chief city (Acts 18:11-12). We are able to join this date to a reference to Lucius Junius Gallio, friend of Claudius Caesar and governor of Achaia, and from a source outside the New Testament, dated from the year A.D. 52. It is thus possible to arrange the events of Paul's life forward with a modicum of surety. If, as Acts 18 reports, Paul had been eighteen months in Corinth while Gallio was governor, and if not less than six years had elapsed between A.D. 52 and Paul's final departure for Jerusalem, and if (!) Paul was martyred by Nero in A.D. 65 or 66, and under house arrest two years prior, the date of the composition of Romans could not be set later than A.D. 59, in all probability, A.D. 58. As to the place of composition, Corinth appears the least objectionable. Not long after Paul wrote 2 Corinthians, he had arrived at Corinth from Macedonia and rested there before his collection trip to Jerusalem (Rom. 15:25). We know of no better time during Paul's Greek and Asia Minor mission better suited for the writing of such a comprehensive letter than the time of his sojourn in Corinth.

Finally, my indebtedness to Paul's interpreters, early and late, is beyond telling. The dependence will often be obvious to the practised eye, as will the errors. Errors written down, take on a kind of permanence. The din from a beginner's ravaging a Brahms Intermezzo or Chopin Ballade soon dies away, thank heaven! but a book can remain an everlasting monument to its author's shame, provided God allows length of life enough to get him to his senses. Still, though the author of 2 Peter wrote that there were things in Paul "hard to understand," he did not on that account exclude those pieces from his repertoire. Nor have I. Romans needs "playing," if for no other reason than that it must be remembered, kept close to the consciousness, handed on, till another great spirit comes along can do it justice. The race would be infinitely poorer, had not these glorious sounds been passed from one novice to another over two thousand years!

The stanzas prefixed to relevant sections of the commentary are taken from Luther's hymn, *Nun freut euch, lieben Christen g'mein* ("Dear Christians, One and All, Rejoice"); the text of the Revised Standard Version of the Bible appears in bold face, and the author's translations from the original in quotation marks.

Introduction

Selected Bibliography of Commentaries available in English

1. William Sanday and Arthur C. Headlam, *The Epistle to the Romans, The International Critical Commentary*, Edinburgh: T. & T. Clark, 1st edition, 1895. As a series, the I.C.C. is still the most complete and technical in English. As the date of this volume suggests, however, the bibliography is old, and the results of current biblical interpretation are naturally not reflected. C. E. B. Cranfield, *The Epistle to the Romans, The International Critical Commentary*, Edinburgh: T. & T. Clark, Vol. I, 1975, Vol. II, 1979. Cranfield's two volumes have recently appeared as the successor to Sanday-Headlam's commentary.

2. Karl Barth, *The Epistle to the Romans*, trans. Edwyn C. Hoskyns, London: Oxford, 1950. A classic of "spiritual" or "pneumatic" interpretation, this single work, as no other, effected that change in twentieth century theology and scripture interpretation.

3. Anders Nygren, *Commentary on Romans*, trans. Carl C. Rasmussen, Philadelphia: Fortress, 1949. In this text, examination of the Greek is at a minimum. Although I do not agree with Nygren's structuring of the epistle in Part II, his commentary is nonetheless a readable and lively piece.

4. *Luther's Lectures on Romans*, trans. Wilhelm Pauck, *The Library of Christian Classics*, Philadelphia: Westminster, 1961. I list this edition of Luther's lectures in preference to the translation contained in the American Edition of Luther's Works, for the simple reason that I know it best, and it carefully reproduces Johannes Ficker's edition of the original.

5. C. K. Barrett, *The Epistle to the Romans, Black's New Testament Commentaries*, London: Adam and Charles Black, 1962. The use of the Greek in this volume is also reduced to a minimum. Barrett is a keen scholar, though at times he may steer clear of the difficult decisions.

6. Ernst Käsemann, *Commentary on Romans*, trans. Geoffrey W. Bromiley, Grand Rapids: Eerdmans, 1980. At last available in English, and the translation carefully examined by Prof. Duane Priebe of Wartburg Theological Seminary, Dubuque, this is without doubt the greatest commentary on the epistle produced in this generation.

R. A. H.

THE PRELUDE
1:1-17

■ **1:1-7**   **Paul, the Servant**

According to the usual letter-style in the Greek speaking world, the epistle begins by immediately naming the sender. Paul's self-designation stands midway between salutations in which he throws down the term "apostle" like a gauntlet, and those in which he simply names himself. Paul was unknown to the Roman congregation. He neither founded it nor experienced anything in the way of pain or pleasure from it, but he did regard it as lying within the legitimate sphere of his apostolic duties (1:5, 14, and 15:15-16). The apostle begins by naming himself **servant of Jesus Christ.** Nowhere else in the Pauline collection is there such emphasis on the divine initiative, such stress on human passivity in face of the divine activity, nowhere else such a continual hammering away at the thought that what we are accustomed to call the "human response" is of a piece with the divine activity, to the effect that the term "response" is robbed of any real purport, and the question as to whether or not any room is left to human responsibility in face of all this everlasting emphasis upon the initiative of God is crucial. Let **servant** stand for all that is called, done and attempted by Paul. But the term must still take its definition from the context. There is nothing servile and mincing in this opening line.

Called to be an apostle, set apart for the gospel, give the peculiar shape of this service as well as its purpose. Paul's apostleship was not of his own choosing. Like a "vessel" he was

17

set aside for the gospel of God. (Cf. 9:21-22; in Gal. 1:15, Paul uses the same verb to indicate that the "separation" took place before he was born.) The term **gospel** is ancient, and had been used by the Caesar cult. Was Paul among the first to borrow the term and load it with new content?

This service of Paul is at the end of a long chain of succession. That for which the apostle has been separated out is no novelty. God, the everlasting Subject of this epistle, had announced the gospel **beforehand** through his prophets in the holy writings. It is thus not a single or simple precedent which Paul found for this gospel—he found it in the prophets. (The scope of the precedent will become clear—in a host of instances, Paul makes explicit reference to the Old Testament, and at each significant ligature of this book a prophet is cited.) But it is not at all immediately perceptible that the prophets promised the gospel beforehand. That "beforehand" is written from a peculiar perspective, according to which the promise is neither promise nor uttered beforehand till Christ appears and makes it so (cf. the remarks on 4:23-25; 15:4 and 16:26).

This gospel for which Paul is set apart, which is God's, which was announced beforehand and now is deposited in what is written, is not an idea, but a person, by virtue of physical descent of David's line. (Verses 3 and 4 may well have been a traditional fragment appropriated by Paul—neither the language nor the content appears to have originated with him.) Christianity is thus a *historical* religion, but what distinguishes this historical religion from every other is the assertion that this person enjoys a peculiar and unique relationship to God which only the word **Son** can convey. There is precedent in the Old Testament and in the literature between the Testaments for such an assertion. Israel, Cyrus, a congeries of "servants" were called "my son," but Paul has narrowed the field of contenders for such unique relationship to only one. There was one, **descended from David,** only one such Son. The statement is hardly full-blown, but it is the seed of the church's embracing of the opposites—God's Son, God's only-begotten *and* Jesus of Nazareth.

Now, the assertion that this gospel was announced beforehand becomes infinitely more bold. To this one, and to this one only, Paul contends, all the prophets witnessed. Such things can be said in only one way—*from* the event of Christ *to* the Old Testament. Whatever method of Scripture interpretation Paul will use, he will always begin at the point of Jesus Christ. Only from that perspective can it be said that the gospel was announced beforehand, for it is not at all clear (certainly not to Judaism!) that the Old Testament points to Christ. Indeed, what the Old Testament awaits might be a host of things, as the sects in Judaism testify. Why then from Christ to the Old Testament? What Paul had seen and witnessed was of such unbelievable, incredible consequence to him that it immediately altered his existence, and from that "sight" Paul drew the radical conclusion that so it must be for everyone.

This Jesus was designated Son of God **in power** (the accent lies here, not on **Son of God**) by or because of his resurrection, and this by virtue of **the Spirit of Holiness** (a typically Semitic expression for "Holy Spirit") who raised him from the dead (cf. 8:11). This one enjoys exclusive lordship, due, like his "sonship with power," to his resurrection. That sonship with power, that lordship, are two sides of the same coin—the one touching his own destiny, the other ours. (The verse is a summary of the "ascent" motif in Phil. 2: "Therefore God has highly exalted him and bestowed on him the name which is above every name . . . Jesus Christ is Lord".)

Paul has not yet put the period to the sentence: **Jesus Christ our Lord, through whom we have received grace and apostleship** (or, grace for apostleship, cf. Gal. 2:7, 9). "Grace," then, is the name for Paul's service, his being called and set apart (v 1). What has occurred to him may have occurred as if against his will, but grace is its name! Roman readers have **not** received grace for apostleship (the plural is the "author's plural"), but they have received grace, and its purpose or result is **obedience to the faith.** (Some editions of the RSV read **the obedience of faith.** What moved the translators to their choice, a "Jacobean" correction of an understanding of faith as mental assent to propositions? Let "obedience to the faith" stand; cf. again the Philippians hymn, "that at the name of Jesus every knee should bow," and Rom. 14:11.)

Verse 6 is not a mere amenity. There is more to it than meets the eye. The Romans, yet unvisited by Paul, their community founded by others, come under the range of his responsibility, and their faith fulfills the purpose of his apostleship. If Paul had not believed this, he would scarcely have written to Rome. Rome receives a letter for the simple reason that God has given Paul grace to serve Christ as minister to the Gentiles ("because of the grace given me by God" in 15:15-16 is the interpretation of 1:6). Here is Paul's *reason*, though it is not the occasion for his writing. All the Gentiles fall to his share, whether or not he can claim to have founded a given community. Paul is certainly not the only evangelist to non-Jews, but he is the only witness to the resurrected Christ assigned directly to the "nations," the advocate par excellence of the Gentile mission. A pity commentators have had to hunt for reasons for Paul's writing the epistle, when he stated his reason loud and clear.

Paul's conception of his mission is mammoth, even aside from the wobbly hypothesis that he supposed the end would come only when he had preached to the Gentiles, though indeed the expectation of Christ's return stoked the furnace of his mind. But if we concede his argument, then the concept of his mission answers to the prodigious character of his appointment. Was it merely for his law-free gospel Paul was attacked, or was it also because of the scope assigned to his ministry, a scope calculated to reduce that of the "arch-apostles" to minisize? And, was it the perception of the range of his task which lent him such incredible boldness among those to whom he preached? The occasion for writing was the Jerusalem collection, but the reason was that he had received grace to bring about obedience among the Gentiles.

To all God's beloved in Rome . . . grace to you and peace from God our Father and the Lord Jesus Christ. At last, the greeting and an end to salutations! The final phrase occurs as a refrain or colophon throughout the epistle, ending a thought or section (5:1 and 15:30 are the two exceptions), and corresponds with our chapter divisions. If grace is not an affection neither is "peace." And more clearly in Romans than elsewhere, Paul will spell out their content, occasion, place, reason, and means.

■ 1:8-13   Paul and the Romans

Giving thanks is almost always first with Paul following the salutation (but cf. Gal. 1:6: "I am astonished. . . ."), and the reason is that **your faith is proclaimed in all the world.** There may be a touch of hyperbole here, but Rome was of easy access and those who were financially able or whose professions required it, could travel freely. Paul was not the only one able to get about.

Then follows Paul's oath: **God is my witness whom I serve** (the term is liturgical, sacral, Levitical, and corresponds to the two-fold reference to serving Christ and the gospel as priest in 15:16) **with my spirit.** These words do not mark Paul's service as interior or inward, opposed to what is exterior or outward. For Paul, what is "spiritual" is always concrete. The words rather describe the quality of a service which cannot be measured by any human standard (in Phil. 3:3, worshiping God "in spirit" is contrasted with "putting confidence in the flesh," with taking what can be observed as the norm for one's activity).

Without ceasing I mention you always in my prayers—for Aristotle, memory was applied only to the past; here, Paul joins memory to intercession—**asking that somehow by God's will I may now at last succeed in coming to you.** Clearly, whether or not we construe that little word "by" in v 10 as denoting instrument or cause, if Paul ever gets to Rome, it will be because it is God's will. The original contains a cluster of conjunctions and adverbs here which yield the picture of a man champing at the bit—thankful to God for the Romans; remembering them everlastingly in his prayers; anxious to see them, but not one to undertake an enterprise on his own: "If at all possible I may now at last succeed by God's will. . . ." When will he know it is God's will to depart for Rome? Will it be by a sign from heaven, or by drawing inferences from a chain of events?

Since the verb **impart** in v 11 never has the genitive when the whole is given, and since greater value is given by separation of the pronoun, noun and adjective ("some . . . gift . . . spiritual"), perhaps the gift Paul has in mind at his coming is not just any gift at all. But what might it be? Occasion or circumstance will dictate. Paul always had something specific to share. The mutuality of comfort which he anticipates at Rome can hardly be missed—**encouraged by each other's faith, both yours and mine.** Paul may be apostle to the Gentiles, and on the sheer strength of his apostleship bring the Romans encouragement, but he expects something of them upon his arrival, and to which he gives the clue in 15:24.

The phrase translated **I want you to know,** is common with Paul (cf. 1 Cor. 10:1; 12:1; 2 Cor. 1:18; 1 Thess. 4:13) and occurs twice, here and in 11:25, in conjunction with the mystery regarding Israel. In both instances, Paul needs to make known something of which his readers are unaware. (Its twin, "we know," by which Paul assumes his readers know also what he knows, appears in 2:2; 3:19; 6:6, 9; 7:14; 8:22, 28 and 13:11, and the knowledge shared may derive from primitive Christian preaching and instruction or from the Old Testament, cf. 2:2ff. The negative, "you do not know," used in reproach, and implying a knowledge which his readers or hearers should possess, occurs in 2:4; 6:3, 16; 7:1; 10:3 and 11:2. Only once does Paul admit to sharing ignorance with his readers: "we do not know how to pray as we ought," 8:26. Finally, in 8:38; 14:14 and 15:29, Paul tells only what *he* knows. In each case, what is not known, known or rejected yields no consistent pattern, and in each the usage reflects Paul's preaching technique.)

The phrase, **but thus far have been prevented** in v 13 is a parenthesis, reflecting either the need to tarry with an idea just expressed, or the resistance of a subordinate idea to its inclusion in the sentence already begun. (There are more of these parentheses in Paul than a schoolmaster would allow; his sentence structure is no grammarian's delight.) Paul later expresses this same thought in 15:22: **I have so often been hindered from coming to you,** and the reason he gives is his activity **from Jerusalem and as far round as Illyricum** (15:19). But since that activity was the consequence of what Christ wrought through him, the final cause of the delay is God himself.

Again, as in v 11, and beyond the word in 15:24, we are left to infer what "harvest" Paul may reap among the Romans.

■ 1:14-15   Debtor to Jew and Gentile

The inhabited world, according to the then current, popular division—**Greeks . . . barbarians**—falls within the range of Paul's obligation. So the indebtedness is not incurred by anything which these peoples have done for him—it belongs to his service to Christ.

Again, as in v 11 (**I long to see you**) or v 13 (**I have been prevented**), to say nothing of v 9 (**whom I serve with my spirit**), this service or obligation corresponds to Paul's desire: **I am eager to preach the gospel to you also. . . .** What a curious situation! To be under obligation and yet to desire in consonance with the obligation. Paul is a servant, yet serves God with his spirit; he is under obligation to Greek and barbarian, and yet desires to preach at Rome. Indeed, he is a servant, and for this reason serves God with his spirit; he is under obligation and for this reason desires to preach at Rome.

■ 1:16-17   The Theme of the Epistle

> *Dear Christians, one and all rejoice,*
> *With exultation springing,*
> *And, with united heart and voice*
> *And holy rapture singing,*
> *Proclaim the wonders God has done,*
> *How his right arm the vict'ry won,*
> *What price our ransom cost him!*

For I am not ashamed. The RSV seems to link this verse so smoothly to what precedes, as though it furnished the reason why Paul is so eager to preach at Rome. But throughout the epistle, and with only one exception, that little conjunction **for** does not conclude but begins an argument, with or without any link to what precedes. Here, the introductions are gotten out of the way, and the apostle takes to the pulpit and launches into his theme without bothering with introductions or prefaces—undoubtedly his habit when preaching on untilled soil.[1]

The phrase, **I am not ashamed of the gospel,** does not express the willingness to bear an onus. The phrase is a stand-in for the affirmative "I confess." The object of this confession— **the gospel**—is more than the message actualized in the church; it is God's making salvation known to the world—something not at human disposal, something present over against the church and its servants, a proclamation always realized anew.

That gospel, writes Paul, is the **power of God,** and the word "power" stands in first position. Elsewhere, Paul makes the same identification between "power" and "gospel," variously called "the word of the cross" (1 Cor. 1:18), the Christ "we preach" (1 Cor. 1:23) or "my speech and my message" (1 Cor. 2:4). What an identification! The gospel, a mere announcement, albeit charged with the "conviction" of the herald without whom it would be amputated, the gospel, to all intents and purposes a mere recitation of events, an altogether human word, uttered by human lips concerning a Jew from Galilee, his fate or destiny, is that by which God carries out his purposes despite human weaknesses. (In a host of instances Paul makes such an identification, but nowhere with more elan than in 1 Cor. 1:18ff.)

Human reflection on deity identifies the power of God with visibility. It identifies that power with what is so alien that it can only evoke awe, wonder or terror. For such reflection, this identification is an absurdity. While it is true that Jewish thought about the end of the world furnished the background of the apostle's teaching, an apocalyptic for which God's visible manifestation of himself was the hallmark, that thought underwent a stunning qualification at the hands of what for Paul comprised the heart of the Christian gospel—the death of Christ, an event in which deity, by all human reckoning, was neither visible nor calculated to create anything else but scandal. Whether or not Paul's identification directly influenced the remainder of the New Testament, it is still reflected on every page of the New Testament—in the "shipwreck" of presuppositions; in the description of the fate of Jesus of Nazareth as *the* apocalyptic event, as the manifestation of the power of God "under the sign of its opposite."

This gospel, this power has its inevitable result in salvation. (The same three-way connection is struck between "word of the cross," "power" and "salvation" in 1 Cor. 1:18; in 1 Cor. 1:24, the connection is between "Christ," "power" and "those who are called.") So the difference between this power in v 16 and that in v 20—a power seen by perception of the things made—is that this power "leads to" salvation. It is crucial, then, that we read "power for salvation" in one breath. And as for **salvation,** the term is from that collection of images used to describe the end of time, and brings to mind all those yearnings associated with final deliverance, ultimate victory for God and his own. The term is frequent in the Greek Old Testament (the Septuagint), found in the messianic expectations of Judaism, and occurs often in the New Testament. It denotes the salvation already become a reality through Christ, not merely an anticipation of the future. Its scope is as broad as the images used for it in the Old Testament and in the literature between the Testaments: one thousand stems on a single vine; one thousand grapes on a single stem; one thousand goblets of wine from a single grape! "Salvation"—a word carved from the longing of millions of the oppressed who still could dream, both Jew and Greek.

It is the power of God for salvation to every one who has faith. The fat is already in the fire! This early formulation of principle as a beginning point is designed to arouse the objection of the hearer. It contradicts the popular conception that ultimate joy or victory may somehow be earned; it erases all distinctions between persons created by systems of merit and reward, since faith, from the purely "horizontal" level, is what everyone can give. But the phrase reflects exclusivity as well. For if the gospel is God's power leading to salvation, this cannot be perceived by the normal, human organs of perception. Another "sense" is required, another faculty enabling one to see God at work where the senses and all the instruments created to assist them perceive nothing at all, enabling one to cling with certainty to something which one's science may even deny, or which the evidence of the eyes can at best only describe as probability, to see with "the eye of faith."

Faith is not an absurdity which opposes sight or understanding but which is present before ever there is sight or understanding; a prejudgment in the light of which we see and understand. To such a faith, everyone not only has the will, but supremely the right. The risk, the venture, remains, but the venture of Christian faith is not so totally unlike other ventures that it cannot be called the risk par excellence—from a "horizontal" point of view.

To the Jew first. That heretic of the second century, Marcion of Sinope, erased that **first** wherever he encountered it in Romans. If the gospel is what it is to every believer alike, why to the Jew first? The answer is not that one must begin somewhere, and since the activity of God is pitched to a world of beginnings and endings, the gospel happened to begin with the Jew. That "first" means something more than a first in time. Popular preoccupation with a history of salvation, with viewing the biblical account of God's mighty acts as a series of points on a line leading from the time of the Jew to the time of Jesus to the time of the church, aside from reducing the redemptive activity of God to the horizon within which it occurs, leaves little to the Jew beyond a mere "first" in time.

The answer is not that Israel deserved to be first. Studies which distinguish the categories of thought in Judaism from those of its pagan neighbors, leaving one to assume the Jew came first because, e.g., he thought in linear fashion or put the accent on being up and doing, whereas the Greek thought in cyclic fashion or put all the accent on the abstract, assume a Judaism which is monolithic, uniform, indivisible, and in the last analysis renders talk of its greatness open to contradiction. Neither answer is true, either is calculated to make that "first" something else, something less than a "first."

The innumerable introductions to this epistle to the contrary notwithstanding, the "problem" of Romans is that of the Gentile, not of the Jew. It is a thousand-year-old Gentile reading of the epistle which has set Paul's discussion of justification in the context of a polemic against Judaism, and out of high-nosed pity for the Jew has dubbed that discussion provisional, temporary. It is the Gentile reading which has confused the

apostle's constant appeal to the Old Testament Scripture—an
appeal unrivaled by any other New Testament author—with a
heaping up of prooftexts designed to serve a limping dog-
matic. It is a Gentile reading which can see in Chapters 9-11
nothing more than a disturbance in the flow of the letter's
argument,[2] and in the word of predestination at its core, only
a harsh and bitter doctrine.

It is true—Judaism will be attacked, its advocates scorched,
its bastions reduced, thus leaving the way clear for anti-Semi-
tism with a host of Christians from Barnabas, Cyprian, Greg-
ory of Nyssa and Eusebius to Martin Luther and beyond, but
the assumption beneath it all, and without which the epistle
will never be understood, is that the Jew is first, not merely in
time, nor by virtue of any inherent right, but *by reason of God's
call*. **To the Jew first** is the explanation for setting forth God's
justifying act as gift and not reward. And was this not Israel's
true experience with God, that he had indeed chosen it for no
earthly reason? "How odd of God to choose the Jews" (Ogden
Nash)—odd indeed, but the oddness is mercy's obverse side!
To the Jew first is the explanation for allegiance to a Scripture
which Judaism and Paul received as norm, canon, and rule.
To the Jew first is the explanation for that peculiar exposition
of Scripture, which, if not totally unknown to Paul's Gentile
readers, was certainly unknown in such astonishing breadth—
gathering Old Testament quotations under a key word or concept; concluding from the "easy to the hard"; arguing from silence and from opposites; furnishing "chain-explanations" and
line-by-line or "pesher" commentaries; adding decisive words
to the text; arguing from the sequence of verses or narratives;
using parable, and all despite or in the teeth of good, Greek
style:

> The impression of dissimilarity is greater than that of simi-
> larity. . . . True enough, the mantle of the Greek orator hangs
> about Paul's shoulders, but Paul has no feel for artistic drap-
> ery, and the lines of the alien shape are evident everywhere.[3]

To the Jew first explains Paul's notion of election, a notion
that becomes unpalatable when mercy and grace are no longer
at issue, when a "response of faith" is conceived independently
of God's will. God called Israel first—there is no getting around
it.

That phrase, **to the Jew first and also to the Greek** means
also "to the Jew first *in order to* the Greek." Israel was called to
be a light, a light to the nations—that was her "advantage"
(3:1), and there lay the reason for Jesus' mission to the lost
sheep of Israel's house. But that is scarcely a reason for Gentile
pride (cf. 11:17-24), and there is more to this thought than that
"in order to the Greek." The phrase is not complete till it
reads: "To the Jew first, in order to the Greek, *and thus, in
order to the Jew.*" The proper reading and interpretation of
Romans is not a matter of being "nice" to Jews, but of acknowledging the choice and election of this people, of recognizing the
"firstness" of this enigmatic and empirically undefinable community as sign of the Godhead of God.

Again, in v 17, **righteousness** appears in first position, just as
power in v 16. The reason why the gospel is God's power leading to salvation is that in it God's righteousness is revealed.

Aeons ago, science had concluded there was no such thing
as a world of spirit. Indeed, nothing was real that was not tan-
gible. Socrates stormed against such "atheism." It was doctrin-
aire. Worse, it was useless, for it did not give one a knowledge
of self or of the proper way to live. So he put a rare question:
What is the end of life? And his answer was: "Perfection of
soul," a perfection disclosed to knowledge. Socrates said: "I'll
not know this or that is good till I see it for myself; I'll not take
others' word for it." In this fashion he undermined the ethics
of constraint at the base of Athens' moral structure, and was left
with a choice between exile or death. This "new morality" was
the chief thing for Plato, who expanded it into a system-cum-
religion, accessible only to the philosopher king. "What every
schoolchild knows" is Plato's theory of "forms" or "ideas,"

those indestructible essences in which everything partici-
pates and are apprehended by the mind. But the goal toward
which that apprehension should lead was "righteousness,"
harmony between the functions of the soul. "Righteousness" is
the theme of the whole of the *Republic,* a righteousness obtained by a knowledge with which the immortal soul already
comes equipped, and needing only to be recollected. Plato's
doctrine was the noblest, most eloquent and most thoughtful
statement of an opinion which has seized the race since its
beginning—righteousness is something to be achieved.

Here Paul writes that righteousness belongs to God alone.
This little verse runs counter to all popular belief; it is a denial
of every human enterprise. But if the righteousness is God's,
then all others must be unrighteous, and salvation for the impious. Then, no one has any place with God but the godless—
Jesus' meaning when he said, "I have not come to call the
righteous, but sinners to repentance."

There is more. In the gospel, the righteousness of God is
revealed, its covering or veil removed.[4] Thus, if the power of
God leading to salvation is the gospel, and if the righteousness
of God is revealed in the gospel, then the righteousness of God
is revealed in the power of God which has salvation as its result. Paul is not only explaining why the gospel is God's power,
that is, because his righteousness is revealed in it, but also telling us what that righteousness is—God's saving power. The
power of God to save is the setting for righteousness.

What does it mean that the righteousness of God is revealed
through faith for faith? Faith is certainly not the mediator of
this revelation. The verse could read, "because the righteousness of God is revealed in the gospel at the place of and tend-
ing toward (or, for the purpose of creating) faith." If Paul
writes in v 16 that the recognition of the gospel as God's power
leading to salvation falls to that organ of perception called
faith, here he states virtually the same thing: Faith is the place
at which God's righteousness is revealed in the gospel.

Paul draws his introduction to a close with the quotation from Habakkuk. The prophets, through whom God announced his gospel beforehand, thus stand at the beginning and end of the epistle (cf. 15:21). The phrase, **as it is written,** is used either to signal the end or actually to close a major section in the epistle, just as here; cf. 3:10; 8:36; 11:26 and 15:9. In 2:24; 9:33; 15:3 and 21, the phrase is followed by a new theme within a major section.

The setting of the Habakkuk passage is the "community" or "national" lament, rooted in Israel's wilderness wanderings, later used at occasional cultic "fasts," and for the purpose of imploring God's help in the face of crisis, here, of Israel's bondage to the Babylonian empire, now at its zenith. Paul's quotation is lifted from that section of the lament called the "salvation oracle" in which the priest responds to the complainant in God's name. After Habakkuk has sung Israel's bitter complaint against its enemies, heard Yahweh's first word that the Babylonians are his tools for punishment, and repeated his complaint by an appeal to the divine justice, and after the brief pause in which he awaits a second reply, he hears again the oracle from which Paul has taken his quotation. Oddly enough, the oracle does not speak of Yahweh's grace to Israel, but of his coming wrath in midst of which the righteous must stand fast.

When a great number of oracles in happier contexts were at his disposal, why does Paul seize on precisely this one for his opening argument? From his use of the passage here, his earlier use of it in Galatians 3:11, and from its subsequent appearance in Hebrews 10:38 and James 2, it is easy to conclude that the verse played a role in early Christian preaching and instruction. Why it should have done so has been a mystery until the discovery of the Dead Sea Scrolls, among them a "pesher" or line-by-line commentary on Habakkuk. The pesher reads:

> "But the righteous through his faithfulness shall live." This refers to all in Jewry who carry out the Law [Torah]. On ac-

count of their labor and of their faith in him who expounded
the Law aright, God will deliver them from the house of judgment.[5]

One trait above all was shared by the community at Qumran
and the early Christian fellowship—the conviction that it lived
at the end of days; that the judgment of the world was imminent, and that "he whose soul is not upright in him shall fail."
This conviction in "sectarian Judaism" falsely so-called, spurred
a cherishing and interpreting of portions of the Old Testament
which were ignored in other sectors of Judaism, and reflected
a faith which furnished the background for Jesus' understanding of himself and his mission. Because Jewish-Christians
aimed at continuity with Old Testament faith, it was natural
for them to draw strength from the same source as did their
non-Christian counterparts. Once, Christian choice of Habakkuk may have been accidental; later, it was deliberate, calculated to summon up a world of yearning. The tiny passage
thus marks Paul as standing within a tradition from which
every movement in Judaism, enraged by the status quo, has
taken its occasion—all the way from the Maccabean wars still
remembered at Hanukkah, to the passive or active resistance
of Pharisee or Zealot in Jesus' time, to the crushing defeat
under the armies of Titus in A.D. 70, to the final tragedy at
Massada, where new recruits swear allegiance to a new Israeli
state.

There is more. Paul's intent is not merely to display his continuity with the tradition. A comparison of his use of Habakkuk here and in Galatians 3:11 reveals that his purpose is
polemic. He is opposing to a life oriented to law a type of existence which relinquishes all expectation on the basis of deeds.
And indeed, if the ancient author—as certainly his interpreters
at Qumran—conceived "faith" as in some sense equivalent to
keeping the law, then Paul was at odds with the tradition.
Finally, that such faith should have its object not in the vic-

tory of "Sons of Light" over "Sons of Darkness," but in a cruel, lonely death, yet a death which would render all human history after it its epilogue—on that question, Paul and Habakkuk, and Paul and Qumran were worlds apart.

Judaism knew enough to make the connection between Habakkuk 2:4 and Genesis 15:6: "And [Abraham] believed the Lord; and he reckoned it to him as righteousness." Why then does Paul reject the doctrine of justification, as taught in certain sectors of Judaism such as Qumran, and in light of the latter's appeal to "grace alone"? The answer is that God himself is present in what he gives. But if that is true, then the entire message of Romans can be summed up in the terse and paradoxical statement that righteousness, justification, is God's gift of Christ to believers.[6] For this reason, the debate as to whether or not "the righteousness of God" marks God primarily as possessor or as author, and whether or not "righteousness" characterizes God's "might which establishes salvation" and stresses the future aspect in the tension between present and future—an accent rooted in Judaism, or whether it characterizes God's gift and stresses the present aspect in the tension— an accent unique to Paul—is an attempt to divide what for Paul was indivisible: Justification as oneness with Christ. In the one instance, the "fracture" of Paul's conceptuality in light of his coming to faith is minimized, and in the other his retention of that conceptuality is minimized, however fractured.[7]

THE WRATH OF GOD
1:18—3:20

■ **1:18-32**   **On the Gentile**

1:18 The Thesis

There is a gap between vv 17 and 18. Verse 18 is a doctrinal statement, and requires what follows for its explication. God's wrath is revealed **from heaven** (righteousness, however, is revealed **in the gospel**, v 17). Paul's idea of the divine wrath may not be construed as an emotion, nor may it be set within the framework of a moral world view. The following verses in which humanity's guilt is identified with its fate, make clear that the phrase "from heaven" is metaphorical—it indicates that the revelation of wrath originates with God. The phrase also conjures up the notion of inevitability, if not of suddenness, dispatch. Paul writes that God's righteousness is opposed when people "bind" or "ban" the truth. The definite article prefixed to the noun "truth" refers to something discrete, specific, to something known—*the truth*. But what is *the* truth? The answer is given in what follows: It is what can be known of God. "The truth" then, has to do with the conditions which ought to prevail between humankind and God.

1:19-20 God's Knowability and the Human Response

Paul now advances to the reason for the revelation of God's wrath. **For what can be known about God is plain to them, because God has shown it to them.** God does not demand what

34

he himself has not made known.[8] Thus the individual is responsible. With this little word, Paul raises the bitterly debated problem of a "natural theology." What is striking, however, is what he omits from the complex apocalyptic tradition on which he draws, and how he limits what he does use. He speaks of God only in his relation to humanity and to the world *after* the Fall, and does not refer to the created world in order from that point to establish a knowledge of God. For Paul, the possibility of knowing God is not a question.

Verse 20 indicates when and in what manner God's knowability was revealed, and wherein it consists: **Ever since the creation of the world his invisible nature, namely, his eternal power and deity. . . .** In other words, God's invisibility, his eternal power and deity are seen by bringing to consciousness or reflection what is before the eye—the created order. For the one who understands the **things that have been made** in their appeal and claim, God is Lord and oneself a creature. Thus, though God himself is not seen, but only what is his, what is his cannot be toyed with. In Paul or in Judaism, there is the conviction that God may be perceived in his works, but that the creature refuses him reverence, commits idolatry and ignores his judgment. God thus gives to humankind the possibility of knowing him, in order that at the final judgment there may be no charge of a mistrial. Paul is not explaining; he is preparing a "brief."

1:21-32 The "Exchange" and the Hidden Judge

Verse 21 does not introduce a second reason for the revelation of God's wrath. The reason is still the refusal to glorify or give thanks to the One who has made himself known in the created order: **Although they knew God they did not honor him as God or give thanks. In this lies the ungodliness and wickedness of men.**

The phrase in v 21, **although they knew,** repeats the thought of vv 19 and 20, this time not from the aspect of the divine initiative, but of the "human response." In what follows, Paul contrasts what those who "bind" the truth did with what they did not do. Their response to "the truth," to God's knowability, invisibility, eternal power, and deity was not to glorify or give thanks, but to become futile in their thinking. At the very place where "the truth," where what is knowable can be perceived and thus held in awe, they **were darkened.**[9]

If v 18 is a general statement, so is v 21. The shape of the revelation of the divine wrath, and the shape of the refusal to glorify or give thanks, of being darkened, is clear from v 22 onward. Paul's argument here is anticipated in 1 Corinthians 21: The wisdom of the world which opposes God's wisdom, embraces not merely intellectual learning, but a type of existence—the world, though able to acknowledge God as Creator and thus to honor him, actively rejects such knowledge as is manifest in the creation, and attempts to create its own. Again, it is not the possibility, but the actuality of a knowledge of God which is asserted. Paul's entire argument hangs on that.

Verse 22, like v 21 containing an antithesis, leads from the human response to a description of the shape the response assumed: **Claiming to be wise, they became** (were made) **fools.** The thought here is not unlike that in 1 Corinthians 1:20-21. In both instances, it is God who makes folly of human wisdom, though here it is the route to folly that is described, not folly as the end result. Verses 23, 25 and 26b also contain antitheses, and in each case the antithetical human response is introduced by the term **exchanged** (echoed in the phrase **God gave them up** in vv 24, 26, and 28). In v 23, the antithesis lies in the exchange of the glory of the immortal God for the "likeness of an image" of mortal man (RSV: **images resembling mortal man**). *Stage one of mankind's Fall!* Clearly, Paul is shaping his argument in Romans 1 after the biblical account of Adam's sin.

God's glory (the "weight" of his eternal power and deity, able to be perceived by means of or in the created order) is bartered off not merely for a mortal, but for the likeness of an image of a mortal—for that which is twice removed from what is human!

Paul's argument is strikingly similar to the penitential Psalm 106, which lists by turns Israel's sin and God's judgment (cf. e.g., Ps. 106:14 and Rom. 1:24, or 106:48 and v 25). The Psalm begins in hymnic fashion, but fastens a long recitation of God's mighty acts on Israel's behalf to a brief, general petition for deliverance. In the foreground is the recital of Israel's sins, for which the Psalmist accuses his people ("they exchanged the glory of God for the image of an ox that eats grass"), and for whom he makes confession, concluding with a call to save. (In the phrase which Paul has substituted for "the image of an ox that eats grass," that is, **images resembling mortal man or birds or animals or reptiles,** every word but one, "mortal," appears in Gen. 1:20-26, and in the same order.)

What relevance has this narrative to the Gentile world? Paul not merely regards Israel's history as a model, believing that in the matter of rebellion against God "there is nothing new under the sun." To make such a point, texts from the Wisdom literature which link Israel closest to the moral philosophy of her neighbors would have better suited (cf. again Wisdom, Chapter 13). Rather, Paul conceives the history of Israel as somehow regulative for all other nations—a bold concept, introduced in that phrase **to the Jew first,** and accented and exhausted in Chapters 9-11. Use of Psalm 106 is appropriate also because the Psalmist links his confession to a cry for deliverance since he is convinced that our relation to God and our external fate are two sides of the same coin. Paul's argument, however, is finer, subtler—our guilt becomes our fate, and God becomes the hidden judge.

From v 24 onward, Paul marks out God's judgment on the Gentiles in a threefold way. He first refers to the impurity and violation of the body; then to blasphemies and sexual aberrations, and finally to the ruin of knowledge, judgment, and action. The strong and repeated **God gave them up** in vv 24, 26 and 28 marks the transition from guilt to fate.

To the term they **exchanged** in v 23 corresponds the phrase, **God gave them up** in v 24, a word which recurs like the old refrain in Genesis 5—"and he died"! The result of the refusal to glorify God and give him thanks is to dishonor the body, an "exchange" effected by God himself. (In the RSV the refrain **God gave them up** is clumsily sandwiched in between two clauses). From this verse to the end of the chapter, Paul will hammer home his point by way of that repeated **God gave them up.**[10]

With v 25, we have reached *stage two of mankind's Fall:* Exchange of the **truth about God** (the **glory** of v 23) for a **lie** (the **images** of v 23); the worship of the creature (the **images resembling mortal men** of v 23) rather than the Creator (**the immortal God** v 23) results in an unnatural use of the sexes. (The RSV eliminates result from v 24, and reintroduces cause in v 25: **to the dishonoring of their bodies . . . because,** but we need not spare Paul the repetition of thought—idolatry and sexual perversion were for the Jew the most grievous sins of the Gentile world.) The blasphemy is horrible enough for Paul to append a benediction, in accord with good Jewish custom. The position of the relative pronoun **they** in v 25, together with the formula of blessing, give the entire verse an exclamatory cast: "Such as these exchanged the truth of God for *the* lie, and worshiped and venerated the creature rather than the Creator, who is blessed forever!"

Paul continues his description of stage two with a reference to lesbianism and homosexuality in vv 26-27. The link between the Fall and reference to the unnatural use of the sexes derives from rabbinic tradition which associated Adam's sin with sexual desire. Homosexuality appeared to the Jew to be typically pagan, though in the Gentile world it was widespread, and often praised as a higher form of love. [11]

The phrase in v 27, **receiving in their own persons the due penalty for their error,** introduces a thought which Paul has had in mind till now but has merely allowed the reader to infer —what the transgressors are delivered up to is that to which they have delivered up themselves. Hence, **God gave them up** is not merely the divine response to humans' "response" to God's knowability—their fate (**God gave them up**) is their guilt (**they exchanged**). For Paul then, God's wrath occurs with a remarkable indirectness, in the surrender of the guilty to what results from their guilt. Cause and effect are thus paradoxically interwoven—moral perversion is not merely the cause but also the effect of the divine wrath. None of this is immediately perceptible, and for this reason the Creator is the hidden Judge. But for Paul everything hangs on the fact that in all this God himself is hiddenly at work. Here lies the radical difference between the revelation of righteousness and the revelation of wrath. In the one instance, the place of revelation is in the gospel; in the other, it is interpersonal, though this obviously does not exhaust the scope of judgment.

Paul then describes the *third and last stage in the Fall*—**God gave them up to a base mind and to improper conduct** (v 28). People assert it is no longer necessary to "hold God in their knowledge" (the phrase, **did not see fit** means that the possibility of knowing God has been rejected), to hear his claim or recognize his revelation. The result is that God delivers them over to a mind without a criterion or norm. When human thought loses its norm, it does what is **improper.** With this, Paul moves to the catalog of vices in vv 29-31. The RSV makes two separate sentences of v 29, but the original is better preserved by linking it with v 28: "God gave up to a base mind and to improper conduct those who had been filled . . . who had been gossips, etc."

The "catalog" has no inherent unity, though there are individual clusters within it, and all the terms appear in their old, popular connections (cf. Gen. 1:20-26!). The catalog differs from old Hebrew registers which tend to accent specific acts, as well as from those "circumstances" tallied up by the Greek preacher, and over which he boasted mastery. In Paul, those sins which are the source of the specific act are set in the foreground—a custom also among the Stoics (other catalogs appear in 1 Cor. 5:10; 6:9-10; 2 Cor. 12:20-21 and Gal. 5:19-21).

In v 32 Paul writes that all this wretchedness results despite the Gentiles' knowledge of the "just requirement," the "ought" (RSV: **decree**) of God. Now the secret is out! Not only is God's "knowability" evident; not only are Gentiles able to perceive his "invisibility," that is, his eternal power and deity—that knowability carried with it an "ought," itself revealed (v 19), itself able to be perceived by means of or within the created order (v 20). Only the negative content of that "ought" is referred to here, but if knowability and "ought" are both evident, then the positive content of that "ought" at least includes glorifying God and giving him thanks. But such as these, **though they know God's decree that those who do such things deserve to die . . . not only do them but approve those who practice them.** They are really then without excuse! Use of the present tense here is a surprise. Paul apparently does not intend to describe a process which has been concluded, but the present ruin of paganism, not only shown in deeds, but in the applause which the guilty give the guilt of others.[12]

The apostle does not assume the Gentiles' knowledge and rejection of the Torah from Sinai in order to establish their guilt. By their existence in the world, they stand before God—even before religion discloses that fact to them, or before they reflect on that fact in a theological way. They are already called to reverence, thankfulness and humanness which does not puff itself up or flee responsibility. The picture here of moral decay in the Gentile world is awesome.

■ 2:1-16   On Gentile and Jew

2:1-5 The "Judge" Judged

Linked to what precedes by that little word-crochet "doing"
in v 32, these verses do not mark an abrupt change but rather
a transition. Thus both Jew and Gentile are addressed. The
Gentiles, certainly, were not without moral consciousness
(1:19-21a). Why might they not be included in that **O man,
whoever you are?** The contention that Paul addresses only the
Jew in 2:1-11 rests largely on considerations of style. But symmetry is still preserved if we regard Paul as moving from
Gentile (Chapter 1) to Gentile and Jew (2:1-16), then to Jew
(2:17-3:8), and finally to all (3:9-20), rather than moving from
Gentile to Jew to all, the argument then rounded off in 3:9ff.
The chapter divisions ought not intimidate us.

Now Paul writes that "because you judge the other you,
the judge, bring charge against yourself." **We know**—the apostle assumes a knowledge of Old Testament revelation, as the
recitation of the tables of the law in vv 21 ff. makes clear:
**The judgment of God rightly falls upon those who do such
things.** The same thought underlying the guilt-fate motif in
Romans 1 **(they exchanged—God gave them up)** is present here:
You condemn yourself corresponds to **they did not see fit to
acknowledge God** in v 28, and the **judgment** corresponds to
the phrase, **God gave them up to a base mind** in 1:28 (or 1:27,
etc.). Again, the judgment is immanent, again God is the hidden Judge, and again, this thought does not exhaust the scope
of judgment (cf. vv 5ff.).

In v 3, the scope of judgment is widened beyond the present
and immanent to the future and transcendent. But these two
significations are not at odds; there are not two judgments, but
rather the same judgment viewed differently. "Or (v 4) do you
despise God's rich goodness, restraint and forbearance, his
holding himself in check in face of evil, because you do not
know, are not aware that all this is a goodness for you, calcu-

41

lated to lead you to a radical transformation of the self? Indeed because of your hardness and unrepentant heart you use the time of God's restraint to heap up one guilt upon another till the judgment day." The background may indeed be that of Jewish teaching of the coming judgment, but whereas such thought never conceived that day as applying to Judaism—mere membership in Israel guaranteed immunity—Paul makes the application to Gentile *and* Jew. However such teaching may have furnished the background for Paul's thought, it does not stand uncorrected, unrevised.

2:6-16 The Criterion of the Last Judgment

The Criterion of Works (6-10)

The paragraph opens with a general, doctrinal statement: In the final judgment God **will render to every man according to his works.** The verses following interpret this statement, first in the series: present existence—future recompense, then in the series: future recompense—present existence: **To those who by patience in well-doing seek for glory** (present) . . . **eternal life** (future); **for those who are factious** (present) . . . **wrath and fury** (future); **tribulation and distress** (future) **for every human being who does evil** (present); **glory and honor** (future) . . . **for every one who does good** (present).

There is an echo here of two identical passages in the Old Testament, Psalm 62:12 and Proverbs 24:12. The first has its setting in an individual lament, specifically, in a song of trust grown out from it. After his complaint, composed in such fashion that any might consent to it, the Psalmist notes the revelation he has received ("once God has spoken; twice have I heard this"), and at the heart of which is the theme of recompense—"thou dost requite a man according to his work." The twin passage from Proverbs enjoins the wicked to rescue their victims, and to feigned ignorance of their victims' innocence

("Behold, we did not know this"), replies that such pretense is futile before the God who knows all, and who will not allow existence to be embellished beyond its deserts.

With Paul, the theme of requital has been torn from its ancient context according to which the recompense occurred this side of the grave—death was, after all, the limit of faith in the Old Testament, so that rebellion against God had to be requited in this life or the basis of faith was destroyed—and set within the context of a final judgment.

If these verses mean that the norm by which God judges consists of deeds done "under the law," then Paul is either yielding to a notion of justification on the basis of works, or he has involved himself in a frightful contradiction. The reader then will be left to infer either that Paul does not take seriously his teaching regarding justification, or that he does not believe God **will render to every man according to his works.** One thing is sure—for Paul, works remain the criterion in the judgment. There lies the impartiality, for faith and unbelief alike. Another thing is just as sure—for Paul, there is *another* function of judgment according to works, that is, judgment according to works done "apart from the law." Without faith, the doer stands alone, but with faith, God himself will be found in the deed at the judgment. The one who is righteous by faith will do the good—for such there will be no wrath (cf. vv 9-10 and 1 Cor. 3:11-15). The impartiality occurs at the point of works, not works "of the law," precisely because God justifies those who believe the gospel.

No Partiality with God (11-12)

Paul next gives his reason for this judgment according to works. The statement in v 6 is thus resumed, and the basis of judgment confirmed. The "ought" of God requires deeds, and from all alike—from the Jew first and also from the Greek. The

43

same thought appears in Galatians 2:6 in which Paul's indiffer-
ence toward those "reputed to be something" at the Jerusalem
council reflects the divine impartiality.

Whether or not Paul is alluding here to 2 Chronicles 19:7
can only be surmised. The "Second Chronicler" sets the office
of judge under the divine seal by referring to the judge's appointment at the hands of the king, who commands that the
judge fear God and allow no party spirit to reign: "For there
is no perversion of justice with the Lord our God, or partiality,
or taking bribes." "Blind" justice is a concept Paul shares with
the Psalmist, sage and ancient chronicler, and in v 12, he indicates how such justice will look: **All who have sinned without
the law will also perish without the law, and all who have
sinned under** (i.e., while having) **the law, will be judged by
the law. . . .**

Doers of the Law Justified (13-16)

If v 6 states the axiom (buttressed by a Scripture-word) that
in the judgment deeds are determinative, and if the following
verses indicate precisely *what* deeds, and done by whom, merit
what reward, and if v 12 lays down a general statement to the
effect that there is no immunity to judgment according to
deeds, then vv 13-16 indicate that the basis of judgment is not
restricted to a legal code. There is thus no ignorance of the law
which might prohibit deeds. Paul is closing the ring! Those who
sinned without a legal code will perish without it—an obvious
truth, but stated to indicate that the code is not needed as a
basis for judgment. Those who sinned while in possession of a
legal code will be judged by it.

It is one thing to state that the basis of judgment is not
restricted to the legal code, and quite another to state that
the legal code furnishes no basis at all. *It does indeed,* to those
to whom it is given. In the last analysis, then, the basis for
judgment is one—*law,* codified or no. This concept in part ex-

plains Paul's curious use of the term **law** with or without a modifier in this section. For him, neither the Mosaic law nor the law written on the heart is a mere refraction of the divine "ought," though the "firstness" of the Jew derives from the *clarity* of the one over against the other, and for which reason Paul appears to concede lesser responsibility to the Gentile (cf. 2:16). But a lesser responsibility does not affect the judgment. Law is law, codified or not. Paul's argument is not with Moses, but with an understanding of the law's function. He may indeed have conceived the function of conscience among Gentiles as analogous to that of the Mosaic law among the Jews, that is, as censor and guide for future conduct, but what creates the analogy is not that the Gentiles come by nature to a knowledge for which the Jew required a revelation. For the Gentile as well, the "ought" or "what the law requires" (vv 14-15) is revealed. It is as good as Scripture, **written on their hearts** (of *both* Gentile and Jew, Paul had written, **God has shown it to them** 1:19). Paul then adds, **while their conscience also bears witness and their conflicting thoughts accuse or perhaps excuse them on that day** (cf. 1 Cor. 4:5; 2 Cor. 5:10). Thus, neither Jew nor Gentile has excuse. Even the Gentile has a law, not codified, but in the vis-a-vis. There is no immunity, there is nothing to prohibit deeds.

■ **2:17—3:8** On the Jew

2:17-24 The Jew Against the Law

Now Paul elaborates on the argument in 12b and 13a (**all who have sinned under the law will be judged by the law. For it is not the hearers of the law . . . but the doers of the law who will be justified),** and in reference to the Jew with whom he deals in bitter irony. Verses 21-23 contain antitheses followed by the Scripture quotation in v 24 which concludes the argument.[13]

Paul does not only speak of the Gentile in the third person, or always directly to the Jew (in Chapters 9, 10, 11:1-12, he speaks of the Jew in the third person, and in 11:13ff. directly to the Gentile). But it is true that in speaking to the Jew—and of course, use of the second person best suits the accuser's style —his language is infinitely harsher than any used of Gentiles. Why this harshness and awful irony? "From whom much is given"—what the Gentile was required to see with the mind's eye, the "ought" (1:32), the Jew had before his eye in the code: **You know his will and approve what is excellent, because** (or simply "and") **you are instructed in the law.** Such knowledge is in contrast to perceiving **his eternal power and deity . . . in the things that have been made** (1:20), or to what is **written on their hearts** (2:15). The law belonged to the Jew's "first." But whereas the Jew tended to regard that "first" as an advantage accruing by virtue of inherent right, Paul construes the "first" as responsibility, as vocation (to the Jew first *in order to* the Greek). And the abandonment of that calling, not merely in taking the law for one's own, which results in the erection of a barrier between Jew and Gentile, and thus in boasting (vv 17-20, 23), but worse, in actual transgression (vv 21-24), Paul describes as dishonoring God, furnishing cause for blasphemy.

In vv 21 and 22 Paul refers to three principles of law in the Decalog: "You shall not make for yourself a graven image", "you shall not commit adultery," and "you shall not steal" (Exod. 20:4, 14-15 and Deut. 5:8, 18-19). In their present setting these statutes appear in connection with Moses' farewell, and thus link the revelation at Sinai with the giving of the law—a tradition anchored in Judaism since the time of the kings. The Israelite did not regard these commandments as arbitrary prohibitions which accidentally achieved importance. This is clear from the manner of their delivery—at the outset, God introduces himself; the commandments thus express his very nature—as well as from their appearance elsewhere in greater series (cf. e.g., Lev. 19) throughout the entire Old Testament. Their sanction was God's covenant with Israel, and their purpose lay in giving content to life within the covenant community. Reduced to their simplest components ("not commit adultery, not steal") the commandments are broad in scope, treaty-like in structure, and deal with what is prohibited without regard to the individual instance.

Paul takes commandments from both tables of the law, one originally directed against kidnapping, one calculated to maintain the sanctity of marriage, and the last, from the first table, prohibiting images and image-worship. Paul thus reverses the order of the commandments in Exodus and Deuteronomy so as to climax the Jews' transgression in an offense against deity himself, and to prepare for v 24 which hides a reference to the command: "You shall not take the name of the Lord your God in vain" (Exod. 20:7 and Deut. 5:11). This word in turn leads the apostle to cite the indictment of Isaiah 52. Paul, of course, believed he had precedent for such attack, as is clear from his reference to a marginal gloss in Isaiah's prophecy concerning the Zion of the future (Isa. 52:5).

It is impossible to give any satisfactory analysis or interpretation of this text, since the origin of the gloss is so obscure and the text so distorted. But the Septuagint translation, on which the apostle depends, is clear enough: "All throughout, my name is blasphemed among the Gentiles because of you." Even in this version, however, the reproach is not aimed at *Israel,* but at her tyrants who shame God's name. Paul understood the quotation as a reproof of Israel: Because of Israel's transgressions, the heathen defame God's name. Here, at least, Paul is not content to fix or even to keep to the context of his text!

See what has happened to the "first" when changed to a "better off" (3:9; cf. Matt. 23:13-15)! Since deeds are determinative in the judgment, deeds described in that Mosaic, codified, written law in which the Jew made his boast and by which he distinguished himself as teacher to the inhabited world, and since he treated that law as his own, measured by his deeds the Jew is a transgressor, no better than the Gentile whom he scorned and despised.

2:25-29 Circumcision—The Last Bastion

The Value of Circumcision (25-27)

The accent in these verses is still on deeds, thus on God's impartiality, but they also introduce a new theme—circumcision. In v 25 Paul indicates when the rite has value (v 25a is put negatively), and in v 26 he turns the other side of the coin, stating that when uncircumcision keeps the law, it is reckoned for circumcision. Finally in v 27 Paul states that the one who is physically uncircumcised and thus "without the law," but who is nevertheless a "doer of the law," will judge the one who with all his observance of letter and circumcision is merely a "hearer."

Why this discussion of circumcision here? It is Judaism's bastion, its "sacrament," the proof in its flesh of its Abrahamic covenant with God (cf. Gen. 17:9-14), the evidence that its "first," its "advantage" is truly a "better off"—the guarantee of its immunity from judgment. If the apostle can score here, at the place of Judaism's great, final, and divinely established institution, the seal, sign and token from which ultimately the law with its requirement derives its explanation and its justification, he will have torn Jewry from its height and leveled it to the status of the Gentile. There is a relentlessness about Paul's argument here which is stunning, blasphemous by Jewish standards; intolerant, irreligious by any other. What has happened to induce this man to tear down the explanation for the religious, political, social and economic existence of a whole people, *his* people, and render him a patron of those intent on its extermination by segregation and the ghetto, the pogrom, the Inquisition, the oven, even of those who shared his faith? Could he have conceived that the Gentile world would ultimately regard the undermining of Israel's faith as rationale for oppression, that such oppression would be the awesome byproduct of the spread of Gentile faith, hideously contrary to its heart and intent?

Paul's argument is that the profit of circumcision is dependent on keeping the law (v 25). So the subject is still deeds! Paul will not allow a separation between the sacramental and the ethical. Where there is no keeping of the law, circumcision "has become and thus is in a state of uncircumcision." What is Paul's precedent? The prophets had long contended that repentance was at the heart of the religion of Judaism. Thus, the difference between Judaism and Christianity does not consist in allowing a separation in the one and disallowing it in the other. To the Galatians about to abandon their faith for a religion oriented to law, Paul makes clear that "every man who receives circumcision . . . is bound to keep the whole law!" (Gal. 5:3). For both Judaism and Christianity any sacramental/ethical separation is an impossibility, and thus the danger to both is the same. The difference between them hangs on the question as to whether or not existence oriented to law can avoid this separation.

The "profit" of circumcision—assuming the possibility of avoiding the separation—is not defined. It no doubt spells righteousness, salvation. But what is the use of defining it when this separation is the reality of life lived according to the law?

If the argument in v 25a is hypothetical, so is that in vv 26-27. This is not a defense of noble Gentiles who keep the law, and thus have the upper hand over the Jew. The point is that circumcision without keeping the law is tantamount to uncircumcision, more, is inferior to an uncircumcision that keeps the law, should such a condition ever exist—which Paul has already argued does not. The argument turns on circumcision, on its validity as conditional upon keeping the law, not on a distinction between moral Gentiles and immoral Jews.

The True Jew (28-29)

Now Paul describes wherein true Jewishness and circumcision consist, first (in v 28) in the negative, then (in v 29) in the positive. If circumcision without the law is uncircumcision, and if uncircumcision which keeps the law is superior to circumcision without the law's keeping, then Jewishness is not constituted by an outward sign but by inwardness, and a **true circumcision** is not public but **a matter of the heart.** That is, what constitutes a Jew is harmony of the self with the requirement of the law. Paul argues the same point from a Christian perspective, when he states that in Christ neither circumcision nor uncircumcision is of any worth, but only "keeping the commandments of God" (1 Cor. 7:19), or "faith working through love" (Gal. 5:6), or when he writes that those who worship God "in spirit, and glory in Christ Jesus, and put no confidence in the flesh" are the "true circumcision" (Phil. 3:3). It is to this Jew that praise belongs—not from those who need proof to convince them of what is true and good, but from God, whose affair is with the heart. What has happened here? A "transvaluation of values." The peripheral, single value has been turned on its head by the central concept. The separation of circumcision and keeping the law has been disallowed; the priority of circumcision over the keeping of the law has been rejected; and by the priority given to the law, circumcision— and Jewishness itself—is made spiritual, a matter of the heart.

Once we accept Paul's major premise, the conclusion is inevitable—what is usually thought to be the basis for Jewishness is not so at all. Or, is it? However effective in theory, in actual practice Paul's argument will not convince. There will still be Jews who see themselves held together by the outward sign, and thus seem to allow a separation between circumcision and the law, despite everything the apostle has to say.

But Paul does not attribute this Jewish unbelief to mere stupidity, but to a "mystery," to the mercy of God on the Gentile's behalf, that is, to the Jews' "firstness," even in their unbelief! This persistence of a Judaism "outwardly" when no earthly reason remains to it, and by divine decree, is the other side of the Pauline coin. But the world cannot live with enigmas, which only means it will have neither cross nor Judaism, since to allow that Judaism "outwardly" to stand is to believe in the God who was in Christ.

3:1-8 Objections and Rejoinders

Verses 1-8 contain objections to Paul's argument (there is the slightest hint of a conversation here; cf. also 4:1): If the profit of circumcision hangs on a keeping of the law, and if circumcision and the law are inward, spiritual, "matters of the heart," then "is it all over with Judaism?" Paul's answer is in v 2: Israel was the crucible of the divine revelation. An **advantage** still remains to Judaism, though circumcision has lost its "profit" (2:25). That advantage lies in the fact that the Jews were entrusted with the divine oracles. (Circumcision is made with hands, but Israel was **entrusted;** the passive voice, clue to the divine initiative, always gets the better of the active!) Here, then, Israel's advantage and profit are viewed from the aspect of the divine—the "history of salvation" commenced with Judaism.

Verse 3 contains another objection: If some disbelieved, will not their unbelief render the faithfulness of God null and void? If God has not bound himself to the conditions of this world signaled in circumcision, is not the covenant a fraud? Has not God given himself to caprice? Paul first replies with a **By no means!** And whenever there is a suggestion of foul play with

God (3:6; 7:13; 9:14; 11:1, 11), or of behavior inconsistent with the Christian "walk" (3:4, 31; 6:2, 15; 7:7), these words tumble out first. They are not a reasoned reply, but an expletive, followed here by a rabbinic-like argument: **Let God be true, though every man be false.** . . . God must win when truth is up for grabs.

Paul's first quotation in v 4 is from an individual lament or thanksgiving Psalm, in which the composer tells of a crisis met and passed with Yahweh's help, and cites in lament form the words he had uttered in his anguish: "Every man is a liar" (Ps. 116:11). The second quotation in v 4b is from the Septuagint translation of one of the best known psalms in the Psalter, but one of the few in which a plea for forgiveness stands at center, and at the core of which is the psalmist's painful consciousness of having sinned (Ps. 51:4). The petitioner, perhaps defending himself against the suspicion that blood clings to his hands ("against thee, thee only, have I sinned," thus challenging the old interpretation of the Psalm against the background of David's adultery and homicide) concludes from the acknowledgment of his guilt that Yahweh's indictment is just: "So that thou mayest be justified in thy words, with the result that thou mayest prevail when thou art judged." Thus, to support his argument, Paul reaches into the history of Israel's psalmody for clear admission of communal, universal culpability before God.

The second objection seems to concede the first round to Paul: "Agreed, let God be true—but if our unrighteousness serves to accent God's justice; indeed if our very existence witnesses to the fact that only God is true, is he not unjust to bring his wrath to bear?" **I speak in a human way.** There is more here than an attempt to ingratiate oneself with an objector by assuming the objector's point of view. **I speak in a human way** means to speak from a perspective that allows no transcendent good or meaning (1 Cor. 15:32), for which the only authority is human (1 Cor. 9:8)—it is that which is not from God (Gal. 1:11; 3:15). The argument really is "human"; it assumes that the same egotism which moves humans must also move God, that at the heart of deity lies jealousy for its honor. And if that is so, why is it not unjust for God to bring wrath to bear when our unrighteousness fuels that jealousy, when it serves to demonstrate the vast difference between us and him? Is that not what it means to be God, to be jealous for one's honor, dignity, integrity? Paul rebuts: **By no means!** For if God were unjust, how could he judge the world? When no other expedient is ready at hand, the opponent is struck dumb with a word that God would not be God if he were right!

Question four (vv 7-8) comprises a more or less subtle transition from the objection to Paul's statement regarding the sacramental/ethical separation to the objection that it is precisely this separation which Paul's "new religion" serves. If God's truth abounds to his glory through my falsehood, why am I still judged a sinner, indeed, why do I not draw the practical conclusion from this curious state of affairs and assist the comparison—do evil that good may come? To the suggestion, Paul retorts: "Their judgment is just." But the alternative to caprice is not yet offered.

■ 3:9-20   On All

3:9-18 Scripture Florilegium

The fifth and last question, put by Paul's imagined objector— **Are we Jews any better off?**—and summarily answered, leads to the assertion that in the face of the requirement of deeds both Jew and Greek are caught in the same dilemma, **are under the power of sin.** Then follows a Scripture florilegium (cluster of quotations) gathered under a single viewpoint. (Elsewhere Paul will cluster his quotations under such key words as "my people," in 9:26; "stone," in 9:33; "snare" in 11:9; or "the Gentiles" in 15:9-12. This method of combining Torah and Prophets and

Writings reflects an intimacy with late rabbinic use of Scripture.)

In heaping up his Septuagint quotations—all but one (Isa. 59) taken from the same section of the Hebrew canon—Paul has linked to Psalm 14:2-3 (= Ps. 53:2-3) lines from Psalms 5, 140, 10, Isaiah 59:7 (= Prov. 1:16) and Psalm 36, and in that order.[14] All the Psalm verses are from complaints against enemies—by far the most frequent motif in individual laments of the Psalter. The Isaiah quotation is from a community lament, expanded by the complaint motif of the individual lament in its description of transgressors. If 3:10b is an allusion to Ecclesiastes, then the merged quotations are framed by texts (Eccles. 7 and Ps. 36) in which the complaints progress from the old contrast between Israel and its enemies to a new contrast between the pious and transgressors within Israel itself.

Ecclesiastes cautions its reader against two extremes: All too righteously laying the words of others in the scale, and all too godlessly dreaming one may win the game of life with the card of unrighteousness. Whoever fears God avoids both extremes, since an excess of righteousness does not exist—"surely there is not a righteous man on earth who does good and never sins" (Rom. 3:10b). In the verses from Psalm 14 (= Ps. 53), 5, 140, and 10, the singer describes God's vain search among Israel's enemies for those who act wisely and seek him: All have strayed, all are corrupt, "there is none that does good, no, not one" (Rom. 3:11-12). The sufferer urges his integrity in contrast to enemies who slander him and though appearing to give comfort have only his ruin at heart—"their tongue is an open sepulchre (the ruin of their victims is as sudden as if they had passed through the jaws of death), they flatter with their tongue" (Rom. 3:13a-b). His foes stand in battle array against him, their tongue is "sharp as a serpent's," and under their lips is the "poison of vipers" (Rom. 3:13c).

The psalmist knows, as did Job, that his "friends" intend him violence—"their mouth is filled with cursing and deceit" (Rom.

3:14; were they magicians whose spells brought the singer ill-
ness or calamity?). Then follow two verses from a "baroque"
lament in Isaiah 59, in which the prophet heaps up accusation
against the transgressors within his own community: "Their
feet run to evil . . . they make haste to shed innocent blood . . .
desolation and destruction are on their highways. The way of
peace they know not" (Rom. 3:15-17).[15]

The florilegium concludes with a verse from Psalm 36, an
individual lament concerning Israel's enemies, but when linked
to Isaiah 59 gives a summary of universal transgression—**there
is no fear of God before their eyes** (Rom. 3:18). There is only
one difference between the apostle's argument and that of his
Old Testament sources. In Isaiah 59, the accusation against
Israel and hence the judgment is softened by the promises that
conclude the chapter—a breach or rupture in traditional prophetic style. But Paul's argument is unrelieved—weighed by
the criterion of works, none escapes indictment or sentence.
In Galatians 3:22 Paul speaks of "Scripture" as consigning "all
things to sin," and may have had in mind just such a cluster
as appears here.

3:19-20 Conclusion

Paul resumes the thought of 2:12—those who sinned **under
the law** will be judged "by the law." Deeds, deeds and more
deeds are what the law is after! In v 20, Paul will draw his
conclusion respecting the law's function, but not before he
aims one last salvo at the Jew: **Whatever the law says it speaks
to those who are under the law** (v 19). There is no wriggling
free of the indictment respecting deeds by pleading misap-
plication of the criterion. Judaism, its existence oriented to
law, stands accused by law, and as a result **every mouth** is
stopped and the *entire cosmos* (once divided into Jew and
Greek) guilty before God. What remains of advantage to Judaism is extrinsic to it **(they were entrusted,** v 2), but the law

demands what is intrinsic, and since none can yield harmony of spirit with letter (2:29), inner with outer (2:28-29), circumcision with keeping the law (2:25)—note the antitheses again in 2:17-24; cf. 1:19ff.; 2:1, 3, 13—no "flesh" will be justified before God because of works of the law.[16]

Paul alters the Septuagint quotation of Psalm 143:2 from which he draws his conclusion, by adding the phrase **by works of the law.** The apostle will occasionally swerve from his text because he is quoting from memory and thus inexactly, or will do so for reasons of style. But here the alteration is for theological reasons. Indeed, the decisive portion of Paul's text is his own addition! In the lament which Paul handles in such sovereign fashion, the usual progression from complaint to petition is reversed, and the latter constructed in such manner as to suggest that the petitioner is in an agony from which he cannot get free. In other words, the complainer and his enemies belong to the same community.

The picture which results is a body torn by contrasts, in which one group has the upper hand and oppresses the other because of its attitude toward God. Together with his petitions, and as though in passing, the psalmist admits to a consciousness of his own sin and cries: "Enter not into judgment with thy servant." This verse from Psalm 143 really completes the progression reflected in the florilegium of 3:10ff., since it not merely (with Isa. 59) erases the distinction between devout Israel and its pagan neighbors—the petitioner all the while enjoying "prophetic" distance from the transgressors (cf. the quotation from Ps. 106:20 in 1:23)—but to the extent he admits his guilt, identifies him with his enemies.

But what is incidental to the psalmist is for Paul the chief thing—"nothing that lives, nothing which is called 'alive' will be justified in thy sight." And for Paul it is but a step from admitting a breach of the law—by now demonstrated to be universal in scope—to contending that **no human being will be justified in his sight by works of the law.** If this is not true, Paul concludes in Galatians 2, "Christ died to no purpose" (Gal. 2:21). So the law's work is to give knowledge of sin. Its limit thus is drawn, and Jew and Gentile are caught in the same dilemma. Written on their hearts or entrusted with the oracles, the end result is the same.

Paul might be accused of concluding in Aristotelian fashion from humanity's inability to keep the law (and certainly, use counts with Paul!) that the law was never intended to produce righteousness, so that another way of achieving righteousness must be found. But this would construe Paul's understanding of righteousness in psychological fashion, and open the door to that 19th century portrait of the apostle as a man torn between the "is" and the "ought," fractured on the demands of the law and his inability to keep it. Paul, however, asserts that his apostleship and gospel resulted from encounter with the risen Christ, and that prior to that encounter he was "blameless" as touching the law (cf. Phil. 3:6; Gal. 1:14). The apostle's reflections on the law root in that encounter, not in any moral shipwreck, and are thus to be understood as conclusions drawn from what he believed God had done in Jesus. For this reason, Paul does not hear those numerous voices from the Old Testament which praise the study of the law or speak of its fulfillment, or he reinterprets them, as in 10:6-9.

THE RIGHTEOUSNESS OF GOD
3:21—4:24

■ **3:21-22a**   **Apart from Law,**
Through Faith in Christ

But God has seen my wretched state
Before the world's foundation,
And, mindful of his mercies great,
He planned for my salvation.
He turned to me a father's heart;
He did not choose the easy part,
But gave his dearest treasure.

This is a new section, clearly joined to the proposition in
1:17. Paul's style has also altered. He is no longer turned to
the outside, bringing his viewpoint to sharp expression, treating practical consequences in that mobile, preaching style. His
gaze is turned inward. The structure has become cumbersome.
The apostle is writing now, not preaching: **But now the righteousness of God has been manifested apart from law. . . .**
(There are seven "but now's" in Romans variously translated—
in 3:21; 6:22; 7:6, 17; 11:30; 15:23, 25, cf. 16:26. In each case,
a contrast is drawn with what precedes. Most often, that contrast is between two types of existence—here between existence
according to **law** and **apart from law**.) [17]

An alternative to **law** has appeared, an alternative to deeds,
and to that entire discussion **in a human way** which it occasions
—a righteousness of God **apart from law** in which the law
played no part. How odd that over against the massive charges

58

in 1:18-3:20, the argument beginning here and continuing till
v 31 should be so tersely stated! The history of interpretation
reveals an inability or unwillingness to come to terms with that
phrase, **apart from law.** The heretic Marcion's radical separation of law from gospel had Paul's distinction between the two
for its father. Marcion's exposition of this verse in an unquali-
fied disparagement of the law was a matter of vital concern to
the young church, since it appeared to hack off at the root the
conviction that God's revelation in Christ was in direct continuity with the revelation in the Old Testament.

The troops were mustered out against Marcion, but it all
served to reduce to a minimum Paul's opposition to righteousness on the basis of law. With his six senses of the law, Origen
of Alexandria contended that an increase of sin could not be
attributed to the Mosaic code. Cyril wrote that the law did not
incite but merely revealed sin. And when the author of the
article on "law" in Kittel's *Theological Dictionary,* states that
for Paul the law's weakness consists in the fact that none keep
it, that it can counter sin only with prohibition and judgment,
and that precisely here the Good News makes its entry, he
adds only a grace note to the ancient chorus.[18]

For the apostle, however, God did not intend the first covenant with its law to be the ultimate expression of his will. That
first covenant was provisional. For this reason a promise was
linked to it which (enjoying priority in time over the law, cf.
Gal. 3:17) pointed to the end of life ordered according to judicial decree, and heralded the advent of a new existence by
which Israel's destiny would be shared by all who believe. God
thus ordered his relationship to Israel in such fashion as to
make any particular and exclusive attainment of that goal impossible. It is this provisional character of the law, not merely
the breach of it, that sets the stage for the coming of the new.

Paul next writes that this **righteousness** was first proclaimed
in **the law and the prophets.** (For the RSV **although** in v 21b,
read "moreover"; the RSV translation removes the accent from a

major point with Paul.) That this **righteousness of God** is not a novelty will be proved from a host of instances in the Old Testament. But the proof will lie only this side of the revelation in Christ. As a Jew, Paul was only too keenly aware that the Old Testament had one reading in the synagogue and another in the Christian gathering. According to him, the Old Testament—like Moses' face following his descent from the mount—was veiled, obscure to non-Christian Jews, and he wrote, "to this day, when they read the old covenant, that same veil remains unlifted. . . . Yes, to this day whenever Moses is read a veil lies over their minds" (2 Cor. 3:14-15). Contemporary Christians, with the moral dilemma of six million deaths between them and Judaism, will prefer to describe the Jewish attitude toward Christianity in quite different fashion. Christians must concede to the Jew the possibility of an interpretation of the Old Testament other than their own, and admit that a "historical" reading of the Old Testament, free of presuppositions, conceived as a basis for common discussion, is a chimera, and leave off commencing the dialog with Judaism at the point of a "science" bereft of faith, hope, and love.

Why then does Paul trouble to address himself to the Jew from the Old Testament? The nature and progression of his argument in Romans gives the answer. Nowhere does the apostle attempt to "prove Christ" from the Old Testament, and nowhere does he assume he and his "kinsmen according to the flesh" agree in matters of history or interpretation. Whether or not he keeps to the true context and meaning of a given text—and he does so to surprising degree—Paul's tactic is to point to what the Jew himself regards as the heart and core of his canon and to exclaim: "There! Torah, Prophets and Writings all bear witness to a righteousness of God!" and then to show that it is manifest apart from law in Jesus Christ. The modern Christian interpreter is obliged to be as honest toward his Jewish neighbor as Paul was toward his. Such a faith, Paul concludes in v 22a, is of Jesus Christ (the first reference to Christ since 1:1, 7, 8), and is for all (cf. 1:16).

■ 3:22b-26 The Need, Gift, Means, and Purpose of God's Righteousness

In v 22b, Paul replies to the question why this faith is for all. In the verse following he elaborates, summing up the argument in 1:18-3:18. In v 24, he then turns the other side of the coin: If righteousness is not effected by works, then it is manifest as **gift**. In this fashion, the "how" of righteousness is explicated. And, in the same verse, the means or instrument, as well as the place of God's righteousness is spelled out—**through the redemption which is in Christ Jesus.** Verse 25 then interprets the **Christ Jesus** of v 24: He is Lord (1:7-8), but he is also *God's,* subject to his Father's will; it was God who "put him forward" (v 25a).

Verses 25 and 26 have long been a problem for interpreters. The terms here are not at all characteristic of Paul. Indeed we could move from v 24 to v 27 without interrupting the argument. Might vv 25 and 26 comprise another of those traditional fragments appropriated by Paul into which he, or even a later editor, inserted phrases such as **by faith** (v 25), **at the present time,** and **who has faith in Jesus** (v 26), which sum up the major themes in vv 21-22? The language of the verses is strikingly similar to that of the doxology in 16:25-27. Are they from the same hand?

At any rate, the terms **redemption** and **expiation** in vv 24 and 25 are parallel. The latter term may not be a reference to the "mercy seat" sprinkled with blood on Yom Kippur—such was never open to public gaze—but should perhaps be read against the background of such a passage as 4 Maccabees 17:22, in which the death of seven brothers is viewed as a propitiatory offering (KJV: "propitiation").

Verse 25a might then be translated: "Whom God publicly set forth with expiatory effect by means of (or, for the price of) his blood. . . ." In v 25b, the reason is given for this display of God's righteousness: In his **forbearance** God had forgiven (not as the RSV reads, **passed over**) **former sins**. This clause is then interpreted in v 26. It is *now* that God's righteousness is manifest (the verb translated **show** in v 25 is the equivalent of what is **revealed** in 1:17); it is for the sake of the present that sins earlier committed were forgiven. God showed **forbearance** because of the death of Jesus yet to come. And again, v 26 states the reason Christ was set forth as propitiation—it was **to prove . . . that he himself is righteous.** The conclusion of v 26 is thus a variation on the theme of v 25c. So, the justice of God depends on Christ the propitiation. It is to the present, to **gift,** to grace, to Christ, that has tied his justice.

■ **3:27-31**   **Questions and Answers**

QUESTION: **Then what becomes of our boasting?**

ANSWER: If righteousness is not on the basis of deeds, but appears **as a gift,** we are then no **better off,** and boasting (cf. 2:17) is excluded.

QUESTION: **On what principle . . . of works?**

ANSWER: **No, but on the principle of faith.**

QUESTION: Why should the principle of faith exclude boasting, but not the principle of works? Because not all would be eliminated if the principle of works excluded boasting? Because Paul has shut the door to doing "works of the law"?

ANSWER: Because the law is excluded from the revelation of righteousness, **for we hold that a man is justified by faith apart from works of law.** (Here occurred Luther's famous interpolation of the word "alone"—"by faith *alone*," cf. again Gal. 2:16.)[19]

"Or," Paul asks in v 29, "would you prefer a tribal deity, seeing that the law erects barriers between Jew and Gentile?" Paul's answer to the effect that God is also God of the Gentiles rests on the assumption that to be God of all, to justify **as a gift** through faith **in Christ,** is all of a piece. If God is one, that is, God of all, he will justify all alike through the instrumentality of faith (the RSV: **he will justify the circumcised on the ground of their faith and the uncircumcised through their faith,** is a distinction without a difference, occasioned by the use of two different prepositions in the Greek which in this instance have the same force: "by faith").[20]

To the question, is it all over with the law now; are we to embrace an anti-law position? Paul responds with another **By no means!** then adds, **we uphold the law.** That is to say, we uphold the law, not as a means to justification, but as agent of the **knowledge of sin** (3:20). To exclude is also to define, thus to uphold. But there is more to be said; there is also something to be included—the law is kept, and "by faith." But a law kept by faith, without constraint and thus without division in the self, a law "upheld" and to the point of an exhaustion of its possibilities in a radically new existence, is to Paul's mind a law of a radically different sort!

■ 4:1-25 Abraham's Faith

4:1-8 Abraham Justified

To support his thesis, Paul now turns to the example of Abraham. The apostle has taken to his pulpit again, and the question about Abraham is put to those **under the law.** So the audience has not changed since 2:17. Why all this Jewish concern in a letter to a Roman congregation? Or, is the "Jewish" argument pertinent also to Gentiles?

If we allow the interpolation omitted by the RSV—"what did Abraham find?"—then Genesis 18:3 seems to have been in

Paul's mind ("My lord, if I have found favor in your sight, do not pass by your servant"), and the way for **gift** in vv 4 and following already prepared. The "our" in **Abraham our forefather** gets its proper interpretation here! What the patriarch found or did or experienced is qualified by the **justified** in v 2 (note the use of the passive voice—the dice are loaded), so that if Abraham had a boast it was not **before God!** How then was it with Abraham—**what does the Scripture say?** Paul answers in a word which played a large role in late Judaism, though not in the Christian community before him (cf. e.g. 1 Macc. 2:52).

The reply, afterwards three times repeated, is from Genesis 15. In a vision, the paradox of Abraham's childlessness and God's promise to make of him a great people is heightened by God's command that Abraham leave his tent and gaze at the stars: "So shall your descendants be" (Gen. 15:5). Leaving the patriarch tested to the limit of his endurance and staring at the sky, the narrator turns to the reader and describes Abraham as "fixing himself on Yahweh," concluding with the terse remark that God marked down such trust for righteousness.

The aptness of this narrative for Paul's argument is obvious. Abraham's faith, never described but only asserted, was passive —it was merely a listening and looking. And the "reckoning of righteousness" occurred solely on the ground of Abraham's consent. For the writer of Genesis 15, and so for Paul, it is only in that negative, passive submission to the promise that any relationship to God can exist. This is how it was with Abraham, this is what he "found."

In v 4, Paul states his position in the negative, and in v 5 in the positive, but with one great, alarming addition: "Faith" is now faith in **him who justifies the ungodly.** This is a bolder variation on the phrase, **I have already charged that all men . . . are under the power of sin** in 3:9. Obviously, the reference is not to Abraham's cultic impiety, nor to his definition of God. Learning of God's intention toward Sodom and Gomorrah, Abraham had exclaimed: "Far be it from thee to do such a thing, to slay the righteous with the wicked, so that the righteous fare as the wicked" (Gen. 18:25). But the apostle may have had the Genesis passage in mind precisely because allowing the wicked to fare as the righteous belonged to *his* definition of God!

In vv 6-8, Paul turns briefly aside from the story of Abraham to a rabbinic argument from silence. Since the Psalter mentions nothing of works, "David" may also be rallied in support! By attaching Psalm 32 to the Abraham narrative Paul's argument moves from the particular to the universal. In Genesis 15:6, it was *Abraham's* faith which was reckoned for righteousness. Here, by virtue of the Psalm superscription which lacks reference to any specific person, the experience of the singer corroborates the general principle first set down. The blessing on the one whose transgression is "forgiven," and sin "covered," to whom the Lord "imputes not iniquity"—and all this despite the acknowledgment of guilt, indeed, all this constituting his "virtue" or righteousness—is a blessing all should come to share.

4:9-12 Abraham's Faith and Circumcision

Now the theme of 2:25ff. is dealt with from a new perspective, and from Scripture. In effect saying, "let's get the passage before us again," Paul returns to his text in Genesis 15:6, and like a rabbi lays stress on every detail of the sequence in the Old Testament narrative. In v 10 he asks: "How then was the blessing reckoned to him—while circumcised or uncircumcised?" Again, the question is "prejudiced" (note the passive: **was reckoned),** and to it Paul replies that the blessing came first, before Abraham had done anything. Indeed, Abraham received circumcision as a sign of what he already possessed in uncircumcision.

In v 11 Paul may be alluding to Genesis 17:10-11, a passage to which he makes direct reference later in 4:17-18, and which combines various traditions about the covenant of God with

Abraham. Following vv 1-8, which describe what God will do and which combine the change of name from "Abram" to "Abraham" with the making of the covenant, the document turns to the act required of Abraham as a sign of his acceptance of the divine mercy. The author of Genesis 17 may be preoccupied with Israel's worship regulations, but he would have agreed with Paul that Abraham's circumcision followed and thus added nothing materially to the covenant "cut" between himself and God. The sense of the passage is that Abraham's circumcision is not a legal performance by which the patriarch becomes signatory to a treaty, but is rather a witness to God's mercy and a sign of its acceptance.

This view which makes the Genesis writer such a fit source for Paul is all the more striking since he constructs his narrative in a period when the great cultic rites could no longer be observed communally and a "personal decision" was required of the individual or family. Whether or not the writer's attitude toward circumcision was influenced by an older, "prophetic" element anchored in the tradition, the fact remains—for him as for Paul, circumcision was only a **sign or seal,** a witness to what Abraham had already received.

In the latter half of v 11, Paul then states the purpose or result of this "reception"—that Abraham might be father of those who in a state of uncircumcision are yet believers, in order that righteousness might be reckoned to them. Having laid the axe to a Jewishness or circumcision which is "external and physical" (2:28), what other alternative is there? The progression in the argument is as follows: Abraham believed God; his faith was reckoned for righteousness; it was reckoned to him while in uncircumcision, that he might be father of all who believe while in uncircumcision, and father of the circumcised who share the faith which Abraham had while uncircumcised! The argument here is anticipated in Galatians 3, though there the story of Abraham is first applied to Gentile faith, whereas here to the faith of both Jew and Gentile.

4:13-17a The Promise to Abraham

In this section Paul gives the reason why Abraham was reckoned righteous while uncircumcised: **The promise . . . did not come through the law.** The law creates distinctions; it cannot embrace the cosmos; it leaves the promise half fulfilled. For this reason, Abraham cannot be **our father** through the law, and the promise must be **through the righteousness of faith.**

Paul may be alluding here to Genesis 22 which, like Genesis 17, has been lifted from its original, ceremonial context which may have legitimized the substitution of animal for human sacrifice. The "oracle" in Genesis 22 follows God's summons to Abraham to sacrifice his only heir, and, more terrifying still, to live without the promise and the covenant. Once Abraham has stood the test, the promise is repeated that his descendants shall be as numerous as the stars of the heaven and the sands of the shore, or, to use Paul's summary, shall **inherit the world.** If indeed Paul is referring to the Genesis "oracle" here, and not merely to the Abraham story in general, he and his source agree that God's promise cannot be retained by virtue of any legal title or with the help of any human demand--**the promise . . . did not come through the law.** God's promise may only be kept by acknowledging it as a sheer, pure gift; by enduring God's apparent contradiction of himself; by giving up the promise; by allowing it to be torn from history, and striking out on a path of God-forsakenness. Paul hopes to awaken in his reader the ancient recognition that Israel must root its existence in the will of God who in his freedom allowed Isaac to live, for **the promise . . .** (came) **through the righteousness of faith.**

Paul then in v 14 enunciates the principle that a promise on the basis of law and a promise on the ground of faith are mutually exclusive. Indeed, a promise on the basis of law is no promise at all. (In contrast to the RSV, the following reading is to be preferred: "If the heirs are such because of the law, faith is null and the promise void"). Adherence to law is one thing, but a righteousness by way of the law is another (cf. v 16).

Paul gives support to his axiom in the curious statement of v 15 that **the law brings wrath, but where there is no law there is no transgression.** What does this mean? If Paul is referring to a time or situation in which the law had not yet emerged, and in which transgression did not exist, or was not counted, then he is in clear contradiction to the Old Testament which refers to a reckoning and punishment of pre-Mosaic sins—Cain, the flood, Sodom and Gomorrah! But the argument is not historical. It is legal: Where there is law, there is wrath because of transgression; but law, transgression, and wrath are not the soil of promise or inheritance. If the promise to Abraham came by virtue of his obedience to the command, then the promise was given in exchange for a deed, and was no promise at all. For where there is law, wrath, and transgression, there is no faith, promise, or inheritance—these are mutually exclusive. Since God will not place us under his wrath, but will give us the inheritance, he has not bound it to law, but made faith the means of its fulfillment. Now the promise rests on God's grace. Now it is sure.

In v 16, Paul recapitulates his arguments from vv 11 onward. The strength of the promise to Abraham rests on grace, that is, by **faith.** Law, however, cannot secure the promise because it sets limits to the promise. The first 16 verses of Chapter 4 contain essentially two arguments. The first is that Abraham achieved nothing but was reckoned righteous prior to his circumcision, and is thus father of the uncircumcised who believe, or of the circumcised who believe as he did. The second argument is that the promise to Abraham is a promise to **inherit the world.** For this reason, the promise must be "by faith." The law, however, creates distinctions, so that if the promise is not "by faith," neither is the inheritance. But the promise is "through faith"! (In v 16, the RSV introduces the **promise** earlier on than does the Greek which reads: "Thus by faith, that it might be according to grace, so that the promise might stand firm.") Believing Jew and Gentile both trace their ancestry to Abraham; but with the former, the paternity is dual.

Paul brings the section to a close with a direct quotation from the narrative merely alluded to in 4:11: "I have made you the father of a multitude of nations" (Gen. 17:5). If the author of Genesis 17 thought to limit the interpretation of that "multitude" to Israel and her proselytes (unlike, say, the author of Gen. 15:7ff., who links Abraham's call to a hope far beyond Israel's confines), Paul's reference to the great ceremonial document here exposes an element in the tradition which it hoped to keep under wraps, but could not suppress, that is, the promise that Abraham would be **father of us all.** Again, the argument is the same in Galatians 3 and Romans 4: "There is neither Jew nor Greek, there is neither slave nor free, there is neither male nor female; for you are all one in Christ Jesus. And if you are Christ's, then you are Abraham's offspring, heirs according to promise" (Gal. 3:28-29).

4:17b-22 Reprise: Abraham's Faith

In v 17b, Paul again describes the object and content of Abraham's faith: **The God . . . who gives life to the dead and calls into existence the things that do not exist.** The extent to which the narrative of the sacrifice or "binding" of Isaac in Genesis 22 influenced early Christian description of Christ's death can be seen from contexts in which a New Testament author refers to the Abraham story (cf. e.g., Heb. 11:19). But that influence can be traced beyond those contexts, e.g., in Paul's description of God as the one who "chose . . . things that are not, to bring to nothing things that are" (1 Cor. 1:28; cf. also 2 Cor. 1:9, in which Paul's designation of God is set in a context reminiscent of the Abraham story. Cf. v 18, **In hope he believed against hope,** with Paul's word in 2 Cor. 1:8-9: "We were so utterly, unbearably crushed that we despaired of life itself. Why, we felt that we had received the sentence of death; but that was to make us rely not on ourselves but on God who raises the dead.") These names for God as the one who **calls into existence the things that do not exist** or who **gives life to the dead** occur in extra-biblical Jewish literature, and their combination has a striking parallel in 2 Maccabees 7:23, 28-29:

> The creator of the world, who shaped the beginning of man and devised the origin of all things, will in his mercy give life and breath back to you again. . . . Look at the heaven and the earth and see everything that is in them, and recognize that God did not make them out of things that existed. Thus also mankind comes into being. . . . Accept death, so that in God's mercy I may get you back again.

In v 18, Paul describes the manner in which Abraham believed—**in hope . . . against hope.** (Note the correspondence of the *how* of Abraham's faith—**in hope . . . against hope,** with the *object* of his faith described in 17b—**the God . . . who gives life to the dead.**) This verse also yields the *content* of Abraham's faith: **That he should become the father of many nations.** If in 4:3, 9, 22, 23, Paul's interest lay in the note of the Genesis author to his reader following the complaint and oracle in the lament (Gen. 15:6), here his interest is in the word of the oracle itself: "Look toward heaven, and number the stars . . . so shall your descendants be."

Verse 19, like 18a, accents the *manner* in which Abraham believed—**He did not weaken in faith when he considered his own body** . . . (or, "with no weakness in his faith, he considered his own body, etc.") and again, as in vv 17b and 18a, the *how* of Abraham's faith corresponds with its *object:* **The God . . . who gives life to the dead!** Verse 20 then furnishes the negative parallel to v 18, and again in reference to *manner:* **No distrust made him waver . . . but he grew strong in his faith as he gave glory to God.** This verse is highly reminiscent of 1:20, and may

form its positive counterpart—Abraham, while in uncircumcision, Abraham the "Gentile," **perceived God's eternal power
and deity,** and gave thanks! In v 21, the manner, object, and
content of Abraham's faith, treated in vv 17b-20, are all com-
bined: He was **fully convinced that God was able to do what
he had promised.** In the last verse of the reprise, Paul again
states the reason for Abraham's justification, once more concluding with the text from Genesis 15:6.

4:23-25 Recapitulation of the Theme in Chapter 4

Now Paul reiterates the theme of vv 11, 12, and 16: We are
that world which Abraham should inherit, since **the words, "it
was reckoned to him," were written not for his sake alone, but
for ours also.** For Paul it was not only an *understanding* of what
once occurred which gave the past its meaning for the present
(cf. Luke 24:31-32). It was not only that in light of the new the
old derived its true significance. It was not only that the old
had occurred *because* of the new, and thus remained inferior
to it. It was not only that the old took on meaning for the present because it foreshadowed the new. Paul did not plunder the
Old Testament for every conceivable prediction of the event
of Jesus Christ—though indeed the riddle of the death of its
Messiah had forced the primitive community before him back
into the Old Testament for its explanation. With all his subordination to the ancient texts, and despite the similarity of his
method of interpretation with that of late Judaism, for Paul
the new had gathered the old into itself, had recreated it, so
that the "once" became the "now." This consciousness, this recognition in Paul furnishes the explanation for his reading of
the Old Testament summed up in that easily misunderstood
phrase, "written . . . for our sake" or "our instruction" (4:23f.;
15:4; cf. 1 Cor. 9:10; 10:11).

Such a reading was indeed a bold stroke, but it was not without precedent. In Judaism as well, God's word, like his name,

71

always "is" or "will be," never "was." The literal character of the long-ago event remained intact, even when "allegorized" (cf. e.g., Gal. 4:21-31). The apostle's reference to Old Testament persons, places and events as "types" or as "typical" (cf. 1 Cor. 10:6) did not deny that they were historical. But for Paul there was only *one* particular, nonrepeatable, unassimilable, concrete event worthy of the name (cf. 1 Cor. 2:2), and whatever else happened took not only its meaning but also its life from it.

Verse 24b supports the statements in vv 23-24a: The raising of Jesus and faith in that event establish what was written as **written not for his** (Abraham's) **sake alone.** So the argument has moved from "type" (Abraham's body, Sarah's womb) to "antitype," and leans toward the Adam-Christ correspondence in Chapter 5. The object of Abraham's faith is next given discrete, explicit description: **Who . . . raised from the dead Jesus our Lord.** The title often occurs in Paul's epistles (cf. Rom. 8:11; 10:9; 1 Cor. 6:14; 15:15; 2 Cor. 4:14 and Gal. 1:1), and with the relative clause in v 25 is part of an ancient Christian creed, for which reason it often appears in the context of faith or confession (4:24; 10:9; 1 Cor. 15:15; 2 Cor. 4:14). The use of the title **our Lord** here not only assigns to God the initiative for the saving event but also marks the continuity between the God of the old and new covenant. (Paul persistently uses the passive voice in referring to the resurrection, as do the synoptic narratives that reflect the ancient tradition on which Paul drew, Mark 16:6; Matt. 28:6 and Luke 24:34.) The God of Abraham, **who gives life to the dead and calls into existence the things that do not exist** (v 17) is the God who **raised from the dead Jesus our Lord.**

It may well be that v 25 once distinguished the cause of Jesus' death (**put to death for our trespasses**) from that of his resurrection (**raised for our justification**). But as used by Paul, the dying and rising is inseparable from the trespass and justification.

Paul's description of the death of Christ here seems to echo two verses from the Septuagint version of Isaiah 53: "But he was wounded for our transgressions, he was bruised for our iniquities" (v 5), and, "he will divide the spoil with the strong, because his soul was delivered up to death . . . he bore the sins of many and was delivered up for their sins" (vv 5 and 12). The "poem" to which these verses belong comprises what is commonly called the "Fourth Servant Song," a report contrasting the humiliation and exaltation of the servant (Isa. 53:1-11a), framed by a word from God (Isa. 52:13-15 and 53:11b-12). The poem differs from the lament or thanksgiving in at least two respects: The one delivered does not tell his own story, and those who report his distress and rescue acknowledge that what occurred to him was caused by their own guilt.

The report is thus in the nature of a creed or confession, and its uniqueness is not due to the idea that the servant's suffering is caused by God himself—this had always been the view of the orthodox and pious in Israel—but that the sins of the nations as well as of Yahweh's own people are atoned for in the suffering of a man whose disfigurement brings him contempt and loathing. How the poet could have advanced to such a thought is as great a mystery as is the identity of the servant himself. Isaiah 53:12, together with 11b which continues the word from God begun in 52:13-15, then gives the reason for the servant's exaltation: "Because his soul was delivered up to death."

Paul found this poem particularly apt. First, it recognizes in the profane and loathsome existence of a common, innocent man the capacity to take the sins of others to himself and thus avert their consequences. Whatever may have occurred in Israel to effect this recognition, for Paul the death of Christ was its supremest truth. (If we keep strictly to a rabbinic interpretation of Isaiah 53, then a Messiah who atones for sin was probably unknown to Judaism before Jesus' time.) Second, the structural line of the creed encompasses an entire existence and thus corresponds to the concept of Christ's suffering as extending throughout his career—in the words of the

Apostles' Creed, "born . . . suffered . . . died . . . was buried" (cf. Rom. 15:3). Finally, since the "Song" conceives the suffering and death of the servant as a single action which abolishes the yearly atonement-offering, it corresponds to the apostle's concept of Christ's death as once-for-all.

RIGHTEOUSNESS AND
CONFORMITY TO CHRIST
5:1—8:36

■ **5:1-5**   **Peace with God**

The solemn and confessional character of 4:23-25, as well as
the content of Chapter 5 mark this chapter as a new beginning.
Paul first wants to show that in justification are contained the
gifts of peace and love (5:1-11). He then contrasts the old and
the new, the way to death and life (5:12-21). Verses 1-5 comprise the first, and vv 6-11 the second half of section one. As
to form, the whole is a psalm of praise. For this reason, a "we-
style" dominates, with the exception of v 7.

The reading of Romans 5:1 has been disputed since earliest
times. Ancient Greek and Latin fathers, orthodox, heterodox
and heretical—Marcion, Origen, Chrysostom, Theodore of
Mopsuestia, Anselm, Tertullian, Ambrose, Oecumenius and
the Vulgate—read: "Let us have peace with God," as do many
modern editors and interpreters. Let Chrysostom speak for
them all:

> What does "let us have peace" mean . . . ? I think it refers
> to our behavior, since Paul penned it after he had said much
> of faith and righteousness on account of works. That none
> might suppose what was said had to do with becoming lax,
> he writes: "let us have peace." In other words, "let us no
> longer sin; let us not return to the former things, for such
> makes war on God." . . . If we are liable for all the things
> from which we were freed through Christ, how much more
> for things in which we shall be able to abide through him?
> Unable to make peace, but once given it to keep peace are

not the same, since the creating is harder than the keeping. But just as the harder thing became easy and was done, so we will be able to do what is easier. . . . It seems to me, not only what is easy is referred to here, but also what is reasonable. For if he reconciled us while we were enemies, it is reasonable for us to remain with those who have been reconciled, and yield him this recompense, lest it seem the clumsy and ignorant have been reconciled to the Father. The force of this is, "have peace among yourselves." [21]

From the standpoint of the external evidence, "let us have peace with God" appears the best attested reading. But it is important to keep in mind that the indicative and subjunctive moods were easily confused in the manuscript tradition (e.g., in 14:19, the better witnesses read the impossible, "we then pursue what makes for peace," an obvious error of the ear). Further, attention to such internal evidence as the immediate context and harmony with Paul's teaching elsewhere tends in the direction of the alternate reading. (In 5:2, Paul writes that **we *have* obtained access,** and in 5:10, **we *were* reconciled.** Indeed, the passives in vv 5, 9, and 10, and the reference to Christ as having died "*while* we were still weak," or *yet* **sinners** in vv 6 and 8, as well as the reference to the reconciliation received through him, all indicate that something has transpired which is out of our hands; only later does Paul refer to what the believers should be and have, for which reason the subjunctive mood is not used till the argument in Chapters 5-8 is complete.) Yet, when all is said and done, the critic's conclusion ultimately depends on the answer given to this question: What has Christ done—reconciled us and thus given us peace? Or, has the reconciliation been won, but is the peace uncertain? To answer "yes" to the latter question is in effect to moralize faith.

The difference between the believer and the unbeliever is not that the one strives after the noble life whereas the other pursues a life of immorality. Moral zeal is not lacking to the unbeliever; it is rather that the unbeliever lacks the power to live the life needed. The accent in Chapters 5-8 is thus not on human endeavor, but on God's gifts. It is clear, justification cannot be interpreted as though it were nothing but a verdict in the "heavenly forum."

Paul's word concerning justification is his first word respecting God's activity in Christ (cf. vv 8 and 9—an intimate connection—and vv 18 and 19!). From that activity, everything flows as consequence. For others in the New Testament collection, there may be other "first words" by which to describe that activity, but for Paul "righteousness," or "justification" is the first word. It is neither a mere "polemical doctrine" nor a smaller declivity within the larger crater of a "Christ-mysticism" or "salvation history," something time-conditioned and provisional, so that one could describe all of Paul's religion without taking notice of it. When it is a matter of describing God's reclaiming what is his, of describing humanity before God and others, no other word will do for Paul. But unless the message of justification is apprehended as the good news that God not merely acquits but heaps on the sinner undeserved riches in abundance, indeed, hammers the sinner into the shape of the One who died and rose, it lies amputated.

That word **peace** in ancient times marked a paradisiacal condition, a peace among the peoples introduced by a humble king, never merely an inner state or condition. "Shalom" is a social concept, and for this reason Paul does not confine it to the unifying of two formerly hostile parties. "Peace" means that life has become life with Christ; it thus marks much more than a "relationship." Whether or not people will ever tire of reducing the whole of the divine activity in Christ to the single denominator of a "new relationship," for Paul **peace with God** spells infinitely more—those who are Christ's are not merely set in a relationship to him, have not merely "taken Jesus as their personal Savior," but are held together by his life! Hence Paul's disciple will write: "For he is our peace" (Eph. 2:14). In characteristically dialectical fashion, Luther comments on the sequence of the words **justified** and **we have peace:**

Note how the apostle does not speak of this spiritual peace ahead of righteousness. He says first, "justified by faith," then "we have peace." . . . Men's perverseness first seeks peace, then righteousness; which is why they never find it. So the apostle points up a beautiful contrast in these words. The righteous man has peace with God, but tribulation in the world because he lives in the spirit. The unrighteousness man has peace in the world, but tribulation from God because he lives in the flesh. But as the spirit is eternal, so will be the peace of the righteous and the tribulation of the unrighteous. And just as the flesh is transitory, so will be the tribulation of the righteous and the peace of the unrighteous.[22]

In v 2, Paul describes the further gifts of justification: **We have obtained access to this grace in which we stand,** and not only that (something is missing here; Paul as is often his wont, expresses his thought in a manner that is grammatically incomplete) but we boast (RSV: **rejoice**) **in our hope of sharing the glory of God.** Paul next writes that we boast in our **sufferings** ("tribulation" was a term often used for the "footsteps of the Messiah," those woes which should precede the final judgment) since suffering produces **endurance, and endurance . . . character, and character . . . hope.** The shape of the argument in vv 2 and 3 is circular—from hope to hope! The intent of the passage is identical to that of 2 Corinthians 10-12, in which Paul speaks of "boasting" in his weakness (2 Cor. 11:30; 12:9).

This suffering or weakness is not a quality adhering to the believer by historical accident. It is the mark of the Crucified reflected in the believer's existence by inner necessity. Life in Christ is discipleship with the Crucified. The risen One is removed from the sphere of suffering, but for the moment weakness is the only reality of fellowship with him, since he still makes his way in the world through those shaped to his suffering. This means that Christian existence, an existence characterized by a dynamic movement toward a goal, is an existence **by faith,** and precisely because weakness and suffering are capable of misinterpretation.

By faith then means that the justified person is at one and the same time the actual person. Either the whole person, the flesh-and-blood-human being, the sinner is justified, or there is no justification; either God makes human existence the scene of his activity or there is no God at work. For, there is no other humanity, no other world to be conceived beyond this humanity, this world; God is present here or he is nowhere; justification occurs on the earth or it occurs not at all.

By faith then means that the essential mark of Christian existence is hiddenness, since its progression from suffering to endurance to character to hope of sharing the glory of God cannot be measured. And again, the event which establishes such existence, renders it hidden in contrast to the apocalyptic vision, or in contrast to the ideal visibly achieved and waiting to be applauded, is the cross of Jesus Christ. For this reason, all boasting beyond a boasting in God is excluded, since nothing achieves visibility but weakness, cross, and death. For Paul, to be justified means nothing at all if not to be the epiphany of the risen Christ in the shape of his suffering. This is his boast!

The climax figure begun with v 3, a device in which each subsequent term takes up the chief word in what precedes, is concluded in v 5, which then yields the underlying reason for this boasting: **hope does not disappoint us, because God's love has been poured** (the verb here denotes a process, not an existing state) **into our hearts.**

Paul's language is an echo of two individual Psalms of lament in Book I of the Psalter. In the first, Psalm 22—together with Psalm 69 the lament most used in all four Gospel accounts of the Passion—the singer attaches to his complaint ("My God, my God, why hast thou forsaken me?") a brief, hymn-like recitation of the history of his people, intended to move Yahweh to intervene on his behalf. The double movement from complaint to retrospection in the first 10 verses of the Psalm suggests a rhythm in the psalmist's mood. His trust sinks, he recalls Yahweh's past deeds; it sinks again, and he remembers once more God's earlier saving work. In the lament of Psalm 25, wisdom-like in its orientation and acrostic in form, the verses cited are an affirmation of confidence ("O my God, in thee I trust," v 2a) and a petition: "Let me . . . let none that wait for thee be put to shame . . . let me not be put to shame, for I take refuge (or, as the Septuagint reads, "I have hoped") in thee" (vv 2b, 3, 20).

If in either Psalm the sudden change of mood following complaints and petitions (cf. Ps. 22:22: "I will tell of thy name to my brethren; in the midst of the congregation I will praise thee") is to be explained in terms of a "salvation-oracle" promising that the complainant will not be put to shame, then the propriety of the quotation is obvious. But what for the psalmist was effected by a word, was for Paul achieved through an event—Jesus Christ, the "salvation-oracle" par excellence (cf. e.g. 2 Cor. 1:20: "For all the promises of God find their Yes in him"). God has his glory now (1:23), but those who are Christ's will come to share it.

If Paul's doctrine of justification hinges on the conviction that **by faith** the disciple of Jesus has come to share his life in hiddenness, cross, and death, it hinges no less on the conviction that the disciple will come to share visibly and unveiled what God will win back from the world he created—**because God's love has been poured into our hearts through the Holy Spirit.** Here, a nod to Homer Rodeheaver, to that alien tradition, from which Norwegians in Chicago, a hundred years from Europe drew a bit of sustenance on Sunday evenings:

> When by his grace I shall look on his face,
> That will be glory, be glory for me!

■ 5:6-11   God's Love

Paul presses toward a description of God's love in vv 6-11. While we were still weak, **at the right time**—not in the time that we make for ourselves, but in God's own good time—

Christ died for the ungodly, for those who do not work but
trust the One who justifies (4:5). The two awkward-looking
phrases in v 7 are best read as taking their meaning from what
precedes and follows. The first phrase in v 7a forms the antithesis to v 6: While we were still weak, at the right time Christ
died for the ungodly. Why, one will hardly die (the future here
describes what might happen under certain conditions) for a
righteous man. High time for the cross! Verse 7b then forms
the antithesis to v 8, which reverses the poles in vv 6 and 7a:
Though perhaps for a good man one will dare even to die. But
God shows his love for us in that while we were yet sinners
Christ died for us. How much more in that love on the cross
than in human deeds of sacrifice! Rabbi Hillel's first of seven
rules, calculated to bring methodological order out of the
chaos of Jewish Scripture interpretation was called "the easy
and the hard," an argument from the lesser to the greater, and
here it has left its trace in Paul.

In vv 9 and 10 the "hard" or "greater" aspect of the argument
is developed: Since . . . we are now justified by his blood, much
more shall we be saved . . . from the wrath. . . . For if while
we were enemies we were reconciled to God . . . much more,
now that (or, because) we are reconciled, shall we be saved by
his life. The reference to his blood in v 9 is to the event of the
cross. Paul would have regarded all talk of the blood of Jesus,
apart from the actual crucifixion, as an offense against the
God who in sovereign freedom made known his final purpose
in this event (the author of Ephesians has the very same thing
in mind when he refers to Christ's "abolishing in his flesh"
the law of commandments and ordinances, Eph. 2:15). The
reference to the death of his Son in v 10 (as well as the reference to his cross in Eph. 2:16) makes that amply clear. Again,
as in 2:5, 8, the wrath of God is not limited to a revelation in the
near future, but is used of a final condemnation at the end of
time from which Christ will deliver the faithful. This description of Jesus' saving work from a negative point of view ap-

pears elsewhere in Paul, e.g., in 1 Thessalonians 1:10 (cf. 5:9).

In vv 9 and 10, Paul accents the "greater" aspect of the argument by including a **much more.** The comparison between what one might do for a righteous or good man and what God has done for us is antithetical, a comparison between what cannot be compared. Since we were *not* righteous (cf. 2:10-18) but rather "weak," "sinners," "enemies," none for whom one would scarcely die or dare to die, what God has done lies beyond contrasting and comparing. Much more! To be justified **by his blood,** reconciled to God **by the death of his Son,** spells our peace with God. (So the verb in v 1 must read: **We have peace with God.**) Reconciliation with God through Christ has been achieved prior to any human recognition of it, indeed, in the teeth of human rebellion against God. This is the obverse side of the priority of the contingent event, and is anticipated in 2 Corinthians 5: "God was in Christ reconciling the world to himself . . . we beseech you on behalf of Christ, be reconciled to God" (vv 19-20).

Finally, in v 11, Paul resumes the boast motif begun in v 2, and in the same elliptical fashion: "And not only that, but we boast in God."

■ 5:12-21   Free from Death for Life

Fast bound in Satan's chains I lay,
Death brooded darkly o'er me,
Sin was my torment night and day;
In sin my mother bore me.
But daily deeper still I fell;
My life became a living hell,
So firmly sin possessed me.

Paul now advances to his Adam-Christ analogy, and as in 3:21-26, the pulpit has been abandoned for the writing desk. In 1 Corinthians 15:21-22, though in abbreviated fashion, and in a quite different context (that of a dispute over the resurrection), Paul anticipates his argument in this section. Here, the argument is set in the context of trespass and gift, and the contrast between these two is heightened by the contrasts in vv 9 and 10.

Sin came into the world through one man. . . . According to Paul's contemporary, Philo, God at creation first made a heavenly creature, a pure soul unburdened with a body, and lofted above law and sin. After this "primal man," the angels or lower powers modeled the man of clay, that "second Adam," a clumsy imitation of the first. But for Paul, as well as for his teachers, the man of clay was the only Adam there ever was and made by God with both his hands! The man of clay came first, and with that assertion all bizarre talk of Adam or Christ as invisible, immaterial and all-souled, is dispensed with and both Adam and Christ are set in the world we know. It makes little difference whether or not we regard Adam as a historical person; the name still stands for a historical occasion—death's entry.

In Genesis 2:17 and 3:12, Adam's sin and punishment are described as lying outside experienced history. God addresses Adam directly, first in the prohibition, for which no reason is given ("of the tree of the knowledge of good and evil you shall not eat," 2:17), then in the curse or sentence of punishment ("in the sweat of your face you shall eat bread till you return to the ground," 3:12). Nowhere else in the Old Testament is the judgment on human mischief so clearly God's, precisely because historical existence as we know it is characterized by ambiguity, and evil as punishment from God can only be believed or denied. Of course, the difference between the Genesis narrator and Paul is that for the former death is relief from drudgery, whereas for Paul and for Judaism between the Testaments, it is the consequence of Adam's sin (cf. the apocryphal Wisdom of Solomon 2:24, or Sirach 25:24; the pseudepigraphical 4 Ezra 7:16ff.; the Syriac Apocalypse of Baruch 48:42ff.

and 54:15-19; the Apocalypse of Moses 32:2; and the Qumran Thanksgiving Hymns, e.g., 5:36f.).

Paul had precedent enough in Judaism for combining the idea of death's entry through Adam with that of death as due to everyone's sin. Even in Genesis, Adam's guilt and punishment are set in the context of all human history, and 4 Ezra says of Adam: "What hast thou done! For though it was thou that sinned, the fall was not thine alone, but ours also," and in the next breath, adds, "Whereas we have done the works that bring death" (7:116-120). But that phrase, **and so death spread to all men because all men sinned,** has more the earmarks of a correction than an addition. For, despite Adam's bringing into the world something that touches all, Adam is not fate and his sin is not imitated (v 14). No principle of solidarity can ever support Augustine's translation: "Sin came into the world through one man . . . *in whom* all sinned." That phrase, **because all men sinned,** cancels out the idea of death by congenital apple poisoning. It harks back to Paul's complaint in 1:18-3:20, and for which he drew support in the law. Here, too, the law is present as silent accuser, for it is on the basis of law that all have sinned. The analogy between Adam and Christ has thus broken down. It is not possible simply to say: "As with Adam, so with Christ," for Adam is not "up to" the analogy. Between him and Christ there stands the law marking him a transgressor, together with all his posterity.

The phrase, **death spread to all men because all men sinned,** is supported by vv 13a and 14: **Sin indeed was in the world before the law was given. . . . Yet death reigned from Adam to Moses, even over those whose sins were not like the transgression of Adam.** But what of v 13b—**sin is not counted where there is no law?** Does it not contradict everything said before and after it? Does it not disconnect law from the real way of things, and thus give Adam a "leg up," making him equal to the analogy? True enough, the law is not needed to prove that sin is everywhere, but if death reigned **from Adam**

to Moses (v 14), then *law there must have been,* before Sinai, before the Torah was given, before sin was **counted,** before men saw in their deaths anything else than release from drudgery. (The difference between Paul and the author of Gen. 2 and 3 is that for the apostle death is not part of the natural order of things, but a terrible frustration of human possibilities, God's revealed wrath in the present as well as a last and final decree.) The law still stands between; the Adam-side of the analogy still limps. The analogy between Adam and Christ is that of opposites, not equals.

In vv 15-17 Paul sharpens the contrast, this time not from the viewpoint of law, but of justification. On the side of Adam, **transgression;** on the side of Christ, the **free gift** (v 15a)—because if many died by the transgression of the one, **much more** did the free gift abound for the many by the grace of the other (v 15b). On the one hand, judgment follows the one man's sin to condemnation; on the other, the free gift follows many transgressions to righteousness (v 16)—because if by one man's transgression death reigned through the one, much more will those who receive grace and the free gift reign in life through the other (v 17). On the one side, deeds, activity, people at work! On the other, free gift, passivity, and the justifying God at work. On the one hand, the person as subject, as sinner; on the other, the person as object, recipient of grace.

Adam is no match for Christ. For this reason Paul dare not simply write that just as the decree of death was handed down from Adam, and yet all chose to share his rebellion, so the life which is in Christ comes as gift, but as gift which all must receive. There is no such unresolved tension in Paul—human activity is no match for grace.

After wrecking the analogy and hammering away at inequality, after that one great ellipse in vv 12b-17, the thought begun in v 12a is finally completed in v 18: **As sin came into the world through one man and death through sin, and so death spread to all men because all sinned . . . so one man's act of**

righteousness leads to acquittal and life for all men, and its support is given in v 19, with its reference to Jesus' story.

Why the analogy, why the comparison, when the Adam-side of the likeness is reduced to caricature? No other "type" on earth would fare any better, since "Adam" spells human history, our history, the arena into which death makes its entry. But not only death. Since the law stands between, cripples the analogy between Adam and Christ, renders it antithetical, the law announces Adam, sin, and death as the place where grace and gift appear: **Law came in, to increase the trespass; but where sin increased, grace abounded all the more, so that, as sin reigned in death, grace also might reign. . . .** (vv 20-21)!

> Utterly separated by the contrast of what is encountered in them, but indissolubly united . . . in that the sin and death of the one and the righteousness of the other cover the whole range of human life in all its dimensions.[23]

In v 19 Paul may be alluding to Isaiah's "Fourth Servant Song," specifically to Isaiah 53:11b, which together with v 12 continues the word from Yahweh framing the report of the servant. If v 12 gives the reason for the servant's exaltation, the "oracle" in v 11b makes clear *in what* that exaltation consists: "My servant [shall] make many to be accounted righteous; and he shall bear their iniquities."

There is a striking difference between Paul's description of the effects of Christ's obedience here and in the great hymn of Philippians 2. There, Jesus' obedience results in his exaltation to lordship. Whatever implication that exaltation may have for the life of believers is left to inference, or waits to be spelled out in the Pauline "autobiography" in Philippians 3. But here Christ's obedience is intimately linked to the existence of the believer: **By one man's obedience many will be made righteous.** The difference may lie in the fact that Paul was not the author of the Philippians hymn, which, despite the possible apostolic revision ("obedient unto death, even

death on a cross," Phil. 2:9) still seems to subordinate the theme
of Christ's passion to his exaltation. For Paul, these are not two
stages in a sequence but rather a single event. The section
closes with the colophon: **Through Jesus Christ our Lord.**

■ 6:1-23 Free from Sin for Righteousness
6:1-14 Buried with Christ

To me he said, "Stay close to me,
I am your rock and castle.
Your ransom I myself will be;
For you I strive and wrestle;
For I am yours, and you are mine,
And where I am you may remain;
The foe shall not divide us."

The "abounding" of grace where sin "increased" in 5:21 leads
directly to the question in 6:1. It is *the* question, raised
obliquely in 3:8, but now put squarely: Since deeds are excluded, why not moral laxity? If grace does not hinge on what
I do, indeed, if grace has the upper hand, why not continue
in sin so as to demonstrate its power?

> "I will explain to you now how everything stands. I tell you
> that people may sin up to the age of thirty; but then it is time
> to turn to God, do you see? And when you have once learned
> to surrender your thoughts completely to God, you may sin
> again, for that is a sin of a special kind—do you follow?" [24]

Following his usual expletive, **By no means!** Paul lays down
a general axiom: A death has occurred. The possibility of moral
laxity is out of the question because the existence which allows
for such a possibility has come to an end. So it is not a matter
of "ought" or "must" or "should not," but of "does not"! Paul
then refers to baptism. Because of the connection between baptism and justification, the one may be used to interpret the

other: "You ought to know that baptism into Christ Jesus, or into his name, is in actuality a baptism into his death." The first half of that statement is no doubt pre-Pauline; the second half is Paul's "correction" or qualification.

Prior to Paul, Christians had somehow hit upon the notion of transferring life "with Christ" at his second coming to the act of baptism as granting a divine and glorious existence in the here and now. For this reason the Corinthians set such great store by the officiants at their baptism—they transmitted the cosmic, divine life—to which Paul replied: "Thank God I baptized none of you . . . !" (1 Cor. 1:12-14). Paul, with an eye to the cross as touchstone of the faith, altered the pattern, bent the idea to the mundane, to the believer's life; forced it to read that life with Christ, however much the future penetrated the present, was in essence still a daily suffering, and baptism a "dying with Christ."

In combating behavior inappropriate to the Christian **walk,** Paul will use one of two types of argument, each derived from the context of the baptismal renewal. In the one type, the accent is on what has occurred to the believers in their baptism and thus ill suits the behavior indulged in or contemplated. From this may follow a series of appeals, as here in Chapter 6 (vv 12, 13 and 19). In the other type, the stress is on the behavior to be shunned or adopted, and often in the setting of a catalog of vices or virtues (cf. 1:29ff. and 12:9ff.).

In the one instance, there is reference to "putting off" and "putting on." Galatians 3:27 yields the closest parallel to our verse: "As many of you as were baptized into Christ have put on Christ." In the other instance, the accent is often, though not always, on abstention from lusts, signaled in the term "immorality." This latter type has been termed a Christian "code," back of which lies the idea of the church as a neo-Levitical community, based on the Holiness Code of Leviticus 17-26. Apart from the question as to whether or not actual written manuals underlie the material, the first type may originally have been addressed to catechumens about to receive baptism, and the second to those who had already received it. With its description of what has occurred to believers in their baptism, with its reference to the **old self** (v 6) and to **newness of life** (v 4), Romans 6 seems to fall in the first category.

Paul, however, applies either type to his Christian readers. Further, in Paul's hands the catechetical material does not exclude the Christian from the world. The purity of the community does not consist in cultic separation, but in incorporation into the Body of Christ. This means that the "Christian ethic" is legitimized by a new authority, the Lord, and its exercise applied to the other, the neighbor. This eliminates the distinction between things sacred and profane, and concentrates on their *use* for the other. This is a more radical posture than that of Paul's Jewish or Gentile-Christian opponents. It leaves intact whatever is natural or good in Judaism or Hellenism. *Use* is all-important, because Christian faith is not a new moral doctrine, but a new life—righteousness, justification as life in Jesus Christ, hidden though inevitably hastening toward its goal.

Paul's argument is that the believers have been put to death with Christ. The assumption here is that the "I" is never self-contained, but has its identity and its life only in community. The Stoic, with his notion of animate creation as a single organism or "body," indwelt by Reason or Soul, need not have furnished Paul his language or conceptuality. There is ample evidence that Judaism also conceived existence as corporate. For the Jew, to be "cut off" from his community constituted a fate far worse than a cessation of biological functions. Hence, even in death he had to be placed "with the fathers" (bench-graves discovered in Jerusalem attest to the practice of communal burial even past the time of Jesus). The same idea is present when Yahweh addresses the nation of Israel as "my servant," or when Hosea likens the entire people to an unfaithful wife— the list of such figures is endless.

Paul's reference in 12:5 to the believers as **one body in Christ,** a designation frequently occurring in the Corinthian correspondence (cf. 1 Cor. 6, 10, 11, 12, and 15), his reference to their existence **in Christ** or **in the Lord** reflects the same concept of corporate existence and corresponds to his description of Christians elsewhere as a "new creation" (Gal. 6:15; 2 Cor. 5:17) or a "new lump" (1 Cor. 5:7)—a theme appropriated and expanded in the description of the "new man" (Eph. 2:15; 4:24 and Col. 3:10). For Paul that Body into which believers have been incorporated was established by the historical event of Christ's death (cf. 6:6; 14:9 and 1 Cor. 12:13).

Occasionally, a scholar commenting on Romans 6:1-4 suggests that the believer's participation in Christ's death is "ideal" or "objective." But the position of the phrase, **we who died** (v 2), and its expansion in the phrase, **we were buried therefore with him** in v 4, indicate that for Paul the relation of the baptized to the death of Christ is real, actual. Further, the little conjunction **so that,** and the untranslated correlative adverb in v 4, make clear that it is only by virtue of an actual death that real life can occur. It is an error to interpret Paul's understanding of baptism as analogous to Christ's death, or of participation in Christ's death as merely "ideal" or "objective," and in this fashion to suit the relation between the baptized and Christ's death to a notion of justification conceived merely as a celestial transaction. (Cf. *The Living Bible* translation of v 5: "and so you died with him, so to speak, when he died"!)

Does the latter part of v 4 (**so that as Christ was raised from the dead,** etc.) reveal a contradiction in Paul's thought? Is he attempting to wed two theologies here, the one characterized by dying with Christ, the other by walking in newness; the one, perhaps, reflecting a "sacramental" theology, urging present sinlessness, the other a "Spirit" theology regarding sinlessness as a future goal? And, is the way out of this dilemma simply to regard Paul as viewing what the believer has received in baptism from two points of view—"under the aspect of the divine" a dying, and "under the aspect of the human" a walking in newness of life?

The relationship between what the believer already possesses, and what the believer will possess is to be explained in terms of the dynamic quality of the new which does not remain static but involves a "walking." This character of the new life prevents Paul from viewing participation in Christ's resurrection as identical to participation in his death. He thus corrects the conception in Colossians 2:12, according to which believers in their baptism "were also raised with him." [25]

Finally, the problem does not lie in the contrast between what believers now possess and what they will possess in the future, but rather in that which hinders them from reaching their goal. Here is where the contradiction belongs—not within the new itself! From this point of view, the purpose of Paul's exhortations—those revelations of the possibilities in which the new life already won can further manifest itself—is not to indicate the incompleteness of the believers' present possession, but to encourage them in their warfare against what tends to hinder them. For Paul, the sacrament did not guarantee immunity. Most of Israel, "baptized into Moses" and drinking from "the supernatural Rock" was "overthrown" in the wilderness (1 Cor. 10:1-5). Paul's preaching of justification was thus a continual call to appropriate the gift given in baptism ever anew.[26]

If the conjunction introducing the phrase, **we too might walk in newness of life** only indicates purpose, then the dying is somehow not complete. But result is also aimed at here—the distinction between the passives in vv 3-4 and the subjunctive mood in v 4b, **we . . . might walk,** ought not be missed. Rather than opening the door to moral striving as supplement to the death in baptism, use of the subjunctive marks the character of a new existence which has not yet achieved its goal.[27] Such existence, however, will surely reach its destination—that

is the force of the phrase, **in newness of life** (indeed, v 5 makes
that crystal clear).

The term "likeness" in v 5 ("for if we have been united by
the likeness with his death"; RSV: **if we have been united with
him in a death like his),** an occasion for great confusion and
misinterpretation, is parallel to the phrase, **by baptism** in v 4,
and notes the similarity between the plunging and emerging
of the baptized with Christ's death and resurrection. The term
translated **united** in v 5 is thus not connected with the term
"likeness," but rather with the phrases, "his death" and "his
resurrection" (RSV: **in a resurrection like his).** The baptized, by
means of what they have experienced in the baptism, have become participants in Christ's death.[28] Now it is clear that the
"walking" in v 4 does not refer to a situation which *might* exist
provided certain conditions are fulfilled, but rather to a situation which does indeed exist: We do indeed walk **in newness
of life,** and we shall indeed be raised!

In his description of what has occurred to believers in their
baptism, Paul has heaped up the figures—"dead," "buried,"
"united with him in his death"—and now in v 6 adds another:
"Our old man was crucified." That term "man" (RSV: **self!**)
makes clear Paul has corporate, not individual existence in
mind. The "old man" to which Paul refers only here, a designation taken up and expanded after him (cf. Eph. 4:22 and Col.
3:9), belongs to that cluster of terms which he uses to describe
human existence as in community, in this instance as a corporate existence enslaved to sin, death, and the law, elsewhere
called existence "in Adam" (1 Cor. 15:22). Accordingly, when
Paul describes "our old man" as crucified with Christ, he is referring to an action completed in the past. Galatians 2:20 and
5:24, the closest parallels to our verse, express the same
thought: "I have been crucified with Christ; it is no longer I
who live . . . those who belong to Christ Jesus have crucified
the flesh with its passions and desires," but without use of
"body" language.

When next Paul writes that this crucifixion occurred with the result that the "body of sin" (RSV: **sinful body**) might be destroyed, he is merely expressing in negative fashion what he had stated earlier in v 4. This same negative aspect is repeated in 6:12 and in 8:13—the "old man," the old "I" or "flesh" has been crucified, but as long as the believers live in this world sin requires constant fending off. It is not the physical body as such which Paul calls his readers to throw off—he is unable to conceive existence now or in the resurrection apart from the physical. Indeed, such existence spells "nakedness," a being "unclothed" (2 Cor. 5:3-4), hence the "body" of the believers is to be redeemed (8:23). What is to be put off is rather an existence marked, characterized, and stamped by sin.[29]

Paul's reference in the singular to that against which the believers struggle—"the body of sin," "the deeds of the body"—again has its explanation in his idea of existence as in community. Thus, though the "old man" and the "body of sin" denote existence as corporate, the terms are not identical. The "old man" has been done to death. The struggle against the "body of sin" is the struggle of the new, redeemed "man." Any interpretation of Paul that construes the "old" and "new man" in terms of two "natures" in the believer offends against the apostle's use of the one or other term to describe existence in community. In his lectures on Romans, Luther does not refer to the coexistence of the "old" and "new man," but when elaborating on the meaning of baptism in the Large Catechism, he clearly assumes it.[30] This virtual identification of the "old man" with the "body of sin," and thus the failure to identify the "new man" with the Body of Christ results from inattention to the terms "old" and "new" as expressive of a totality of existence— a curious error, in light of Luther's understanding of justification and the renewal as simultaneous, thus of justification as a being conformed to Christ.

The phrase, **that we might no longer be enslaved to sin** in v 6b no more introduces possibility than does the phrase, **as**

Christ was raised, or **we too might walk** in v 4. What characterized the "body of sin" or **sinful body** was its servitude to sin, not its servant-character as such. The Christian is also servant (1:1). Next, v 7 is to be read in light of the "old man's" crucifixion **with him** in v 6, the death **with him** in v 8, and Christ's death **to sin** in v 10. Paul, then, is not stating a general principle (death *as such* does not free from sin) but rather reiterating that the believers' death *with Christ* in baptism has set them free from death. That phrase, **with Christ** in v 8 does not denote an *imitation*—it is shorthand for everything stated earlier in the chapter: **baptized into Christ Jesus . . . baptized into his death.** It is a summary word which needs interpretation, an interpretation which preserves the once-for-allness of Christ's death as well as the distinction between Christ and the believer. **We believe,** Paul continues, **that we shall also live with him.** In v 9 the apostle cannot say of Christ that **he who has died is freed from sin** (v 7), but he can refer to death's lordship over him. Within sin's reach, though not its slave, he died to sin **once for all** (v 10), a word which prepares the way for v 11.

In v 11, the result clause of v 4 (**so that . . . we too might walk**) gets its explanation. The call to **consider yourselves** is not merely an appeal to think in a certain fashion, but a summons to acknowledge the reality: "You are such, come to terms with it!" The believers' death and life, however, are **in Christ.** That is the one condition, apart from which there is no "considering." (This concept of existence in community is clearly reflected in Paul's reference to his own death to the law as a death with Christ in Gal. 2:19, or in his reference to the believers as having died because of the death of the One for all in 2 Cor. 5:15. Even the curious, "rabbinic" exposition of the promise of a "seed" to Abraham in Gal. 3:16 serves the same motif. Because the promise to the patriarch was of the seed which is Christ, and because we are Christ's, we are Abraham's offspring and heirs.)

From v 12 it is clear that the alternative to moral laxity is not moral striving. The reason is simply that the content of the indicative and of the imperative is the same. Why then the imperative? It is proof that a real death has occurred! If not, there is no point to it—servitude to sin is the only possibility, and one does not call a servant to reject his servanthood. But does this not suggest that what has occurred is really only a "metaphysical basis for an ethical reformation of life," or worse, that we are dealing with two theologies here? The answer is that the appeal in v 12 corresponds to the phrase, **consider yourselves** in v 11: "Face up to the reality!" What might prevent one from doing so? The mortality of one's body (that "body of sin," or **sinful body**), the fact that we still live in this world which makes possible an obedience to the **passions.** So it is not a summons to "become what you are," but a summons to disallow that to which we have died, which does not exist for us who are **in Christ.**

The same thought is expressed in v 13, though made more specific: **Do not yield your members to sin as instruments of wickedness.** For Paul, the possibility of allowing the non existent is always present! The language of the verse is that of warfare. In the verse following, the future tense in the phrase, **sin will have no dominion over you,** does not express what might occur given the conditions, but rather marks an event about to take place—a death has occurred, therefore sin *will not* reign! The Pauline imperatives are a call to recognize what *is*, not a summons to be what one is not yet or might be.

Despite the marginal references in standard Greek texts of the New Testament, the warning to Cain in what has been called the most difficult verse in Genesis (Gen. 4:7), has little in common with Paul's appeal. Whatever the origin or purpose of that word in Genesis 4, its present meaning is that Cain, morose and petulant at God's approval of his brother's sacrifice, may lift his face again if he does well, but if not, "sin is couching at the door." Everything depends on Cain—"sin's desire is for you, but you must master it." Paul's argument moves in the opposite direction—everything depends on God, and for this reason sin shall not reign. If the verse in Genesis 4 is a later editor's interpolation, intended to allay the suspicion that God's regard for Abel's offering was capricious by raising the question of Cain's moral character, then Paul might well have used the unexpurgated edition of the narrative in the Isaac-Ishmael, Jacob-Esau section of Romans 9. The decree to which Romans fleshes out ideas expressed in earlier epistles can again be seen from the fact that the argument in Chapters 6-8 appears in abbreviated form in Galatians 5.

6:15-23 Bound to Righteousness

Paul now repeats the question put in v 1. If the imperatives are a summons to moral striving, and not rather a call to recognize a truth of Christian existence, why the question a second time? Clearly, Paul anticipates repeated objection. Because he does not regard the imperative as a summons to moral effort, his opponents see the danger of moral laxity. Again, the same expletive is used here as in answer to the first response in v 2: **By no means!** Servanthood there will be—there is no escape from this truth of existence. The question is only service to whom or what?

Paul's readers have no choice; their servanthood is for righteousness. But what a strange picture of the believer's existence! Once described as dead, buried, "planted" with Christ, they are now spoken of as handed over to a "standard (type) of teaching." Even if the reference is to instruction concerning baptism following conversion, the description of the change in lordship from sin to a "standard of teaching" is odd. The phrase may be traditional, pre-Pauline, used for the sake of its association with baptism, and on which Paul performed a bit of minor surgery by adding **to which you were committed** (delivered). With that addition, the phrase becomes a virtual cipher for the One at the heart of that teaching, and to whom the Romans have now been delivered.[31]

In v 19 Paul writes: **I am speaking in human terms.** Does this mean that vv 16-18 with all their talk of yielding and hearkening are written from a "horizontal perspective," from the attempt to describe in human fashion what God has done? Curious, then, that a "hearkening from the heart" should be classified as "humanly speaking"! Apparently, there is a way of speaking of faith or existence in Christ which is a concession to the flesh. (RSV: **Because of your natural limitations.** This is the first instance in Romans in which that term *flesh* is used in a pejorative sense; till now it has been used of physical descent, cf. 1:3; 4:1; of what is corporeal, 2:28; or simply of humanity, 3:20. From now on, with but four exceptions—9:3, 5, 8; 11:14—Paul will use the term to characterize what in mankind or its environment is hostile to God, cf. 8:7). Like the terms *law, sin,* and *death,* Paul does not conceive "flesh" only as the totality of human rebellion, but as a transcendent power that holds everyone in its grip. For that reason, as with law, sin, and death, the apostle assigns to "flesh" a personality. The "climate of opinion" from which such peculiar use derives is that of Hellenism or Judaism whose sages could assign a transcendent and personal quality to e.g. "wisdom." The language stems from discontent with describing things in merely quantitative terms or in a fashion which regards an object merely as the sum total of its parts. It is the language of art, poetry, philosophy, and religion.

But why should Paul speak **in human terms** here? In 3:5 he spoke **in a human way,** but there the question was obviously of a human sort. But here? Is he breaking a lance with a theology accepted in the church, but which he nonetheless believes is wide of the mark?

Suppose we link the phrase, **in human terms** to what immediately follows in v 19b: **You once yielded your members** (servants) **to impurity and . . . iniquity,** and **now yield your mem-**

bers (servants) **to righteousness for sanctification.** The usage is certainly not characteristic of Paul, but is one which a later generation took to be eminently Pauline, and thus moralized the revelation of righteousness. The term **sanctification** in v 19 is no more Pauline than the phrase "standard of teaching" in v 17. One might indeed conceive the new life in **human terms,** as obedience to a standard, as yielding one's members to righteousness **for sanctification,** though in reality what the imperative requires has already been accomplished. On that aspect Paul has put all the stress.

Paul next writes that **when you were slaves of sin, you were free in regard to righteousness** (v 20). He might also have written: "Now that you are slaves of righteousness, you are free in regard to sin," but his intent here is to show the futility of servitude to sin—there was no return from allowing sin to reign, "humanly speaking!" Ezekiel 16 contains an allegory of Jerusalem, the ungrateful foundling, whose scorn for God's free act of love cannot annul his eternal will for her good, and whom he will shame by the abundance of the grace he gives her: "Then you will remember your ways, and be ashamed . . . and never open your mouth again because of your shame, when I forgive you all that you have done, says the Lord God" (vv 61, 63). Had Paul this figure in mind? At the core of his argument in this chapter lies that concept of corporate personality, of baptism as into the Body, and it was from that same idea of an entire people incorporated into a single person that Ezekiel's figure grew. Paul shares at least one conviction with that ancient "father of allegory": God has led his readers to this point, and not shame, but conformity to Christ will lead them to receive others till now rejected, just as Jerusalem would some day take Canaanite Sodom for a daughter and acknowledge God to be the One he is.

In v 21b, Paul writes that the end of such servitude is **death.** The term is comprehensive, and spells not merely a cessation of functions adhering to this life, but a judgment beyond the death of this life—corporeality is never annihilated. Verse 22 then contains the antithesis to v 21. One would have expected Paul to rouse his readers here in one last, great summons, for which vv 20ff. might have served as motivation, as the "indicative" waiting for its twin. This is not the case—"you *were* freed," Paul writes, "*made* to serve God; you *have* the reward, and the end *is*, etc." The argument in human terms has been abandoned. The Romans are not called to perform moral gymnastics but to acknowledge the truth of their existence, something vastly different from arriving at a new "self-understanding," predicated on the assumption that the structures of existence remain the same. They have not remained the same! An actual death has occurred; the **but now** at the opening of the verse heralds the new! The final verse in this section states the principle that sin earns death, but life is given **in Christ Jesus our Lord**—the colophon which closes the section (cf. 1:7, etc.).

■ **7:1-25**   **Dead to the Law**
                  for Union with Christ

7:1-6 The Marriage Analogy

My own good works all came to naught,
No grace or merit gaining;
Free will against God's judgment fought,
Dead to all good remaining.
My fears increased till sheer despair
Left only death to be my share;
The pangs of hell I suffered.

The thought of Chapter 6 is not broken off, but illustrated from the marriage bond. Paul singles out his Jewish hearers, **those who know the law,** earlier addressed in 4:1 and 2:17. The argument in Chapter 7, prepared for by the little word-crochet in 6:14 (**not under law but under grace**), is identical to that in Chapter 6, though in regard to another aspect of existence

apart from Christ—adherence to Torah. Only a death can break
the reign of law, just as only a death can break the reign of sin
(6:2). The movement is thus not so much from freedom from
sin to freedom from law, as a treatment of the same theme
from a different perspective, since the idea of servitude to sin
is every bit as evident here as in Chapter 6. (Note the recurrence here of motifs in Chapter 6, of being **destroyed** or **discharged** in 6:6 and 7:6; being under **dominion** or **bound** in 6:9,
14 and 7:1f.; of **return** or "bearing fruit" in 6:21, 22 and 7:4, 5;
and of slavery or service in 6:20, 22 and 7:6. The transition from
you in 7:1, 4 to **we** in 7:4ff. repeats the alternation in Chapter 6.)

**A married woman is bound by law to her husband as long
as he lives; but if her husband dies she is discharged from the
law concerning the husband** (v 2). The same principle is laid
down in 1 Corinthians 7:39, though there the context is not of
law, but of an apostolic counsel in view of the imminent "tribulation." Paul's purpose here is not to protect the sanctity of
marriage, but to illustrate freedom from the law by way of
analogy. The analogy, however, breaks down: Whereas the
husband dies and his wife is free to marry another, Christians
have died to the law so as to be joined to Christ. The illustra-
tion of the principle of the marriage relationship is therefore
executed in only one respect: Now that death has dissolved
their relationship to the law, believers are free for union
with Christ. The analogy breaks down again in v 3: **She will
be called an adulteress if she lives with another man while her
husband is alive. But if her husband dies she is free from that
law. . . .** Why then the analogy? The answer, first, is that the
gospel is in some sense analogous to the law: Like the law, the
gospel has to do with events and occurrences, not feelings.
Second, there is an "ought" to the gospel, just as to the law.
Third, Paul's intent is to indicate that a death disposes of obligation to the law, and finally, the analogy of the marriage relationship makes clear the law's power as well as its limitations.
Its power consists in its binding the woman to it as long as her

husband lives. Only death puts an end to its force (that verb **discharged** in v 2 has an element of finality about it!). While her husband lives, the woman would be "plying a trade" if she were to break the law.

In v 4 Paul draws his conclusion from the analogy: **Likewise, my brethren, you have died** ("were made dead") **to the law through the body of Christ.** The verse summarizes what was said in 6:33ff. of the death, burial, and crucifixion of believers with Christ in baptism. Whatever the origin of that term **body,** and whatever associations it might have conjured up, it *now* takes its definition from what was said of the union of the believer with Christ in Chapter 6. This passage, then, makes sense only within the context of baptism. It is baptism that gives participation in the cross-event—not in that dead body on the cross (not even in 1 Cor. 10:16f. does Paul speak of participation in Jesus' dead body). The "Body" rather signifies the gift of the risen Lord who gives a share in himself, and to this Body is opposed the realm of law.

The phrase in v 4, **so that you may belong to another,** is the truth for the sake of which the marriage analogy in vv 2 and 3 was introduced (cf. v 6). The subsequent phrase, **that we may bear fruit for God** is to be interpreted in consonance with the phrase in 6:4, **that we too might walk in newness of life.** 2 Corinthians 5:15 yields the same futuristic sense: "That those who live might live no longer for themselves but for him who for their sake died and was raised."

Verse 5 is parallel to 6:20-21, though here Paul includes himself among his addressees. **While we were living in the flesh**—the word must have been a blow to Paul's Jewish readers; in such fashion to describe life under the law! This is Paul's second use of the phrase, but the first usage (in 2:28) was sufficiently vague to suggest a mere reference to the physical. Here, it is clear that life under the law is life **in the flesh.** For the first time, the law and sin are set in an unholy alliance. Till now, the law has been described as revealing sin (e.g., 3:20), as working wrath (4:15), its entry the occasion for reckoning or "count-ing" sin (5:13). Now it is described as sin's occasion (Paul will soon ring the changes on that theme): **While we were living in the flesh, our sinful passions, aroused by the law.** . . . And, since these passions were at work so as to yield fruit unto death— death is thus the culmination of existence under the law! (A parallel to this thought appears in 6:21b.)

Paul then draws the contrast between the *then* (v 5) and the *now* (v 6) just as he had done in 6:20-21 and 22: **But now we are discharged from the law** (the language of the analogy is retained; v 2: **if her husband dies she is discharged** . . .). This is the obverse side of that truth for the sake of which the analogy was used (cf. v 4). Paul writes of the law that it **held us captive,** but again the marriage analogy breaks down. What is striking here is that humanity is not merely viewed as pas-sive over against God and his activity, but also in face of law, sin, and death. Indeed, there is no alternative to slavery (cf. 6:6). Verse 6 then concludes with a parallel to v 4: To be dead to the law through the Body in order to bear fruit for God means to serve in newness of the Spirit and not the oldness of letter.

In 6:4, the reference was to **newness of life,** but here "life" is replaced by "Spirit," that name which gathers up into itself all that "newness" means. Since participation in Christ's death occurs by activity of the Spirit, walking **in newness of life** in 6:4 and "serving in the newness (RSV: **the new life**) of the Spirit" are identical. It is this new situation effected on the basis of Christ's death which creates that "ministry of the new covenant" to which Paul refers in 2 Corinthians 3:6. In 2:28f., the contrast was between that which is "in the flesh" (RSV: **physical**), and that which is "in the Spirit" (RSV: **spiritual**), though there the terms were used obliquely. Now the contrast is specific—to be "under the law" or to be "in the flesh," that is, in "that which held us captive," is now described as "oldness of letter" (RSV: **the old written code**).

This identification of the **written code** with the law was alien to Judaism. For Jewish authors, the law not merely appeared in letters, but was written on the heart—a sentiment Paul himself shared (cf. 1:18ff.). And when Paul writes in 7:14 that the law is spiritual because the written code and the law are identical in content, he might as well have said the same of the written code. How then explain the inconsequence of thought in vv 6 and 14? The explanation lies in the alteration of viewpoint. The viewpoint expressed in v 14 is that the word is always a union of letter and spirit. Here, in v 6, Paul views the law from the standpoint of the dissolution of that union, when the word becomes mere legal code, a thing external and with killing effect. And whether, as in Chapter 6, the addressee is viewed from the standpoint of "lawlessness" (RSV: **iniquity**), or as here, from the perspective of captivity to law, the result is the same—death.

In ancient times, it was customary to read the change Paul describes as a being freed from one law for another. The place of Christ, as of Moses, was construed as of a lawgiver. But such a reading ignored the element of the totally new in the new life, since the contrast is not between two laws which differ in quality or degree, but between two ways of life, one dominated by its relationship to the legal, and the other by its relation to Christ which puts an end to the necessity of life ordered according to judicial decree. When, Paul writes, **we were living in the flesh** (v 5), he means that the time prior to baptism was part and parcel of the old reign of law. But since Christ as bringer of the new "discharges" us from the law, we have died to it; life **in the flesh** is now at an end.[32]

Those "passions of sin" or **sinful passions** to which Paul refers in v 5 may denote passions leading to or connected with concrete sins, but in either case, Paul has in mind a power, and in this distress, the law is not an aid but a threat, since the full power of the passions (whose home is **in our members,** in our corporeality, v 5), is only realized and made effective through the law. The law then does not give life, but marks the helplessness of the human situation before God. Yet, it is not simply because the law is everlastingly transgressed that it cannot give life. There is no talk here of a transgression of the law. The case is rather that the passions are aroused by the commandment, *whether or not* the commandment is fulfilled. We are thus sinners even when we keep the commandment! Paul contends that it was precisely his own adherence to law that made him a persecutor of the church and thus "least" of the apostles (cf. Phil. 3:6 and 1 Cor. 15:9). For this reason, deliverance must be from the law as such, and not merely an annulling of transgressions.

If then we have been made free from the law, we now live in a sphere in which God gives life. But "newness" and "oldness" are not merely contrasted in temporal fashion. Service "in newness of the Spirit" is a dynamic movement, in harmony with that "walking" in 6:4. And its antithesis is that service in "oldness of the letter" (RSV: **the old written code**) which "kills." [33]

Romans 7:1-6 has an earlier parallel in Galatians 3. There, the relationship to law is defined as a bond-relationship, corresponding to that between Abraham and his servant, Hagar (Gal. 3:23). There too, Paul maintains the sanctity of the law: It was "ordained by angels" (an inter-testamental doctrine appropriated by the New Testament authors; cf. Heb. 2:2). But the law is nevertheless provisional; the activity of the "custodian" is temporary (Gal. 3:24), and Hagar is eventually driven from Abraham's tent (Gal. 4:30). By indicating the priority in time of the promise attached to the law (Gal. 3:17), Paul argues that it never was God's intention that the law should be the ultimate expression of his will.

The differentiation of the content of the promise from the law in Galatians is identical to the contrast between the two types of existence and the conditions prevailing under them in Romans 7 and in 2 Corinthians 3:6—the Spirit is the content of the promise. Thus in Galatians 4, because Isaac, son of the free

woman, is heir of the promise, he is the one "born according
to the Spirit" (Gal. 4:29). By virtue of their relation to the promise, Ishmael and Isaac embody life under the old and under
the new order. In contrast to the old covenant which is Hagar,
"the present Jerusalem" (Gal. 4:25) and bondage, Paul describes
the new covenant as the "free woman" (Gal. 4:22), which is
Sarah, "the Jerusalem above" (Gal. 4:26) and mother of us all.

Paul also assigns the same significance to Jesus' death in
Galatians 3 and 4 as in Romans 7. Bondage to the law has been
"discharged" with Christ's death. And just as in Romans 6, baptism grants participation in Christ's death, so in Galatians 3:26-
29 such participation grants believers equality with Abraham
as inheritors, and equality with Isaac as sons of the free woman
(Gal. 4:30), children of "the Jerusalem above" (Gal. 4:26).

7:7-25 Existence Under the Law

The Law an Occasion for Sin (7-12)

Who is speaking here? From earliest times to our own, Scripture interpreters have given at least four answers to the question. Some have contended that there is nothing of Paul in
Romans 7, that he speaks in the first person merely because he
prefers to express "odious" things in such fashion.[34] Others
have written that Romans 7 reflects Paul's Christian experience, and in one instance have leveled their argument with the
proviso that the chapter must not be read in such a way as to
assign sin to Paul. Augustine originally interpreted this section
of humanity apart from grace, then changed his mind and
linked it directly to Paul's experience as a Christian. Luther
followed suit, contending that the "old man" never recognizes
such inner conflict as Romans 7 describes, since he is com-
pletely under the domination of the powers of the old age.[35]

Scholars in the 16th and 17th centuries suggested that Romans 7 reflects Paul's pre-Christian existence, but not till the

modern period did this view gain popularity, due principally
to its advocacy on the part of the History of Religions School.
Accenting religious personality as the conjunction of divinity
and historical reality, thus as medium of transcendence and
shaper of history, this school opted for the psychologically
explicable and put to the blade whatever smacked of the
miraculous or prodigious. Since Luther research and the study
of Paul were not merely coincident, but concomitant, the ten-
dency was to regard the "spiritual struggles" of the one in light
of the other. One American scholar wrote:

> We . . . recall the story of Luther, a kind of second Paul vainly
> seeking relief for the anguish of a conscience that will not
> down, by climbing on his knees the Holy Stair at Rome. With
> muttered prayers he nears the top, thinking at last to lay to his
> soul the unction of indulgence, when lo, a voice, so seemingly
> outside himself he can hardly believe that others have not
> heard it, proclaims aloud, "The just shall live by faith"; and
> Martin Luther the penitent rises from his knees, and delib-
> erately walks down the stair through the midst of the aston-
> ished worshipers.[36]

The propriety of such a psycho-religious interpretation of
Paul, though not of Luther, has been challenged. In face of the
vast amount of literature, it is difficult to keep in mind that
Luther was sufficiently vague and contradictory respecting his
"tower experience" to raise doubt regarding the correctness of
the popular view. Indeed, Luther's attack on the theology he
inherited may not at all have derived from a "tower experience," but from a painstaking study of Scripture which only
later moved him to break with Aristotle and the scholastic
system.

In the Pauline letters, there are only two passages in which
the apostle makes explicit reference to his situation prior to
faith (Gal. 1:13-17 and Phil. 3:5-6). Neither of these passages
supports the argument that he underwent "inner preparation"
for his conversion (the narratives in Acts 9:1-9; 22:4-16 and

26:9-18 are similar in that respect). Paul's encounter with the crucified and risen Christ did not involve a man torn by conscience and broken on his own insufficiency, but rather a robust Pharisee whose boast was the law of God, his membership in the elect community, and his own righteousness. We cannot ignore the force of the confession in Philippians 3:6: "As to righteousness under the law blameless," or the description of its implication in Galatians 1:13: "I persecuted the church of God." It was not an unbeliever suffering under the "evil impulse" whom Christ met on the Damascus road, but a zealot!

Thus, if in Romans 7 Paul is outlining the plight of the non-Christian from the perspective of Jewish faith, there is nothing to support the notion that he is linking this outline with his own conversion. In recent years, the majority has abandoned the application of Romans 7 to Paul's pre-Damascus existence, and has interpreted vv 7-25 as the description of a life under the Torah when viewed from the perspective of Christian faith.

In any answer to our question, it should first be noted that the description of existence in Romans 7 is not unique to the Christian. The author(s) of the Thanksgiving Hymns of Qumran experienced sin as a frightening reality:

> When I called to mind all my guilty deeds and the perfidy of my sires—when wicked men opposed Thy covenant, and froward men Thy word—trembling seized hold on me and quaking, all my bones were a-quiver; my heart became like wax melting before a fire, my knees were like to water pouring over a steep. (IV, 33-34)

> Lo, for mine own part, when I mark the nature of man, how he ever reverts [to perversity and wrongdoing], to sin and anguish of guilt, a fountain of bitter mourning wells up within me; [my tears flow like rivers], and sorrow is not hidden from mine eyes. These things go to my heart and touch me to the bone, that I raise a bitter lament and make doleful moan and groan, and keep plying my harp in mournful dirge and bitter lamentation, till wrongdoing be brought to an end. (XI, 19-22) [37]

107

It is possible, of course, that such an emphasis on human sin-
fulness roots in a "conversion" which regards any former existence as nothingness. But Socrates' portrait of the ideally just
and unjust state, mirrored in the philosopher-king and despot
reflects nothing of the sort:

> Just as a state enslaved to a tyrant cannot do what it really
> wishes, so neither can a soul under a similar tyranny do what
> it wishes as a whole. Goaded on against its will by the sting of
> desire, it will be filled with confusion and remorse. Like the
> corresponding state, it must always be poverty-stricken, unsat-
> isfied, and haunted by fear. Nowhere else will there be so
> much lamentation, groaning, and anguish as in a country
> under a despotism, and in a soul maddened by the tyranny of
> passion and lust. It cannot be otherwise.[38]

And it was Ovid who wrote, "I see and approve the better, but
I pursue the worse." This is the kernel of truth in the old History of Religions interpretation.

Paul may indeed be describing his earlier life from the new
vantage point. It is one thing to include oneself in illustrating
a type, and another to cite oneself as an example in autobiographical fashion. In the first instance, the person is not far
from the circumstances described, though the general perspective does not suit in every detail. Any insistence on Chapter 7
as "pre-Damascus" founders on v 9 (**I was once alive apart
from the law**), and on v 14 (**we know that the law is spiritual;
but I am carnal, sold under sin**)—words which might easily
be read in analogy with 1 Corinthians 10:30 and Galatians
2:18, and which hardly apply to Paul. An autobiographical
confession goes beyond such description.

Finally, in contrast to the popular view, the situation of the
Christian is not free of ambiguity. Paul's description of existence is thus not a stage on which one may look back and
heave a sigh of relief. This is the kernel of truth in Augustine's
and Luther's exposition of Chapter 7 (if it was the religious-
psychological interpretation of Paul which influenced that of
Luther, and not the reverse, then that interpretation has no

support here, since Luther insisted that this chapter is the confession of the Christian). For Paul, however, the Christians' assurance does not spring from their consciousness of the tension, but rather from the God who conforms them to Christ in justification: **Thanks be to God through Jesus Christ our Lord!** (v 25). So then, Paul in Romans 7 identifies himself with the sinner, and for this reason uses the "I-style" in vv 7ff., and the present tense in vv 14ff. What he writes, the sinner would have to say if he could speak of himself. But the text is blunted when hastily treated as the introspection of the Christian, or as the confession of the sinner prior to his coming to faith.

Paul begins the argument in 7:7-25 by allowing his imagined objector to ask: "Is the law sin?" and again responds with his usual **By no means!** It is one thing to uncover, reveal, to give knowledge of what *already* exists (cf. 3:20), and quite another to mark it down to evil's point of entry. Then Paul adds, **if it had not been for the law, I should not have known sin. I should not have known what it is to covet. . . .**[39] Paul's reference to the Tenth Commandment (Ninth and Tenth among Lutherans and Catholics) of the Decalogue in Exodus 20:17 and Deuteronomy 5:21 is apt here, since the Hebrew word for **covet** denotes a desiring as well as a taking, thus a passion leading to a proportionate action. Paul is adamant on the point—it is one thing to say that the law uncovers or reveals what *already* exists (cf. 3:20), and quite another to call the law sin. The law gives knowledge of sin because it reveals that one is *already* a sinner. The command or prohibition makes clear that sin is *already* present. It does not need first to take anyone captive.

Sin is the culprit—so reads Paul's argument in vv 8-14—the law's part is passive in this unholy alliance. But this does not erase the fact that the law is the occasion for sin's emergence, or that it even potentiates sin. The statement here is stronger than in 3:20; 4:15 or 5:13. There it was stated that knowledge of sin comes through the law, that law was the bedfellow of transgression, or that sin is not "counted" where there is no law. Here, sin itself is **dead** (v 8) apart from the law. But if so, Paul continues, **I** was alive, the self experienced no conflict; it lived as undivided. It was thus the coming of the law that revealed sin. (Again, the law is conceived as making historical entry; without this connotation, Paul's concept of law becomes a mere principle of order.)

Verse 9b is parallel to 8a, and the idea is not that the prohibition arouses to transgression. The law stands iron-clad against sin! But sin does take its opportunity to test the law, and breaks it as soon as it appears. So the claim to freedom from the law is not only a mark of faith, but also of sin: Thus **sin revived and I died,** and with that "revival" the self experienced a division, a divorce ending in judgment and death. (Note the antitheses in vv 8-10: Verse 8b: **Apart from the law** *sin lies dead;* v 9a: *I was once alive* **apart from the law;** v 9b: **When the commandment came,** *sin revived;* v 10a: **And I died**).

There is a tradition in Judaism according to which life and not death issues from a keeping of the law: "And the Lord said to Moses . . . You shall therefore keep my statutes and my ordinances, by doing which a man shall live" (Lev. 18:5); "it is God who has saved all his people . . . as he promised through the law. For we have hope in God that he will soon have mercy upon us and will gather us . . . into his holy place, for he has rescued us" (2 Macc. 2:17-18; cf. Luke 10:28: "Do this, and you will live"!). It is plain—the law "promised" life, but in "my" case, writes Paul, it had its issue in death. The reason is given in v 7 onward: The law says "thou shalt not covet," but sin, taking occasion in that command works all kinds of covetousness.

There is also a tradition in Judaism which avers that the law can be kept: "Verily, when the law commands us not to covet, that, I think, should strongly confirm the argument that reason is able to control covetous desires" (4 Macc. 2:6). This was Erasmus' contention too, and Paul himself treads close to the notion in Philippians 3:6: "As to zeal a persecutor of the church, as to righteousness under the law blameless." Or is the apostle distinguishing external compliance from inward resistance which makes real, genuine keeping of law impossible? In either case, we are faced with the dilemma that **the very commandment which promised life proved to be death.** But what of v 13: **Did that which is good, then, bring death to me? By no means!?** Is this a distinction without a difference, or does the argument really turn on what actually occurs with the law, and not on the nature of law isolated from its use, not on what it "promises" or intends?

Verse 11 repeats the thought in v 8, and again, as in vv 8 and 9, **commandment** is the shape which the law assumes, **commandment** the agent by which sin does its awful work, and against the intention of the law: **For sin, finding opportunity in the commandment . . . killed me.** Only under the law is it clear that with sin not merely good and evil, but also life and death are at stake. Apart from the law **I was . . . alive** (v 9)—death was veiled. Thus, I did not die *although* I lived under the law, but precisely *because* I lived under the law, for the law encountered me as sinner.

In v 11 Paul echoes the "trial" to which the man and his wife are summoned following their eating of the forbidden fruit (Gen. 3:9-13). To the question, "What is this that you have done?" the wife responds, "The serpent beguiled me, and I ate." In the Old Testament narrative, Adam and Eve (not the serpent) must explain their behavior and reasons are given for their punishment (the serpent is cursed for no reason at all). To the specifically human belongs the quality of intelligibility, answerability, a quality inherent also in God's judgment. Hence the punishment is made to fit the crime. Next, the narrative makes clear that rationality has its limits: The origin of the deed and thus of evil itself is unexplained—the man points to the woman, the woman to the serpent, and the serpent has vanished from the scene!

Paul's reference in v 11 differs from the original text by substituting sin for the serpent as subject of the action—"sin . . . thoroughly deceived me." The substitution is not intended to exchange one excuse for another and is not made because Paul balks at referring to the serpent (cf. 2 Cor. 11:3). The difference consists in the fact that Paul here intends to describe a universal situation—again, by reference to himself as type—in order to trace the activity of sin conceived as cosmic power, and without thought for its entrance into his own personal history or into any time beyond time. But the mere allusion, and in a context treating of human life as presently lived, is proof enough that for the apostle the story of Adam's transgression and its consequences is ultimately that of everyone, whatever the differences in detail (cf. 5:14) and whatever the origin.

In v 12, Paul draws his conclusion. The law is not sin, though I had not known sin without it; though through its commandment sin worked covetousness in me; though apart from law sin is dead; though without the law I was once alive; though sin revived with its entry; though intended for life it issued in death; though through its command sin deceived and slew me.

Willing and Doing Evil (13-20)

Verses 13ff. are the commentary on vv 7-12: If we ought not call the law sin, might we not call it death? Is it not but a brief step from saying the law **proved to be death** (v 10) or sentenced me to death, to saying that it is a "death-bringer"? **By no means!** (In v 7, Paul had refused to call the law sin.) Again, sin is the culprit (the rsv has added the copula: **It was sin,** the implication being that if the law was not death to **me,** sin was), and the function of the law is to reveal sin as such (cf. again 3:20). The law may indeed issue in death, but it is sin which "works death in me." Only in this sense does the commandment which promises life "prove to be death."

The same refusal to disparage the law, and yet the same alignment of the law with sin and death appears in 1 Corin-

thians 15:56, in which sin is likened to the arrow's point at
which death makes its entry, and the law likened to the bow:
"The sting of death is sin, and the power of sin is the law."
Why this overprotective stance respecting the essence of the
law, when sin has the law on its side, so that the sinner must
die under the law? In any case, did not God give Israel a
"wooden nickel"? Or, is such a conclusion impossible because
the law is somehow, after all, really, on the side of life?

In v 14, Paul describes the law as **spiritual,** then adds, **but I
am carnal.** "The very commandment promises life," the law
is **holy and just and good** (vv 10, 12-13), but **I am . . . sold under
sin.** What does this mean? It means confusion, it means that
"I do not know what I am doing" (v 15). That is not to say that
I am unaware of the dilemma I am in, that I am not conscious
of what is taking place, but rather that what *I* do is beyond me
(v 17: **It is no longer I that do it, but sin which dwells within
me;** v 18: **I can will what is right, but I cannot do it;** v 20: **It is
no longer I that do it, but sin which dwells within me**). Not
only the effects of my actions are unknown to me; if I do anything at all in this condition, I am unaware of it, for there is
too much else at work! Indeed, I do not do what I wish but
what I hate. Note again the antitheses. There is a striking
similarity between this verse and the following lines from
Epictetus:

> Every error comprehends contradiction; for since he who errs
> does not wish to err, but to be right, it is plain that he does
> not do what he wishes . . . every rational soul is by nature of-
> fended at contradiction, and so long as it does not understand
> this contradiction, it is not hindered from doing contradictory
> things.[40]

Something at work in me divorces willing from doing, and
produces this inability to understand my actions.[41] In v 16 this
division in the self marks an assent to the goodness of the law
insofar as I do *what I do not want.* Is what I want, then, what
the law requires? For the "moral" person, the person **under**

the law, the answer to that question must be in the affirmative. But how did such willing come about? Did the law effect it? The law brings **knowledge of sin** (vv 7-8), but does it effect a will to do the good? Paul would hardly have denied to all but Christians such a good will.

In v 17 Paul makes clear that if not wanting what I do spells assent to the law's goodness, then doing what I do not want is sin's activity within me. Things are somehow out of my hands; I am **sold. Sin,** not the I is the subject of my activity. But if so, am I absolved of responsibility? Not at all, since sin is not a thing external to me, but **dwells** in me. In v 18, Paul then gives the reason why sin can make such habitation: **Nothing good dwells within me.** But perhaps that phrase, **that is, in my flesh,** spells some qualification, allowing the possibility of contrasting willing and doing, and to the degree of the contrast, absolving me of responsibility? Again, the answer is no: **I am carnal** (v 14), fated to suffer precisely this conflict of willing and doing. And, it makes no difference to the law how much I may will— the law demands **doers** (2:13)—on that hangs my culpability. The law was never content with "hearing" or "willing." The latter half of v 18 gives the reason why there is no good in me: **I can will what is right, but I cannot do it.** Thus, the **good** in v 18a takes its definition, at least in a negative sense, from v 18b: What is **good** is harmony, and the absence of harmony between willing and doing is **nothing good.**

Verse 19 then repeats the thought in v 15, but with the addition of the **good** and the **evil.** Once again, the **good** or the absence of it (v 18) hangs on doing or not doing—there is no other alternative, no other route of escape from this dilemma of willing and doing. Verse 20 almost literally repeats the thought in vv 16a and 17, and just as v 16, it contains a simple condition. The repetition fastens down the argument that to be **sold** means to have something else than the **I** as subject of one's activity; more, that the subject is bent on the **evil,** consent to the law to the contrary notwithstanding.

The Law of God and the Law of Sin (21-25)

The thought in v 18b is repeated, together with the contrast in v 19 between "good" and "evil": **So I find it to be a law. . . .** "Law" here is simply that which is inevitable. (If we look elsewhere for parallels to the "laws" in this chapter, the "desires of the flesh" and "the law" in Gal. 5:16-18 correspond to that "other law" or "law of sin," and to the "law of God" or "law of my mind." Verses 16, 22, 23b, and 25a refer to the latter, and vv 23a, c, 25b—cf. v 20—to the former. Two laws plus a principle of necessity appear here: The law of God, and the law of sin.)

Verse 22 repeats the thought of 16b with a nuance: **I delight in the law . . . in my inmost self.** The phrase is comparable to **what I want** in vv 15, 18b, 19 and 21. This is as close as Paul will come to the Greek division of the person into body and soul, though personhood has already taken its definition from his use of the term "to will." Is this perhaps a clue to the kind of person who is speaking here? Might it be not only the Jew zealous for the Torah, but also the lordly pagan, struggling with the mind to master the spirit and natural cravings, and again, from the perspective of deliverance? The secondary question in this chapter is always lurking.

Verse 23 continues the thought in v 22 without a break, but nuances it as well: **The law of God is the law of my mind.** The thought is the same as that in vv 17, 20 and 21—sin is subject of my activity. There is yet another refinement in v 23. Rather than referring simply to the law of sin which **dwells within me,** Paul now refers to it as "the law in my members." So the verse should read: "I see in my members another law at war with the law of my mind and making me its captive, that is, a law of sin which dwells in my members."

Why this talk of **members?** Is it to allow some distinction, perhaps, between the **members** and the **I,** the self equipped with a modicum of moral consciousness? Quite the reverse!

115

"Doing" needs **members,** and the law demands doing. But doing does not make the person; it is the person that makes the deed, and I am a sinner, doing what I do not want! With *that* "law," that law of doing what I do not want, with that "law in my members" or **law of sin** the "law of my mind" loses the struggle. It takes **me** (!) captive, and what survives is nothing at all—no good will, no reserve of inner moral consciousness. See how what is **holy and just and good** has ruined me!

Now God, it appears, has nothing more to say, and humanity only a sigh: **Who will deliver me. . . .** "My God, my God, why hast thou forsaken me?" (The similarity of the cry here with that in 1 Cor. 15:50 is not accidental. In each case a death occurs through sin's finding opportunity in the commandment, and in each case, the sufferer is trapped: **Who will deliver . . . ?** and "flesh and blood cannot inherit the kingdom of God.") For this **man** to be delivered, he must be saved "in person" (**who will deliver *me*. . . .**)—not through the law, for the law merely requires deeds. But since the law presupposes such a **man** for the deeds it requires, the law is a call to faith which can make such a **man!** Thus Luther's "faith creates the person," his thrust at the scholastic notion that one is or becomes something by doing.[42] And God, who not only requires the good but also gives it, comes to the sinner in faith. And, in order that the sinner may be certain of what faith brings, God reveals his will in Christ—colophon: **through Jesus Christ our Lord!** So that which **proved to be death to me** really was, after all, on the side of life!

> All which I took from thee I did but take,
>   Not for thy harms,
> But just that thou might'st seek it in My arms,
>   All which thy child's mistake
> Fancies as lost, I have stored for thee at home:
>   Rise, clasp my hand, and come! [43]

After the light in v 25a, v 25b plunges into the darkness again. Is the thanksgiving in v 25a an addition? With 8:1-2 might it perhaps be the work of an ancient reader impatient for the happy ending? Or is the verse Paul's own curious way of stating that either side of the deliverance there lies a darkness in the midst of which we must still cling to God?!

■ 8:1-39   The Spirit and the New Life

8:1-13 Spirit and Flesh

Now to my Father I depart,
From earth to heav'n ascending,
And, heav'nly wisdom to impart,
The Holy Spirit sending;
In trouble he will comfort you
And teach you always to be true
And into truth shall guide you.

Romans 8 describes the new in midst of the world of flesh, sin, and death, but substitutes a new contrast between **flesh** and **spirit** for the earlier contrast between law and flesh (cf. the same contrast in Gal. 5:16-25). The chapter is composed of sections that are logically connected but are often independent of each other in respect to content.

In v 1 Paul seems to be drawing a conclusion as well as raising a new issue: **There is . . . no condemnation for those who are in Christ Jesus.** These words set us once more in the context of justification; for where there is no condemnation, there is forgiveness of sin. The personal address (the reading, **the law of the Spirit . . . has set *me* free** is to be preferred) in 8:2 then harks back to the cry in 7:24, an address continued in the purpose or result clause of 8:4.

For the community of Khirbet Qumran as for Paul, our fallenness consists of sin and creatureliness, and salvation is an aid against sin; it is deliverance from nothingness. The Qumran sect already taught the justification of sinners—there are no deeds that can save them; those who have been made righteous and transplanted into eternity remain sinners. Qumran thus shared Paul's premise that both the fallenness of the creature and the initiative of God exclude all boasting. Indeed, self-humiliation in praise of God represents a most characteristic aspect of the Qumran Thanksgiving Hymns.

This thought in Qumran is all the more striking in light of texts that speak of the covenanter's new condition or situation. But when we ask precisely in what do sin and salvation consist, we discover what a constitutive role the Torah plays in Qumran. For the Dead Sea community, sin does not occur within but *alongside* obedience to the Torah, and the justification of sinners frees them for the way of the Torah. The division which the Qumran believer suffers is thus always from without, a thing alien, foreign to one's true self. But for Paul, sin occurs precisely in pursuit of the Torah. Indeed, it is the Torah itself that creates this division in the self—the theme of Romans 7—from which God's redemptive activity sets me free. Thus in Qumran, grace alone is not as for Paul something **apart from law.**

So the question arises, how radically did Qumran understand sin and grace? In spite of the shared premise—humanity as sinful in the extreme; salvation only through divine grace— Qumran did not regard humankind's dividedness as so deep and profound that the keeping of the Torah availed nothing. In spite of its contention that God alone creates salvation, it did not do away with Torah as a way of salvation and with the underlying assumption that faithfulness to the covenant guarantees a right or claim; it did not find in weakness and helplessness a God-given strength. Paul pointed to the incompatibility of real grace with an undialectical reception of power by asserting that salvation lay in Christ alone. The Christological basis of salvation is not just one among many differences. It is the *chief* difference between Qumran and Paul.

In Christian tradition, early and late, Paul's reference to the **law of the Spirit** was mistakenly viewed as a second Torah.

The identification was a tragic error. Paul's use of the term **law** here has its occasion first of all in the parallelism (**the law of the Spirit . . . the law of sin and death**). But there is another, more important reason for his use of the term. He has in mind an existence within a sphere of power that energizes and moves the believer with a necessity every bit as compelling as the law or Torah with its demands. In fact, this **law of the Spirit** is contrasted with and superior to the **law of sin** (7:23, 25). Thus this "law" is not at all equivalent to the first, for over against the first which exerted influence from without, this "law" dominates from within. More, this **law of the Spirit** is equivalent to deliverance, and a deliverance precisely from that which characterized the earlier condition of life. So the contrast is not between two laws which differ in degree or quality, but between two mutually exclusive ways of life, one dominated by its relationship to the legal, the other by its relationship to Christ.

The old "orthodox" doctrine of the "third use of the law" (next to the "civil" use—to restrain the wicked, and the "theological" use—to lead to Christ) as regulative for the life of faith, is only a variation on the ancient identification. In this sense, the cross cannot be a "yes" to the law. Rather, that cosmic, killing power, killing by virtue of its unholy alliance with the "flesh" which will always be only for itself, was the occasion for the cross:

> If Moral Virtue was Christianity
> Christ's Pretensions were all Vanity,
> And Caiphas & Pilate, Men
> Praise Worthy, & the Lions' Den
> And not the Sheepfold, Allegories
> Of God & Heaven & their Glories.
> The Moral Christian is the Cause
> Of the Unbeliever & his Laws.
> The Roman Virtues, Warlike Fame,
> Take Jesus' & Jehovah's Name;
> For what is Antichrist but those

Who against Sinners Heaven close
With Iron bars, in Virtuous State,
And Rhadamanthus at the Gate?
. . . . The Moral Virtues in their Pride
Did o'er the World triumphant ride
In Wars & Sacrifice for Sin,
And Souls to Hell ran trooping in. . . .
The Accuser, Holy God of All
This Pharisaic Worldly Ball,
Amidst them in his Glory Beams
Upon the Rivers & the Streams.
Then Jesus rose & said to Me,
"Thy Sins are all forgiven thee."
Loud Pilate Howl'd, loud Caiphas yell'd,
When they the Gospel Light beheld. . . .
The Moral Virtues in Great fear
Formed the Cross & Nails & Spear,
And the Accuser standing by
Cried out, "Crucify! Crucify!" [44]

The function of the law is not to teach believers "what they ought to be and what they ought to avoid" (Erick Pontopiddan's *Explanation of Martin Luther's Small Catechism;* cf. the *Formula of Concord,* Epitome, Article VI, "The Third Function of the Law").[45] Its function is rather to reveal sin (3:20; 7:7, 13). It is one thing to state that the law assumes faith for its keeping, and thus is on the side of life; one thing to state that the law "drives one to Christ" and thus facilitates the entry of grace; it is one thing to state that the "ought" or **just requirement of the law** is fulfilled through Christ, and quite another to state that the law is regulative of the Christian life. Unless that distinction is rigorously held to, the Pauline concept of justification as conformity to Christ by the power of the Spirit who activates the Body from within apart from external command is perverted, and Christian faith interpreted in a fashion so bitterly attacked by the apostle in the Galatians letter.

From oldest times legalism or existence by external decree has been viewed as the only alternative to moral laxity or anarchy. Paul is of an entirely different conviction—Christian existence is not at all a life oriented to the external demand which can only exact external compliance and thus give rise to a divorce in the self between willing and doing the good. It is rather an existence in which Another is subject of our willing and doing! Note the clues to the divine initiative in this chapter:

- v 2, the **law of the Spirit;**
- v 3, **condemned sin in the flesh;**
- v 9, the Spirit determines what is carnal or spiritual;
- v 10, the indwelling Christ marks the death of the body in respect of sin;
- v 11, the Spirit guarantees life to mortal bodies;
- v 12, **we are debtors;**
- v 15, **the spirit of sonship** is received;
- v 18, the **glory** is to be revealed;
- v 20, the entire creation is **subjected,** and **not of its own will;**
- v 21, the cosmos **will be set free;** cf. vv 28 30!
- in v 32, not even the Son appears to enjoy any initiative— God **did not spare** him;
- in v 33, the elect are **God's;**
- in vv 38-39 what enables us to transcend death or life, etc. is God's love in Christ Jesus.

Paul connects the idea of Spirit with that of conformity to Christ when he writes that this **law of the Spirit** is **in Christ Jesus.** This Christological orientation of Spirit may have been Paul's own work. In the Synoptic Gospels and Acts, the Spirit is in some sense viewed as an addition to faith, but the question for Paul was: How are the Spirit and the life, death, and resurrection of Jesus related? His reply was that Spirit is not merely a power given to announce the good news, not merely a force enabling the community to perform its work in the world, but the One who sets us in that new world which God created when he sent Christ to his cross. Thus, the Body of Christ and the Spirit of Christ—for Paul none else than the earthly presence of Christ following his resurrection—may be distinguished but never separated.

To the question, "Who is the Spirit?" Paul replies: He who witnesses to Jesus as Lord;

- who gives understanding into what occurred for us on Christ's cross;
- who sets us under the lordship of the cross of Christ;
- who is the power of God by which we believe;
- who enables us to live our faith in love for that One who died and for the other.

"Who is the Spirit?" "He is the Power to comprehend in its height and depth and breadth what God accomplished on that rude tree, *and* the norm by which we live from out of that deed of God." That word, "now the Lord is the Spirit" (2 Cor. 3:17) effected a revolution in religion.

In biblical studies, a mortal blow was dealt the notion that the Spirit of the Bible and the human spirit are the same. The miraculous, the prodigious, the alien, and the foreign were discovered to mark the activity of the Spirit of God. But there is more to be said. The quality of finality belongs to the Spirit of God and his activity, for faith is not something which I may possess at will and thus is repeatable. Faith's context is God's own good time in which he creates its occasion and possibility. Of course, the nature of the Spirit's presence is something hidden. "Spirit," contended Paul's opponents, "is what erupts or penetrates from another sphere." "No," Paul responded, "it is not demonstrable," or "yes," Paul replied, "but it is present beneath its opposite—Spirit is where we are conformed to the crucified!" By binding the Spirit to the life and death of Christ, Paul flooded the Christian world with a notion contrary to all sense and expectation.

Verse 8:3 makes clear that sin or its law wars against the **law**

of God, produces a divorce in the self, and that precisely this war constitutes my existence as **carnal** (7:14). So it is by way of the carnal that sin makes its entry and frustrates the law. In the latter part of the verse, sin is no longer the subject, but the God who sends his Son **in the likeness of sinful flesh.** The term **likeness** (cf. Phil. 2:7, in which Christ is described as "born in the likeness of men") is not used to lessen Christ's full participation in humanity, nor to set him apart from a humanity marked by sin. The intention is quite the reverse. Indeed, v 3 may reflect Paul's altering of a motif that originally described only the incarnation of the pre-existent Son. The life of Christ, characterized by association with "publicans and sinners," and culminating in death under a curse ("a hanged man is accursed by God," Deut. 21:23), was not a fact Paul and the Christian community cared to deny. Rather it was the ground of their boast.

The difference between Paul's view of Christ's humanity **in the likeness of sinful flesh** and that of his opponents lay in the fact that for him, this humanity was voluntarily assumed; that sin did not attach to it by any necessity; that such deprivation rather constituted an "obedience" (Phil. 2:8) to the divine will on behalf of the race ("Christ redeemed us from the curse of the law, having become a curse for us" Gal. 3:13). From such a perspective Christ had become the greatest sinner of them all. The picture here is hardly that of a Gnostic Redeemer who as stranger was imprisoned in the material world. Because Christ took on sinful flesh, sin was condemned precisely where it made its attack—**in the flesh,** at the point of its entry. There, the law was powerless. But God did what the law could not, and before we had attempted anything, indeed, while we were still **sold.**

The contrasts between the Spirit and the flesh in Chapter 8, and between the law of God and the law of sin in Chapter 7 are not interchangeable, but are linked to each other as means to ends: To **walk . . . according to the Spirit** (means) is to fulfill the requirement of the law (ends), and to **walk . . . according to the flesh** (means) is to **serve the law of sin** (ends, 7:25). But there is still a *difference* between the Spirit and the law of God, or there is still a *similarity* between the law of God and the law of sin. Because the law of God, not willingly, nor by intention, nor "in theory" but still in actuality furnishes sin its opportunity (7:13), it is thrust into an alliance with sin. To walk according to the Spirit is thus to be free not only from the law of sin and death, but also from the law of God (cf. Gal. 5:18: "If you are led by the Spirit you are not under the law"). On the other hand, there is still a *similarity* between the Spirit and the law of God, or, there is still a *difference* between the law of God and the law of sin. Because God sent his Son in the likeness of sinful flesh that **the just requirement of the law might be fulfilled in us, who walk . . . according to the Spirit,** to walk according to the Spirit and thus to be free from the law does not mean to be quit of what the law requires.

Again, it is one thing to be delivered from the law as an external authority which can extort a mere external compliance, and quite another to carry out the true intention of the law. In the old existence, God's command was impossible of fulfillment because of one's **carnal** orientation, whereas in the new that command is fulfilled through incorporation into the Body of Christ. For Paul, then, being set free (v 2) and having the **just requirement of the law** fulfilled in us are not contradictory. Life always involves service. The question is where is it done— in the mere "willing" or "in us"? Once **nothing good** dwelt **within me** (7:18), but now **the just requirement** is **fulfilled in us.** Thus, **Spirit** is not to be interpreted as a power that grants divinity; it is not a heavenly, impersonal substance, but the power and will which proceed from the risen Lord.

In vv 5 and 6, life **according to the flesh** or life **according to the Spirit** is interpreted in terms of its intention. The phrase, **to set the mind on,** refers not only to mental activity, but also to the focus of one's life. Thus, to **set the mind on the things of** the flesh, or on the things of the Spirit means to focus one's life on that which is in opposition to or in harmony with the just requirement of the law. And just as the one mind results in death, so the other mind spells life and peace (8:6), an end to the war (7:23). If, Paul continues, to set the mind on the flesh is death, then it is enmity toward God, because it is not now nor can it ever be subject to the law of God.

Paul then turns to the baptized in v 9: All that which is carnal, sold under sin, wretched or which serves the law of sin; all that which is according to the flesh, sets its mind on things of the flesh or issues in death; all that which is hostile to God, does not submit and indeed . . . cannot—all that you are *not!* You are everything opposed to it—in the Spirit! The little conjunction in the clause, if (in fact) the Spirit of God . . . dwells in you, does not raise a suspicion. It introduces a simple condition which assumes the reality of the premise.[46] In the verses that follow, and which are linked to the sentence in v 9 by a contrast: any one who does not have the Spirit of Christ does not belong to him, Paul explains the significance of the phrase, you are in the Spirit, if (in fact) the Spirit of God . . . dwells in you.

The difference between the phrase, in the Spirit, and the phrase, the Spirit of God (or Christ) . . . in you is a difference between the object and the acting subject, as v 11 makes clear. Since v 10 is the only passage in which Paul refers to the body as dead (in every other instance, the body of sin is to be destroyed, or the deeds of the body are to be put to death, 6:6; 8:13), and since it is the "old man" which is elsewhere described as crucified, the "body" in this verse is identical with the "old man" in 6:6 (RSV: bodies!). Similarly, the "spirit" here is the equivalent of what Paul elsewhere calls the "new creation" (RSV: spirits!). The terms *body* and *spirit* thus mark two types of corporate existence, neither of which may exist with the other. The one is dead, destroyed, crucified with Christ because of sin, that is, the death was necessitated by slavery to sin; and the other is alive **because of righteousness,** that is, by virtue of God's revelation of his righteousness in Christ to whom believers have now been joined. The singular *body* and *spirit* in v 10 must be retained, since the body is neither the **deeds of the body** in v 13, nor **your mortal bodies** in v 11, but again that corporate personality which has been put off in the baptism.

In vv 9-11, the individual components of the terse statement in 2 Corinthians 3:17 ("now the Lord is the Spirit") are all set down one by one: **You are in the Spirit** (v 9a); **any one who does not have the Spirit of Christ does not belong to him** (v 9b); **if Christ is in you** (v 10); and, **if the Spirit . . . dwells in you** (v 11). In v 11, just as in 12:1, Paul refers to the **bodies** (plural) of believers about to be raised or presented as a **living sacrifice,** because he wishes to accent the totality of persons involved, not their corporateness. In v 23 he returns to the singular, corporate use. Corporeality, then, not "flesh" (1 Cor. 15:50) has a share in the future.

The result of this, writes Paul in v 12, is that we are **debtors, not to the flesh.** The phrase does not suggest obligation, but rather compulsion (just as the statement in 1:14—being **under obligation** belongs to being a **servant,** being **called** and **set apart**). For this reason, Paul in v 13 does not issue a summons, but states a fact: **If you live according to the flesh you will die, but if by the Spirit you put to death the deeds of the body you will live.** The verb *to die* shares with the noun *death* the same comprehensive meaning—a judgment of death beyond natural death. The same thought is expressed in Galatians 6:8.

That **body** in **deeds of the body** is the equivalent of the "body of sin" in 6:6, and not "the flesh with its passions and desires." It is thus not the "old man" (or "dead body" referred to in v 10), not bodily existence as such, but bodily existence as stamped by sin that requires a continual "putting to death." (In 1 Cor. 9:27, Paul speaks of "pommeling" and "subduing" his body.) The reference to *deeds* of the body is calculated to accent the concreteness in action which such bodily existence assumes and against which the "new creation" (or "new man") must still struggle. Hence, that which is "spiritual" or pertaining to the new is a "walking" (8:4). "Putting to death the deeds of the body" is thus not something added to what is "spiritual." There is no separation here of being and doing:

> The sun is not obliged to shine; it does so naturally. Three and seven are not obliged to make ten; they do so in any case. So, faith is not obliged to do good works; if it is faith, it simply does them.[47]

8:14-27 Sonship and Cruciform Existence

In this section Paul describes those who are "in the Spirit" or "in Christ" as "sons," and again, there is no mistake as to where the initiative lies—they are **led by the Spirit of God.** Verse 15, with its contrast between sonship and **slavery to . . . fear** echoes Galatians 5:18: "If you are led by the Spirit you are not under the law." The two passages have the same meaning: Existence under the old, "under the law" or "under sin," is an existence in fear. The same contrast between slavery and sonship is drawn in Galatians 4:5: God has sent his Son to redeem those who were under the law that they might receive adoption.

Paul next writes that in or by **the spirit of sonship** we are made to cry **Abba! Father!** (The RSV inexactly translates the prepositional phrase in v 15b **when we cry. . . .**) This cry then— an old Aramaic invocation preserved by the primitive community in its worship, similar to the Kyrie (or, perhaps retained in glossolalic speech?)—is evidence of our sonship. It is the Spirit who makes us address God as "Papa" (cf. Gal. 4:6: "God has sent the Spirit of his Son into our hearts, crying 'Abba! Father!' "). In the Greek, v 16 begins a new sentence, and as is often the habit with Paul a gap or interval results: "The Spirit himself bears witness with our spirit that we are children of

God." Where two witnesses agree, there is truth! Knowledge of the new existence rests on the agreement between the Spirit's witness and that of the believers. And that witness is not just an inward certainty given with the audible cry, **Abba!** It is not simply to be identified with the believers' psychic states. It is an independent event encountering them from without. The Spirit's witness is thus the presupposition for the witness of **our spirit,** and thus for the believers' assurance. In the Body occurs the awareness of renewal. So it is not at all apparent that we are **children of God.** Indeed, that will be *revealed* (v 19!). The thought in 2 Corinthians 1:21 is similar, and in both passages the context is liturgical. In Romans 8, the cry **Abba!** guarantees sonship with God; in 2 Corinthians 1, the "Amen" marks the gift of Christ's Spirit as seal and guarantee of Paul's preaching and apostleship.

Verse 17 marks the climax in the progression of thought from **sons** and **children** (vv 14-16) to **heirs and fellow heirs** (v 17), to "suffering" and "being glorified with him." Verse 17 thus strikes a new note—sonship, co-inheritance with Christ, being called to the fellowship of his Son (1:6; cf. 1 Cor. 1:9), existence "in" or "with" Christ, "Christ in us," interprets cruciform existence. Elsewhere Paul describes this existence as "carrying in the body the death of Jesus" (2 Cor. 4:10; note again the use of the term "body" to denote not merely the believers' existence in community, but also its physical aspect). The RSV translates the little conjunction in v 17b, **provided,** so as to make the sentence read, **provided we suffer with him,** but the conjunction does not introduce such a condition. Again, it assumes the reality of the premise: "We are heirs of God, co-heirs with Christ, if it is true *(as it really is,)* that we suffer with him. . . ." The "suffering together with" is for the now-time; Christ makes his epiphany in us in the shape of the cross. This is his way on earth till the revelation of the glory. But, as Paul writes, the two events are beyond comparing. (In 2 Cor. 4:17, Paul contrasts the suffering or "tribulation" and "eternal weight of glory" as between what is slight, momentary, and what is eternal, beyond compare, linking the two as cause to effect.)

For this "coming glory," Paul says, the whole creation waits. This is Paul's first and only reference in Romans to what is customarily called "cosmic redemption" (the concept has its most "classical" expression in Col. 1:15-20, and Eph. 1:9-10). At the same time, the concept of a creation-wide deliverance is common to the New Testament. Neglect of this fact or its reinterpretation in terms of human or individual existence drives a wedge between what the New Testament does not separate—between the creation's **eager longing,** and the **revealing of the sons of God;** between the cosmos' deliverance from **bondage to decay,** and the **glorious liberty of the children of God;** between the creation's **groaning in travail** and our waiting for **adoption** (8:19-23). If the Son's revelation—elsewhere called the "revealing of our Lord Jesus Christ" (1 Cor. 1:7), or the "hope of righteousness" (Gal. 5:5)—is something for which the creation waits, then that means that the children and their adoption are hidden now.

If the creation **waits with eager longing,** the reason is that it was subjected to **futility.** There may be a reminiscence here of that ancient warrior against free will who two hundred years before Christ framed his sentences of instruction with the assertion that "all is vanity." But Paul's argument differs from that of Ecclesiastes in at least three respects:

• "Vanity of vanities" (in the Hebrew "breath of breaths"— that which is most ephemeral of all), belongs to the creation, not to humankind (note the contrast in Rom. 8:23: **But we ourselves,** and cf. the reference in 1:21!). The "vanity" exists because of the Creator's cursing of the ground as a result of Adam's sin (Gen. 3:17-18; cf. 5:29).

• Resisting like a watershed Ecclesiastes' torrent of despair, Paul announces that the creation was subjected to futility **in hope.** There is thus a future for the creation after the "sun and the light and the moon and the stars are darkened and the clouds return after the rain."

• Unlike the preacher in Ecclesiastes, Paul knows why the ground was cursed—so that our earth home would not anticipate our future glory. Thus, though like the preacher, Paul knows the vanity was not the creation's but the Creator's doing **(not of its own will but by the will of him who subjected it in hope)**, and stands as inexorable warning against all boasting, against confusing gift with deserving or grace with right, he not merely calls his reader to remember the Creator before the long darkness, but promises glory, glory for humankind and for the earth as well.

In v 21, the **futility** from which the cosmos will be freed is called a **bondage to decay** (the term appears only here in the New Testament). Further, this ruin imposed on it is from without—it was **subjected** to it! The relation of the creation to sin, to the human condition, is therefore indirect. The creation is "innocent," cursed for humanity's sake. But the relation of the creation to humanity's fate is direct and intimate—"cursed" and "futile" for humanity's sake, it will be freed from its servitude for the freedom of the glory of God's children. Now the creation experiences a bondage it does not deserve—but then it will come into its own.

Whether inspired by the idea of oneness with Christ or by that of the creation's sharing humanity's final destiny, Paul heaps up his favorite compounds in v 22: **We know that the whole creation has been groaning** (together) **in** (and suffering) **travail together.** . . . The language is apocalyptic, and everything said of the Christians' possession **until now** falls under the heading of **first fruits** (v 23). On the day after the Sabbath concluding the feast of unleavened bread, the first ripe sheaves were given to the priest who "waved" them toward and away from the altar, symbolizing the harvest as God's from whom one received it back again (cf. Exod. 23:19; 34:26, and Lev.

2:14-16; 23:9-14). The oldest creedal statement known to us from the Old Testament is connected by the author of Deuteronomy with this festival (cf. Deut. 26:5b-9).

Paul uses the term **first fruits** of Christ's raising, of Israel, even of first converts in a given province, and principally to indicate that what is first will inevitably have its sequel in a general resurrection (1 Cor. 15:20-21), in Israel's "grafting" back into its own "olive tree" (11:16, 24), or in the Gentiles' coming to faith (16:5; cf. 1 Cor. 16:15). The term is the equivalent of the "guarantee" in 2 Corinthians 1:22. Even if Paul uses the term here apart from any ceremonial associations, say, in analogy with its use elsewhere to denote the "birth certificate" of a free person, the result is the same: What the Christian possesses is a pledge of what is to come. The creation, however, has no **first fruits**—what is perceptible to it is only **futility.**

In v 23, Paul describes the partner to the creation's "groaning"—**Not only the creation but we ourselves . . . groan inwardly**—and thus resumes the cruciform theme of vv 17b and 18. It is one thing to possess the **spirit of sonship,** and another to possess that sonship itself—in the next breath called "the redemption of our body" (again, the rsv incorrectly translates: **bodies**). In the first passage in which Paul uses the term **redemption** (3:24), he does not refer to something awaited but to something already in existence. Here, however, "redemption" embraces corporeality. Verse 23 thus repeats the thought in v 11.

For in this hope we were saved, Paul continues. (What if we were to translate, "for we were spared for this hope"? Elsewhere in Romans, the verb **to save** is always used in the future tense. To translate in this fashion would accent the end-time dimension of the term.) This hope theme was first struck in 5:4, and the same connection between **Spirit** and **hope** was established there as here in Chapter 8. **Hope** qualifies and restricts what **we know.** In essence, hope equals faith—it embraces the nonperceptible and hidden. Once more, then, the theme of vv 17 and 18 is resumed: The believers' present existence is characterized by hope, because what they endure with Christ appears to be the opposite of glory. But there is more—there is a rightness, an appropriateness to this imperceptibility and thus to this hoping. It is a hope for which we have been spared!

Where there is hope, there is patience (v 25 is an echo of 5:3: **suffering produces endurance**). The creation **waits** (v 19) by **groaning** (v 22), as we do also (v 23), but this **patience** (a flat word!) is not resignation to fate. It is the condition of an arrow poised for release from the bow. If in v 24 the essence or nature of hope is defined (non-perceptibility), here in v 25 its mode or manner is described—**with patience.** In such fashion the cruciform existence behaves.

Verse 26 then indicates the relation between Spirit and this existence: **The Spirit** also **helps us in our weakness.** (The RSV omits the word "also," but the Greek requires it: Just as hope sustains us, so "also" does the Spirit.) "Weakness" is the name for our cruciform existence, for "suffering," "groaning," and "waiting," the name for hope and patience. And all by virtue of that little prefix "together with." Several ancient New Testament manuscripts have botched things so as to make **weakness** in v 26 refer to moral failings. Our cruciform life is not an imitation—this is what Paul intends to say—not an existence by which Christ or the Spirit keeps his distance from us, or we from him. He takes our burden on him (the RSV **helps** is pale by comparison) "at the other end of the log." He must, since it is he who has given this shape to life! That incomparable genius and bear of a man, Johann Sebastian Bach, born at Eisenach, site of Luther's boyhood learning, Thomaskantor and director of university music at Leipzig, father of 20, wrote one of his six great motets on themes from Romans 8, and titled it: *Der Geist hilft unsere Schwachheit auf* (The Spirit helps us in our *weakness*)!

Verse 26b (**for we do not know how to pray as we ought** or, "the problem of praying as we ought we do not know about")

132

was the occasion for those variants in v 26a that equated weakness with moral failings. But not knowing what to pray for **as we ought** does not mean we cannot list our petitions in intelligible fashion. This little half-verse clearly connects with what precedes. So the **praying** must have some relation to the notseen, to that which is awaited **with patience!** The shape of what we hope for, of what we await, for which we and the creation groan, the shape of our adoption, our redemption—how should we conceive it in address to God? In the face of such incapacity, the Spirit must take the suppliant's case into his own hands: **The Spirit himself intercedes for us with sighs too deep for words.** If an utterance in tongues is referred to here, it is not the phenomenon as such which is of importance, but that "praying as we ought" which it reflects or signifies. And God himself guarantees that those **sighs too deep for words,** by which the Spirit speaks to God on our behalf, are **according to the will of God.**

8:28-30 The Hinge of the Epistle

In his *On Christian Doctrine,* IV, 20, Augustine refers to this section and what follows as an example of the "majestic style of speech." Verse 28 may be translated in a host of ways, but expressed or unexpressed, God is subject—the context demands it. Is Paul perhaps revising an old adage here; shaping to his own purpose that old saw about the cloud with the silver lining? In his *Republic,* Plato writes: "So we must suppose that, if the righteous man is afflicted with poverty or sickness or any other seeming evil, all this will come to some good for him in the end, either in this life or after death." [48] In any event, the **weakness** theme is being continued: Though we cannot conceive the shape of our adoption—that in itself is a mark of our cruciform existence—and though we endure, he will bring everything together to the point of good for those who love him. And the good is the glory (vv 17f.), the revelation as heirs and co-heirs (vv 16, 17, 19), the glory of the children of God (v 21), the redemption of the "body." This is the outcome for **those who love him,** despite the weakness, indeed, because of it.

Those who love him (cf. Paul's use of Isa. 64:4 in 1 Cor. 2:9) are now defined in new and striking fashion: They **are called according to his purpose.** (The term is used only here and in 9:11.) For the first time in the epistle, an answer is given to the "why?" Till now, the "what," the "where," "by whom," "under what circumstances," and the "when" have had their innings, but not the "why." Why, then? Why the passive voice; why the impossibility of remaining in sin; why does everything, does God, work for good? Because it is **according to his purpose,** and with this phrase we have come to the hinge of the epistle. These words are finally the only explanation Paul can give to his own existence. He did not bring himself to faith; he did not sustain himself in it one second—and so it must be for everyone, **according to his purpose!**

In any discussion between the divine sovereignty and human responsibility, Paul gives the accent to the former. Still a reading and rereading of the epistle will astonish the reader at the degree of the accent! Does this mean that the apostle neglects the factor of human accountability? Scarcely—the "ought," the **just requirement** remains! But is it possible to give such great emphasis to divine initiative and still affirm human responsibility? If we answer "no," do we then choose the one in opposition to the other? If we answer "yes," must we somehow hold the two in a "tension"—divine sovereignty *and* human accountability? And, if that is so, why does not Paul hold them in tension, treat them as paradox; why does he lay all the emphasis on the divine initiative, and at the same time retain the "ought"? This is the question with which Chapters 9-11 deal at length, chapters prefigured in this little hinge, and which furnish the explanation to those innumerable clues throughout the letter.

Paul uses the ancient "climax" device in vv 29-30—**foreknew . . . predestined . . . conformed . . . called . . . justified . . . glorified** (cf. 5:3ff.). All that "being buried," being "united with him in his death through the likeness," "being crucified with," "dying with him," becoming "slaves of God" (Chapter 6); all that "death of the body" (8:10, 13), that "suffering" (8:17-18), "groaning" (8:23), "waiting" (8:23), "hoping" (8:24-25), and "not knowing how to pray as we ought" (8:26)—all that existence "conformed to the image of his Son," the opposite of "the likeness of the image of mortal man" for which his glory was once exchanged (Chapter 1)—all that he has fixed beforehand, **predestined!** And the purpose? That **he might be the first-born among many brethren.** So it is *that* to which the newness ultimately comes round! We are elected so that *he* might be first-born—as august a statement made of Christ as anywhere in the Paulines (cf. Col. 1:15, 18). But one cannot be **first-born** without his **brethren.** The purpose of this "foreknowing" and "predestinating" is thus that Christ might have his kin, that **we too might walk** (6:4), though himself first-born!

However we read those words **foreknew** and **predestined,** they are derivative of the divine purpose! Without us, Christ cannot be **first-born,** and for this reason the "foreknowing," "predestinating," "calling," "justifying" and "glorifying"! Here lies the **good** the deity contrives. **And those whom he justified he also glorified.** The glory is not yet—the action begun is viewed from its consummation. Our glory is a truth so sure that it might just as well have already occurred.

8:31-39 None Shall Separate

Paul is preaching again, and his speech is raised to a pitch where triumphant self-consciousness lunges after expression in rhetorical questions. The verse clusters in 31-34 and 35-39 are each set within a "frame" (the first **for us,** the second **who shall separate?**). **What then shall we say to this? If God is for**

us . . . ? The simple conditional clause (again, the reality of
the premise assumed!) sums up all the divine activity described
to this moment. It has all been **for us**—God never was anything
for himself. He **did not spare his own Son** (that verb "spare"
will be used one last time in 11:21) is the interpretation of the
phrase in 3:25: **whom God put forward.** It is the proof of his
life **for us.** Verse 32 then turns up the other side of the coin:
He **gave him up for us all,** and conjures up the old battle-cry

- **To every one who has faith** (1:16);
- **For every one who does good** (2:10);
- **God shows no partiality** (2:11);
- **For all who believe. For there is no distinction** (3:22);
- **All have sinned . . . justified by his grace as a gift** (3:23f.);
- **Is God the God of Jews only?** (3:29);
- **Abraham . . . father of us all** (4:16);
- **While we were yet sinners Christ died for us** (5:8);
- **One man's act of righteousness leads to acquittal and life
  for all** (5:18).

That word, **gave him up,** is Mark's favorite designation for
Jesus' arrest, trial, and death. Did he derive it from Paul, or
from earliest Christianity through Paul? In any event, that
which befell Christ at God's hands occurred with the same
necessity as the ruin on those who **suppress the truth** in Chapter 1. **He . . . did not spare . . . but gave him up . . .** gives the
lie to the old "penal" theory, which conceived God in the
role of Monsieur Javert in *Les Misérables* waiting to mete out
justice till thwarted by an unwanted compassion. And since
this is so, **will he not also give us all things with him?** If Christ
is not first-born without his brethren, it is also inconceivable
that we should be or possess anything without him, for we were
predestined for conformity with him.

Verses 33 and 34 are replete with antitheses: **Who shall
bring any charge . . . It is God who justifies** (v 33); **who is to
condemn? It is Christ Jesus, who died** (v 34); **who shall sep-**

arate . . . **No, in all these things we are more than conquerors**
(vv 35-37). Antithesis is highly developed in Paul, after the
fashion of ancient Hebrew poetry. (For the sake of the antithesis, the declarative statement in v 34 is to be preferred to
the interrogative in the RSV: **Is it Christ Jesus who died . . . ?**) [49]

Verses 33 and 34 are a dare, a "calling out": Who will accuse
the **elect**, *God's* elect, since it is God who justifies? To accuse
those whom God is "for," is to arrogate to oneself divinity,
since God is the last court of appeal, but, more presumptuous
still, to overturn his judgment, since he has **justified** (v 30)
those whom he foreknew!

Here Paul uses the same linguistic form as appears in Isaiah
50:4-11, the Third Servant Song (the rhythm of the ancient
text, whether the Hebrew or Septuagint, is also of an alternat-
ing question and answer). The passage is an individual psalm
of trust, and in the verses akin to Paul's (Isa. 50:8-9), the motifs
of confidence and the certainty of a hearing are at the fore.
Isaiah's certainty takes on rich expression in courtroom language: "He who vindicates me is near. Who will contend with
me? Who is my adversary? Let him come near to me. Behold,
the Lord God helps me; who will declare me guilty?" For the
servant's enemies the dispute has been decided, and the servant
judged, but the servant is still confident of his rehabilitation.

Paul's purpose with this psalm of trust is in contrast to that
of its original composer. He does not intend to lay a basis for
the condemnation of the unfaithful but to comfort the elect.
So, the propriety of the allusion can only be seen from the end
of an arc at whose beginning lies the anonymous servant—for
whose portrait Israel, the patriarchs, the prophets, and a host
of others may have sat, but at whose center Paul has set Christ
—the end then embracing all who have been made to conform
to him: **If God is for us, who is against us?**

Second Isaiah's own experience as prophet may have colored
the Psalm, since the one who confesses such unshakable trust
in God is also the one entrusted with the "oracle" ("The Lord

God has given me the tongue of those who are taught, that I
may know how to sustain with a word him that is weary,"
Isa. 50:1), and reflection on his own existence may have conjured up in Paul's mind an association with the servant-
prophet's fate, but he never thought to make a simple identification apart from Christ and all who are his.

Verse 34 heightens the thought of v 33: **Who is to condemn?**
The Christ who died, yes, who was raised, is on the right
("hand" to be inferred) and intercedes. The addition, **who died
and was raised** gives flesh and blood to the old colophon,
Jesus Christ, our Lord. Justification comes by way of Christ's
death, to which we are joined and rendered dead to sin (Chapter 6), and by way of his resurrection which we shall share
(6:5, etc.). Without that death and rising there is no justification, no God **for us.**

With his reference to Christ **at the right hand,** Paul is echoing what may have been a coronation psalm. In an "oracle,"
the court prophet whispers in the monarch's ear the divine
command: "Sit at my right hand, till I make your enemies your
footstool" (Ps. 110:1). Whether or not the synagogue ever connected this psalm with the Messiah or Danielic Son of Man,
Jesus is said to have used it on at least two occasions: In a
temple dispute, in which he subtly challenges the ancient doctrine of Messiah as a mere Davidic heir ("how can the scribes
say that the Christ is the son of David . . . David himself calls
him Lord; so how is he his son?" Mark 12:35-37 and parallels),
and at his trial before the high priest, to whose question, "are
you the Christ?" he replies, "I am, and you will see the Son
of man seated at the right hand of Power" (Mark 14:62 and
parallels). Psalm 110 enjoyed a peculiar position among Christians (in the context of baptism in which the "enemy" was for-
sworn?) for whom Christ, following his resurrection, assumed
the place of honor and authority next to the God who would
some day avenge him on his enemies. In response to the question, **who is to condemn?**, Paul repeats a confession which pre-

ceded and followed him far into the post-apostolic period and
down to our own time. (Cf. the near identity of the references
in Rom. 8; 1 Peter 3:22; and Col. 3:1.)

But while Paul shares with other Christian authors the conviction that Jesus is at God's right hand *and* makes intercession
for us, unlike the author of 1 Peter or Colossians (cf. also Heb.
7:25; Acts 7:55-56; and 1 Cor. 15:27-28, in which Paul quotes
Psalm 110 directly), he does not leave his reader to infer the
connection between Christ's session at God's right hand and
his interceding, but unequivocally connects this psalm with
Jesus' action as intercessor. The reason for the connection is
that Paul intends not only to signal Christ's honor or vindication at the last judgment, but to make clear that the very *place*
of the Christ on whom everything depends is a guarantee of
the believers' safety. The believers are Christ's, and since
Christ is seated at "the right hand of Power," his petition on
their behalf is sure of a hearing. Thus, their present, not merely their future is assured. If earlier Paul could not conceive
the elect One or servant apart from those who are his, here
he cannot dissociate their present, however fraught with suffering, from their future defense and acquittal: **Who is to
condemn? It is Christ Jesus, who died, yes, who was raised
from the dead, who is at the right hand of God, who indeed
intercedes for us!**

The interrogative occurs again in v 35, but this time the
subject is not one who accuses or sentences, but rather those
things which mark existence as cruciform (cf. the lists in 1 Cor.
11:26-27; 2 Cor. 6:4ff.; 12:10; 2 Thess. 1:4). None of these things
shall separate from Christ's love, whose "being put forward"
and "being raised" were voluntarily endured.

Pressing to the conclusion of this section, marked by the
phrase, **as it is written,** Paul describes the believers' existence
in the words of Psalm 44:22: "For thy sake we are being killed
all the day long. . . ." A community lament, composed in the
face of political misfortune, the psalm begins with a narrative

of God's saving deeds, only to launch into a dirge over the nation's ruin and the people's oppression. And since the psalmist interprets the political calamity as a religious crisis, he sees it as endured on God's behalf: **For *thy* sake we are being killed all the day long.** Paul however, shares neither the psalmist's disclaimer nor his mood ("all this has come upon us, though we have not forgotten thee, etc." vv 17-18). The purpose of the quotation is simply and without complaint to note that the existence in which nothing shall separate from God's love is still cruciform, precisely because it has been made to conform to Christ's life.

Further, the crisis which for the psalmist seemed to last an eternity—**all the day long**—Paul regards as the "natural" order of things. Life in the Body, conformity to Christ is never punctiliar, but linear, complexive, recurrent—a daily dying. Here then, as in v 17, the theme of the believer's death in the baptism in 6:4 is given its proper interpretation: **If we have died with Christ, we believe that we shall also live with him.** But above all, by setting the believers' suffering in the context of Christ's session and intercession, and thus of their guarantee of a hearing with God, Paul marks their conformity and suffering as the very ground and foundation of their hope. Paul can describe his own existence as a death-sentence, a daily dying, as a being given up to death (1 Cor. 4:9; 15:31; 2 Cor. 4:11), but our verse makes clear that what he says of himself and his apostolic office as the epiphany of Christ is not restricted to himself. Paul is not a special case. This is also true of the remainder of the Pauline and Deutero-Pauline passages that suggest the conformity-pattern. No distinctions are drawn; the life of the believer is conformed to the life of the Crucified.

Verses 37-39 are a hymnic reprise. Reference is again made to the love of Christ, but this time in a roll of thunder! Christ may have been his Father's servant, but the service was entered willingly, out of love for us. For this reason, "we more than conquer" (a pleonasm), and through the agency of that

One. The list in vv 38-39, like that in v 35, once more characterizes the believers' life as cruciform, as shaped to Christ's suffering. Death, life, angels, principalities, things present and things to come, powers, height and depth—none shall separate! (Cf. 1 Cor. 3:22; 10:5; 15:24; 2 Thess. 2:9.)

> My dear Wormwood. . . . Has none ever told you about the law of undulation? . . . . Humans' nearest approach to constancy . . . is undulation—the repeated return to a level from which they repeatedly fall back, a series of troughs and peaks. . . . Now it may surprise you to learn that in His efforts to get permanent possession of a soul, He relies on the troughs even more than on the peaks; some of His special favorites have gone through longer and deeper troughs than anyone else.[50]

None shall separate, for these things are "creation," things with a specific, discrete beginning and end, but "God is God forever!" From his love nothing shall separate. That sphere of existence into which we have been taken up is finally, when all is said and done, the Father's love! **In Christ Jesus our Lord!** Colophon!

GOD'S RIGHTEOUSNESS
IN ISRAEL'S HISTORY
9:1—11:36

■ **9:1-29**   **In Israel's Past**

9:1-5 The Apostle's Lament

This section applies the theme of justification to the historical entity Israel. What Paul has said till now of justification and faith has been consistent in the realm of speculation. The question now is, how do these themes appear when given flesh and blood? [51]

When proceeding to these chapters, Luther's caution still is best:

> Follow this epistle in its order. Concern yourself first with Christ and the gospel, so that you know your sin and his grace. Next, strive with your sins, as taught in chapters 1-8. Then, when you come to chapter 8, under cross and suffering, providence in chapters 9-11 will rightly teach you what a comfort they are. For apart from suffering, cross, and pangs of death, we cannot manage providence without hurt and secret anger against God. So Adam must first be dead before he allows it, before he drinks the strong wine. See to it you do not drink wine while a suckling. . . . Every doctrine has its measure, time, and age. [52]

First, if Paul is not only checking the Gentiles' pride in these chapters, but also giving new meaning to his Jewishness, interpreting the divine activity within the context of the "Jewish question," then a word is needed here respecting terms and their definitions. With one exception, in which Paul contrasts

142

the *outward* and *inward* Jew (2:28), he uses the term *Jew* in a non-technical sense to designate a stance, posture, or attitude which a Gentile or proselyte may also assume by way of circumcision (cf. 1:16; 2:9, 10, 17; 3:1, 9, 29; 9:24 and 10:12). A kind of "Judaism" may thus derive from Christianity. Again, with one exception, in which Paul contrasts those who are **descended from Israel** with those who **belong to Israel** (9:6), he uses the term *Israelite* in a more technical sense to denote the spiritual, divine choice of a people who "strive with God" (cf. 9:4 and 11:1). And here, the exceptions are of greater significance than the rule, for they clearly indicate that neither of the terms may be strictly applied to race. Indeed, in the Talmud, "Jew," "Israelite," or "Hebrew" (which can denote mere physical descent, cf. Phil. 3:5) marks the synagogue held together by the law. This people, then, is not a phenomenon of nature, as a species of horse or dog, but rather of history. The Christian community is analogously defined.

In 9:1, Paul begins with an oath: **I am speaking the truth in Christ . . . my conscience bears me witness in the Holy Spirit.** That phrase, **in Christ,** not merely reinforces the oath, but designates the sphere in which anything at all can be truth, the area in which conscience and speech or self may unite, that is, "in the Spirit." And, the emotion or passion reflected here ought not be missed: **I could wish that I myself were accursed and cut off from Christ for the sake of . . . my kinsmen.** This is no mere patriotic feeling: That people, still the chosen, still zealous for God (a quality Paul would not concede the Jew in 1 Thess. 2:14-16!), is "hardened," on the outside looking in, and he, Paul, himself an Israelite, of Abraham's seed, from the tribe of Benjamin!

Next follows Paul's confession which answers the question: *What of Israel's past?* In reply, Paul enumerates the marks of Israel's election, and concludes with the benediction: **God who is over all be blessed for ever. Amen.** There is rhyme ("sonship" and "glory," "giving of the law" and "worship" have

identical endings in the Greek); rhyme within rhyme ("Israelites," "covenants" and "promises" all rhyme, one word preceding, one concluding, and still another interrupting the rhyming
of "glory" and "giving of the law"). There is that repetition of
the conjunction dear to the heart of the Greek preacher: *(and*
the **glory** *and* the **covenants** *and* the **giving of the law** *and* the
worship *and* the **promises. . . .**); *anti-climax* (**to them belong the
patriarchs**) and *climax* (**and of their race . . . is the Christ;** perhaps even, *theirs* is the **God who is over all**). Paul has gone at
his recitation with care. The article which in Greek precedes
the phrase "according to the flesh," and which is left untranslated, may qualify Israel's glorious past—"to them belong
the Christ, that is, as far as physical descent is concerned"—
but that past is no less glorious. (Elsewhere, Paul uses such
terms as "sonship," "glory" and "promises" only of believers.)
And at the head of the list stands "Israelites"—name for the
"elect" nation, name for the Jews' **advantage,** for that **much in
every way** (cf. 3:1). So this time, the benedictus appears at the
end of an incline, and not a decline (cf. 1:25!).

9:6-13 To Whom the Promise Belongs

Have God's calling and choice of Israel gone awry? Paul responds: **Not as though the word of God had failed.** There has
been a division—**Not all who are descended from Israel belong
to Israel** (in 2:28-29, the contrast was also between Jew and
Jew)—and the division occasioned by a call: To **belong to Israel,** to have Abraham for a father was contingent upon being
called in Isaac. The reference here is to the strife between Sarah
and her maid following Ishmael's birth, in which Abraham re-
sists his wife's demand that Hagar be thrust out and yields to
her only on God's express command. What is important to Paul
is that "tense moment" in which God pursues his purposes contrary to expectation—the reader of Genesis 21 would have assumed that God was on Abraham's side—and thus to all human

willing: "Do as she tells you, for through Isaac shall your descendants be named."

If to be Abraham's child is contingent upon being *called*, then biological descendance counts for nothing; then only the children of promise are *seed*. With each contrast, Paul becomes more specific:

- In v 6, the contrast is between those **from Israel** and those who **belong to Israel,**
- in v 7 between the **children of Abraham** and his **descendants,**
- in v 8 between **children of the flesh** and **children of God** or **of the promise.**

In the Hagar-Sarah allegory of Galatians 4, the contrast is all but identical to that in v 8: The son of the slave is "born according to the flesh," and that of the free woman "through promise" (Gal. 4:23). Thus the phrase in v 7, **through Isaac shall your descendants be named** and that in v 8, the **children of the promise are reckoned as descendants,** come round to the same thing.

On the other hand, the little adversative (**but**) in v 8 further defines the clause prefaced by the adversative in v 7: It is the *promise*, it is the transcendent which creates identity! Note the progression from **descendants,** used without modifier in v 7, to **children** in v 8. To be a *descendant* requires only physical generation, but to be a *child of God* rests on the calling **through Isaac.** The Jew who cared anything for religion, and thus furnished Paul any kind of debate partner, reckoned himself a child of Abraham, and precisely by virtue of biological descent. Now, Paul must go beyond the two clauses in vv 7 and 8 to explain *why* to be called in Isaac excludes such pedigree.

But for the moment, one thing is certain—Paul is describing a Jewishness to which the ordinary tests or criteria on the basis of which a people is defined do not at all apply. In Galatians 3 and 4, Paul uses the Isaac-Ishmael narrative to accent faith as heir of the promise to Abraham: Since Abraham's inheritance was by way of promise, with the advent of faith all who believe share his inheritance. Here, however, the accent is on the promise in order to prepare for the argument in v 11, according to which the promise roots in the divine decree. In Romans 9, Paul is working at a stage in advance of Galatians 3 and 4.

Paul next gives the content of the promise which creates a child of God: "In the appointed time" (the rsv too casually translates the original) **I will return and Sarah shall have a son.** The quotation is from the story of the visitation to Abraham at Hebron, incorporated into the Abraham-Lot cycle (cf. Gen. 18:10, 14). In the story, three men—a "trinity" representing God's single yet differentiated activity—visit Abraham and Sarah, and relieve the anxiety over their appearance with the promise that Sarah shall have a son. But the promise has been delayed to the point of the absurd, so that Sarah laughs and says: "Shall I indeed bear a child, now that I am old?" Following this contrast between the divine promise and its reception in unbelief, the narrator climaxes his story with the question: "Is anything too hard for the Lord?"

If the purpose of Paul's quotation from the Sarah-Hagar episode was to signal the divine activity in opposition to all human willing, here his intention is to mark its opposition to all human capacity. That curious word for *time*—to mark God's own good time—leaves no question as to who has the initiative! But the content of the promise allows us to infer why biological descendance and true sonship are not the same. Abraham had *two* sons, one by Sarah, and one by Hagar (cf. Gal. 4:22); Sarah's is the child of promise, and the promise involves selection. The physical-natural character of the Jewish idea of covenant is therefore "spiritualized," and the instances of election or choice in the history of the patriarchs are "spiritualized" to the effect that Isaac, the later-born was preferred to Ishmael, since Isaac was son of the promise (Gen. 18:10, 14). For Paul, the events at Isaac's birth are proof that biological descendance is of no value. A wedge has been driven between the empirical Israel and the Israel of promise.

In vv 10 through 13, what was implicit is made explicit:

- To be a "child" is not merely to be a "descendant" but to be called (v 7);
- To be a "child of God" is to be a "child of the promise," to be "named" a descendant (v 8);
- The promise that Sarah should have a son (v 9) assumes a choice, a selection.

Indeed, Rebecca had two sons, but only one was chosen (vv 10-13). (The argument is tight, and a dash should follow v 10, since vv 11-12a are a parenthesis; the subject is not resumed till the phrase, **she was told** in v 12.) This choice took place before the two sons were born, before either had done anything—lest it might be thought the choice was somehow conditioned by an action, whether good or bad—"in order that God's purpose of election might continue" (or, perhaps, "that God's purpose might be according to election"), due not to human instrumentality, but to the God who calls.

Verse 12 resumes the thought begun in v 10. While Rebecca was pregnant by Isaac, she was told **the elder will serve the younger.** Here, Paul reaches into a block of narratives titled *the descendants of Isaac* (cf. Gen. 25:19 and 23). At the head of these narratives a word of the Lord serves as a preface to a series of events grouped about the hostility between Jacob and Esau. The prefatory word roots the destinies of the two brothers in a divine sign—the two struggle with each other in Rebecca's womb—and thus accents the secrecy in which God will carry out his plan. Paul's reference to the purpose of God's election as "remaining" according to his call suits the ancient narrative, which explains Israel's history in terms of the inexplicable, hidden divine will. To this much of Paul's argument, if not to all of it, his Jewish reader must consent, since the patriarchal narratives would never have assumed their peculiar shape had not the Jew been certain his history had originated in the divine willing.

Paul then concludes his initial argument in Chapter 9 (again signaled by the phrase, **as it is written**) with a reference to Malachi 1, which simply recapitulates the Genesis theme. The era in which the unknown author of this prophecy lived was in a sense akin to Paul's own—the great world-change anticipated with the completion of the Second Temple had failed to appear, and the religious community was divided among skeptics and those who held resolutely to their faith. Israel's external and economic situation was no better. She suffered natural catastrophes and threats from her neighbors. The exiles, allowed to return to their homeland under relaxed Persian rule, were confined to such tiny space that some prospered at others' expense. With an eye to the rescue of Judah and Jerusalem, Malachi delivers six speeches that describe an arc from past to future. In the first, the prophet in a sharp and antithetical formula roots Rebecca's preference for Jacob in the divine choice: "I have loved Jacob but I have hated Esau" (vv 2b-3a), a choice from which Israel may derive certainty of its salvation.

9:14-29 Election in Order to Mercy

The Divine Election (14-18)

Is God to be blamed for the fact that most did not believe? The argument seems irrefutable, but Paul responds with his **By no means!** and in v 15 quotes from one of a cluster of Exodus narratives (Exod. 33:19), grouped about the theme of God's presence. In Exodus 33, God answers Moses' intercession on Israel's behalf with the promise to proclaim his name, and in the formula cited by Paul, gives his name and thus his nature definition: "I will be gracious . . . and will show mercy." But if the Exodus narrator's primary concern was to define God's nature in light of his gracious activity, it is Paul's intent to define God's activity in light of his nature, that is, in light of his freedom, signaled in the formula: "I will be gracious to whom I will be gracious" (cf. Exod. 3:14: "I am who I am," or "I will be that I will be"). In this fashion, the Exodus quotation "interprets" the phrase in v 13: **Esau I hated.**

A new note is struck here, but left till vv 17-18 for its exposition—hardening as well as mercy is from God. Paul's submission to God's unsearchable will is reminiscent not merely of prophets or of Qumran, but of such Greeks as Hesiod and Sophocles who sought and found refuge in Zeus, despite his capriciousness. But how can such preserving the notion of a just God win the struggle with logic, to say nothing of the struggle with the ethical requirement? Kant saw the problem as clearly as anyone before or after him:

> Were this faith to be portrayed as having so peculiar a power and so mystical (or magical) an influence, that . . . it is yet competent to better the whole man from the ground up (to make a new man of him) . . . such a faith would have to be regarded as imparted and inspired directly by heaven . . . and everything connected even with the moral constitution of man would resolve itself into an unconditioned decree of God: "He hath mercy on whom he will, and whom he will he hardeneth. . . ." [53]

Paul sums up in v 16. By attraction to the Old Testament quotation in v 15, the "one who calls" (v 11) is now the "one who has mercy." For this reason, the election is "not because of works." For this reason neither "willing" nor "running" (RSV: **exertion**) lies at the base of selection. The Old Testament reference in v 15, and the reference to the God of mercy in v 16 suggest a context for that "purpose according to election" which is in absolute contrast to the setting within which every other deity similarly conceived is supposed to act—caprice! Somehow, the "purpose according to election" comes down to mercy. But can mercy be the opposite of caprice? The hint will be taken up again later.

If in vv 15-16 the theophany in Exodus 33 served to illustrate
the divine freedom in showing mercy, in vv 17-18 the Exodus
plague stories illustrate that freedom in the act of "hardening."
In the latter, Paul refers to the word that God gives Moses for
Pharaoh following the sixth plague. Though a minor skein in
the narrative and difficult to interpret, the sense of Exodus
9:14ff. is that God has allowed Pharaoh to live in order to show
his power and declare his glory. In v 18, Paul then draws his
twofold conclusion: **So then he has mercy upon whomever he
wills, and he hardens the heart of whomever he wills.**

The Old Testament text of Pharaoh's "hardening" which
Paul follows so closely here comprises an explanation of the
signs in Exodus (4:21; 7:3; 9:12 and 14:4, 8). If the term *hardening* was once chosen at random to explain why the signs performed by Moses before Pharaoh did not achieve their goal, or
to indicate the "coincidence" of God's plan with that of Pharaoh, the priestly writer went on to fix the resistance of the
Egyptian ruler in God himself. Threading through all these
passages is the assumption that the plagues do not result from
Pharaoh's hardening, but quite the reverse—Pharaoh's heart is
hardened that God might multiply his signs and further harden
Pharaoh's heart, as a result of which God will deliver Israel
with mighty acts, and all shall come to know who he is.

This total concentration on the theme of God's self-revela-
tion, this gathering up all of Israel's history into one magnifi-
cent act of self-disclosure, furnishes the reason for this peculiar
and unique motif. If Paul's intent was to interpret God's mercy
and now his "hardening" in light of his freedom, his "election," he could scarcely have found better precedent. And if
the plague-narratives were capable of any other reading than
Paul gives them here—his Greek Bible left nothing to the psychological—the mystery of Pharaoh's obduracy lay clearly with
God. But what for Old Testament faith appears from nowhere
only to vanish again, is for Paul at the heart of the matter.

Striking in all this is that Paul does not take his sovereignty theme from the patriarchal narrative (except for Malachi's interpretation of the Jacob saga in v 13), but from the Exodus "hardening" narrative, and not in respect of Israel, but of Pharaoh. In other words, the "hardening" is applied to a figure through whom God showed mercy to Israel! Just as v 16 accents the "God who has mercy," though what preceded did not exclude the opposite idea—**Esau I hated**—so v 18 lays the stress on the God who hardens, though what preceded, at least by implication, did not exclude its opposite—hardening in order to deliverance, mercy!

One scholar who took offense at 9:14-18 wrote:

> Paul's conception of predestination is perhaps the worst of all from our point of view because it seems a denial of the very thing that Paul saw in the face of Christ, that is love. It seems arbitrary. It seems cruel. It cannot be made to look otherwise. It does not seem fatherly. So we are in a region where we are not going to follow Paul unless we want to.[54]

True enough—for Paul, God's election is beyond right and wrong; it gives expression to his sovereign will. At least three things must be kept in mind, however, or his entire argument is misunderstood.

First, the idea of predestination, stated here with such sharpness, does not inquire back into a prehistoric period in which the dice were thrown over human destiny, but has its home within the sphere of the divine grace. Paul is after disclosing the nature of grace, pointing his readers to the place where they belong, and at which every attempt to be righteous before the Creator becomes pride. Justification depends on God's mercy, not **upon man's will or exertion,** or it depends on such willing and running—which for Paul could only mean there is no justification before God.

Second, to allow the truth to stand that God does everything and that humankind cannot resist his will (v 19), is for Paul the greatest comfort. Indeed, it is faith. And when evil, "fleshly" existence or "hardening" is not construed in mythological fashion as a power alongside God and with which he is locked in struggle; when Satan himself is seen as nothing but the mask of the absent God, then the appearance of dualism disappears and the answer to Blake's question is "Yes," though he himself would have shouted "No":

> Tyger! tyger! burning bright
> In the forests of the night,
> What immortal hand or eye
> Could frame thy fearful symmetry?
> . . . . When the stars threw down their spears,
> And water'd heaven with their tears,
> Did he smile his work to see?
> Did he who made the Lamb make thee? [55]

Third, the fact that Paul regards everything which occurs as taking place by God's will, cannot be represented as a theoretical statement, but only as a confession. It can be understood only within the context of faith as praise of God.

But what of the moral factor? If the human will is "bound," how can one be held accountable for one's acts: **Why does he still find fault? For who can resist his will?** (v 19). How can one be responsible, be in possession of any "moral sense" if one is not at the same time free? Is not responsibility the obverse side of freedom which enables us to choose wrongly or well and thus enjoy or suffer the consequences of our acts? The apostle does not address himself to this question, but it is one with which his interpreters have always wrestled (Augustine, Erasmus, Luther, Calvin, Arminius, Swedenborg, Jonathan Edwards, and the Mathers!).

"Freedom of the will" and responsibility are not two sides of the same coin. To regard them so reflects an inability or unwillingness to embrace the grandeur or horror of the natural world, and thus to create a world apart from nature, a world of "spirit." (Luther and his "enemy" Aristotle, were kin in at least one respect—they contended that knowledge must begin with the evidence yielded by the senses.) In this fashion, if God is not hustled out of the world we see he becomes the variable, and the natural world becomes the constant. Free will then spells "salvation" from the natural world—a reversal of the roles of God and the natural world in Paul, for whom God is the constant and the natural world is the variable. But the assumption which underlies the notion of free will, namely, that every deed follows an act of will, is just as shaky as the assumption that choice is mere appearance. For when carried to its conclusion, the notion of free will means that I have somehow willed myself into existence. "Free will" is every bit as much a "faith" as the Pauline belief that what we do or what occurs to us only appears accidental and freely chosen so long as we look away from God.

Predestination is not something that Paul adds to the concept of justification, but rather it is his application of the concept to our entire existence. To view our wills apart from grace as bound, and yet to hold ourselves responsible, means simply to see ourselves as in the presence of God. To see ourselves as bound but delivered by a God of grace, and to see what seems to be our choice as mere appearance, to see God as the One in whom cause reigns, is one and the same act of faith. Indeed, it is a witness to the "glorious liberty of the children of God," since it frees our conscience to set appearance within its proper bounds.

Is not our hatred of the Jew the negative proof of this truth? This Jew, with whose appearing the definition of race or religion has been radically altered, who lives by birth and yet not by birth at all but by the will of God, and thus can never suffer extinction like the Pharaohs; this natural-unnatural someone, a race and yet not at all a race, which eludes all scientific definition and thus causes our view of the world such embarrassment—is he not hated because he is witness to a sovereign God at work in the world, and thus a witness to the truth that we all are in Another's hands; is he not hated because to accept him would be to acknowledge God as God, and at terrible cost?

The Divine Mercy (19-29)

What of Israel's *present?* Paul introduces the objection of his fictional opponent with the formula: **You will say to me then** ... (cf. 11:19; most of the time, Paul will voice the objection in his own words). It is the same question as was put in 3:5 and 7. In 6:1, 15 and 9:14, the question of Paul's opponent was stated in another form, and from another perspective—the revelation of righteousness apart from law or deeds—but with the exception of the question in 8:31 (**What then shall we say to this?**), the questions are all an objection to the notion of God's activity independent of human behavior. Whether or not his choice of Pharaoh to illustrate the hardening was an attempt to catch his audience unawares, Paul is only too conscious that his reader has gotten the point, and voices the objection flat outright: **Why does he still find fault? For who can resist his will?**

Verse 19 is a variation on opening lines from the third section of The Wisdom of Solomon, in which the sage recalls how "Wisdom" led Israel from Adam to Moses, an activity climaxed in God's judgment on Egyptians and Canaanites. The writer's intent is to comfort readers undergoing experiences which they are unable to assign to God, which in reality contradict what they believe to be in accord with the divine purpose, and as a result threaten to shake their faith. In this situation, "Wisdom" announces that faith must not be torn by conflict, but must concede to God's freedom even these experiences which are past reckoning: "For who will say 'what hast thou done?' Or who will resist thy judgment?" (Wisdom 12:12).

Now Paul places in the mouth of his hypothetical opponent a word which "Wisdom" says no one has a right to utter, this time not in face of uninterpretable experience, but in face of the freedom of God. And in answer, he replies: "Who are you, a man, to answer back to God?" Till now, the imagined objection or the response has been oblique. But here the apostle's response is positively frontal, and the usual "by no means!" is replaced with **Who are you . . . ?**

Paul then continues with an allusion to two "woes" in First and Second Isaiah. In the first, Isaiah 29, the prophet laments Judah's plotting against the Assyrians. In the second, Isaiah 45, the prophet enters Yahweh in a civil dispute with his people who have taken offense at the news that God will use the pagan Cyrus to free them. The rhetorical questions in both contexts reflect incredulity that the Artist should be thought of as inferior to his material. ("Shall the potter be regarded as the clay; that the thing made should say to its maker, 'He did not make me'?" Isa. 29:16; "Does the clay say to him who fashions it, 'What are you making?' " Isa. 45:9. The questions are framed in such fashion as to require a negative reply.)

Paul continues his response by harking back to an individual lament from Jeremiah, who uses the same rhetorical devices and potter-clay motif. (To this moment, Paul has deferred any direct reference to the potter, since the sequence of his argument in vv 19ff. is the reverse of that in his sources, that is, from the clay to the potter; the sequence is determined by the question of Paul's "objector" in v 19.) At God's command Jeremiah, in doubt, and scorned by his enemies at the delay of the ruin he predicted for Judah ("Behold, they say to me, 'Where is the word of the Lord? Let it come!' "), pays a visit to a potter. This ordinary event becomes the occasion for a revelation which the prophet shapes into a word of proclamation: "O house of Israel, can I not do with you as this potter has done? says the Lord. Behold, like the clay in the potter's hand, so are you in my hand, O house of Israel" (Jer. 18:6). For Jeremiah, the word is a confirmation—God is sovereign and holds the event in his hand. For the people it is a reprimand—no one may fix God to earlier promises, for the motives and criteria of his activity, the setting of the time for his intervention, are left to him alone. The prophet's lament and the people's scorn are silenced. They must concede, as did Jeremiah's successor, that "we are the clay, and thou art our potter" (Isa. 64:8).

God, the **molder** of v 20, the **potter** of v 21, has the right to do as he chooses with what is his. He has the right over the clay to make of the same lump the one a vessel for honor, and another for dishonor (the rsv softens the harshness of expression: **for beauty . . . for menial use**). The purpose is according to choice, to election. Paul's word in v 21 is reminiscent of a passage in the next to last section in Wisdom, in which the sage, in a reflective exposition on the folly of idol worship, describes the potter as making useful vessels and false gods from the same lump: "He fashions out of the same clay both the vessels that serve clean uses as those for contrary uses, making all in like manner; but which shall be the use of each of these the worker in clay decides" (15:7). However abhorrent to his reader the analogy between the potter and God's election of Isaac versus Ishmael, Jacob versus Esau, Israel versus Pharaoh, for Paul it was a simple inference from the description of Pharaoh as "carefully preserved" for the sake of God's name and glory.

With only a slight alteration of two of the RSV, the original sense of vv 22 and 23 can be restored: "What if God, desiring to show his wrath and to make known his power, has *brought out with much diligence* the vessels of wrath made for destruction, *and, in fact,* in order to make known the riches of his glory for the vessels of mercy, which he has prepared beforehand for glory . . . ?"

If Paul has in mind here not only the Exodus deliverance but also that from exile in Babylon, then Jeremiah 50:25 (to which at least a portion of 9:21 is identical) gives an added light. The author of the great oracle against Babylon (a contemporary of Second Isaiah?) does not see in Nebuchadnezzar the tool of Israel's chastening, but (dependent on First Isaiah 13:5?) prophesies the ruin of Babylon as God's punishment for the unrighteousness done his people (cf. Isaiah 54:16), a ruin which spells the exiles' return. Since Babylon has not reckoned on Yahweh's might, he will muster the nations against it, and Babylon will come to know he is a God of recompense: "The Lord has opened his armory, and brought out the weapons of his wrath, for the Lord God of hosts has a work to do in the land of the Chaldeans."

The sense of Romans 9:22-23 may thus be gleaned from Paul's reminiscence of two deliverances: In order to awaken Babylon to the recognition that he is a God of requital (**desiring to show his wrath and to make known his power, v 22a**), the Lord has opened his armory, amassed the nations against Babylon ("brought out with much diligence the vessels of wrath," v 22b), with the result that he will deliver his people by his mighty acts (**to make known the riches of his glory for the vessels of mercy, etc. vv 23-24**). Or again, God hardens Pharaoh's heart in order to multiply miracles and signs, to the end that he will bring Israel out with a "mighty hand and an outstretched arm." The theme of v 17 is thus expanded in vv 22-23. The word, "I have raised you up for the very purpose of showing my power in you," is now altered to read **desiring to show his wrath and to make known his power . . . in order to make known the riches of his glory.** The antithetical parallels are there for all to see: **To show his wrath and to make known his power** is contrasted with **to make known the riches of his glory; vessels of wrath** are contrasted with **vessels of mercy,** and that which is **made for destruction** with that which is **prepared beforehand for glory.** Finally, the sovereignty motif struck in vv 18-21 is resumed, and what was implicit (hardening in order to deliverance, in order to mercy) is now crystal clear.

All this activity finally devolves upon us: **Even us whom he has called, not from the Jews only** (v 24). "Purpose," "predestination" is not restricted to Israel. Paul then draws support for this contention in vv 25-26. In these two verses, the apostle has merged two quotations from Hosea 2:23 and 1:10, never used by the rabbis of the hardening of Israel and the calling of another people. The two passages are dissimilar in form, the one a hymn, used perhaps at a reenactment of the creation (at a New Year's festival?), and the second an oracle. Hosea, contemporary of First Isaiah, announces to the northern kingdom that a great "day of Jezreel" is about to dawn. Israel, whose judgment had culminated in the annulment of the covenant, is destined once more to become God's people. Her name will be changed from "Not my people" to "My people" or "Sons of the living God." Israel's reinstatement, her being "sown" in the land, will mean the return of rights to the dispossessed and an immeasurable increase, or, in the words of the ancient Genesis oracle, "The number of the people of Israel shall be like the sand of the sea" (Hos. 1:10; cf. Gen. 22:17). In face of Israel's oppression by Assyria, and her insignificant numbers, that "day" had all the earmarks of miracle, a raising of the promise to the fathers to the nth degree in a final deed. For Paul the event of Christ comprised that deed, and from it and from faith in that deed among the Gentiles Paul trajected back into Hosea's promise a word which exceeded the boundaries of Israel: **Even us whom he called, not from the Jews only but also from the Gentiles, as indeed he says in Hosea. . . .**

What then does it mean that the greater part of Israel is hardened and only a remnant follows the Messiah? It means that God has called not only Jews but also Gentiles to his lordship. In 3:29, Paul asked: **Or is God the God of Jews only? Is he not the God of Gentiles also?** and replied: **Yes, of Gentiles also** (Simeon bar Johai, A.D. 185, disagreed, and on Exodus 20:2 wrote: "God said to the Israelites: I am God over all who come into the world, but have joined my name only to you. I am not called the God of the nations of the world, but the God of Israel. This means: God is the God of all, insofar as he has created them and insofar as they will stand before his judgment seat; but God is Israel's God, insofar as only this people is loved by God and destined for bliss").[56]

158

To the Hosea quotation in vv 25-26, Paul next joins two passages from Isaiah 10 and 1. They are not a merger, but a chain-like explanation of v 24, each link in the chain drawn from an independent portion of the Old Testament. The origin of such peculiar exposition lies in Judaism between the Testaments, and appears with considerable frequency in Romans (cf. 10:5-8, 11-13, 19-21; 11:8-10, and 15:9-12). "Purpose," "predestination," and "Israel" are not synonyms. Though indeed God's word did not fail with Israel (v 6), that phrase, **from the Jews** (v 24), signals a "remnant." If Hosea's promise of renewal furnished Paul an occasion for an inclusive, the warning in Isaiah 10 furnished the occasion for an exclusive interpretation of the ancient oracle, the two passages linked in the word of Israel's increase. In Isaiah 10:22f., the author challenges a popular "remnant theology" according to which whoever remained in Zion once Judah's punishment was complete, was destined for life. To the prophet this notion was false. There is no salvation without a "leaning" on Yahweh: "For though your people Israel be as the sand of the sea, only a remnant will return." In fact, if God had not preserved a remnant, there would have been no Israel at all.

To Isaiah's warning, Paul in v 29 adds a portion of an invective or woe, uttered perhaps at a "Zion festival" celebrating the invulnerability of the Holy City: "If the Lord of hosts had not left us a few survivors, we should have been like Sodom, and become like Gomorrah" (Isa. 1:9). The prophet's burning hope that the survivors of Judah's devastation might be a "remnant that remains," that Yahweh's goodness, which alone had prevented their heaping on themselves the destruction of Sodom and Gomorrah, might still surround them, was his sole reason for uttering the woe. But if for Isaiah the survivors' persisting was still an open question, for Paul it was not—a remnant had indeed "remained" (cf. e.g., the references to his "kinsmen" in 16:7, 11, 21). That fact led Paul to interpret the prophet not in

light of his hope but in light of that hope's restriction to the
few, for what remained was only a "remnant."

■ 9:30—10:21   In Israel's Present
9:30-33 The Stumbling Stone

As so many of the preceding, the question in v 30 (**what shall
we say?**) follows the Scripture support and draws the conclusion to what precedes (here, in reference to the calling of the
Gentiles, vv 21ff.). There is an amazing reversal of conditions
here. The Gentiles, though not pursuing righteousness, attained to it, and, in fact, to a righteousness by faith; but Israel,
with all its pursuit of the law, found itself one step behind non-
pursuit. But why? **They did not pursue it through faith** (v 32).
The law, then, cannot be kept through deeds by which one
establishes a claim upon God. The attempt to keep the law in
this fashion frustrates its purpose, construes its keeping as a
human possibility (**as if it were based on works**), when the law
itself points to its keeping as something to be "revealed." Thus,
pursuing a law which aimed at righteousness, but supposing
the object of its pursuit could give what it was never intended
to give, Israel did not "reach to" the law.

Why is this pursuit worse than no pursuit at all? The answer
is given in vv 32-33: Israel **stumbled over the stumbling stone.**
In v 33, Paul quotes from memory, and allows his recollection
of the one passage in Isaiah 8:14 to color his reference to the
other in Isaiah 28:16, in effect merging two passages of contrasting moods. Both speak to the Assyrian danger, challenging
Judah's confidence that its worship or temple will preserve it
from the fate of its sister kingdom to the north, but in the one
instance, the "stone" is a threat, and in the other, a promise.
In Isaiah 8, the temple visitor will encounter the jealous God
of Sinai in that stone which he imagines guarantees his safety:
"The Lord of hosts . . . will become . . . a stone of offense, and

a rock of stumbling to both houses of Israel" (v 14). In Isaiah 28, the stone will furnish protection: "Behold, I am laying in Zion for a foundation a stone, a tested stone. . . ." (v 16). Regardless of how the synagogue may have read the latter verse —of Zion, Messiah, faith, the remnant, or simply of "him who believes"—Paul interpreted either "stone" as referring to "the Lord of hosts," to the Christ, "set" for the Jews' stumbling. God himself initiated that event; he raised the stone for stumbling, for offense and for faith. In Jesus Christ, God, the Handler or Potter, shapes one for honor and the other for dishonor, brings forth vessels of wrath to make known his glory toward the vessels of mercy (vv 20ff.).

10:1-4 Christ the End of the Law

In 9:1f., the apostle referred to his sorrow and anguish for his kinsmen **by race.** Now he writes of his prayer for them: **That they may be saved. They have a zeal for God,** he adds. Write "zeal for God" over all of Judaism! But it is not **enlightened.** Verse 3, in which the themes of Chapter 9 are resumed, gives the reason why. That zeal is not **enlightened,** because Israel *ignored* the righteousness of God and sought to establish its own. (The rsv translates: **For, being ignorant of the righteousness that comes from God, and seeking to establish their own, they did not submit to God's righteousness;** but it is a deliberate act to which Paul is referring; cf. the parallels—9:31: **Israel who pursued the righteousness which is based on law . . . did not succeed;** 9:22: **did not pursue it through faith, but as if it were based on works,** and 10:3: **seeking to establish their own . . . righteousness.**)

In Philippians 3:9 the same contrast is drawn between a righteousness "of my own, based on law," that is, a zealous striving after the Torah by which the attempt is made to wrest for oneself one's due, and a righteousness which has God as its author and occurs "on the ground of faith." (The rsv translates Phil. 3:9: "That depends on faith," but scarcely anywhere else outside the Romans epistle does Paul so clearly mark off faith as ground or instrument from faith as cause.)

Verse 4 corresponds to the "as it is written" in 9:33: **For Christ is the end of the law, that every one who has faith may be justified.** Does this mean

1. that the law has been put an end to, so that everyone who has faith may be justified, or,
2. that Christ is the end of the law as a way of righteousness, "an end to legalism for the attainment of righteousness" to every one who has faith, or,
3. that in respect of righteousness, Christ is the law's goal for everyone who believes?

One thing is sure—the law has not been annihilated. But it is also true that Christ is an end, subjectively viewed, to the law as a way of righteousness, though the law itself was never given for such purpose. Paul may have the second reading in mind—use is always uppermost with him—but the third is best supported by the context (cf. 9:31: **Israel . . . did not succeed**). The law had a goal, but the goal was not the establishment of righteousness through its keeping, but rather Christ through whom we keep the law. (That little phrase in 1 Cor. 1:30, "Christ our righteousness," is, after all, the heart and core of the Romans epistle.)

But then that means that the law aimed at infinitely more than its "keeping," for which reason it neither intended nor was able to establish righteousness. Such was reserved for Another, and with him the law was not rehabilitated, but at last "made to stand" (3:31)! Now that he has come and the goal attained, fulfillment of the **just requirement** (8:4), the "ought" of the law has at last become possibility. But the law as external command, as "letter," loosed from its Giver and shorn of its goal, given independent status as a thing to be "kept" in exchange for righteousness—and by virtue of its alliance with

162

the "flesh" giving sin its opportunity (7:8)—is a caricature of the divine will, an enemy, and existence "under" it marked for death.

10:5-11 The Near Word

Paul begins this section with a word from the Holiness Code of Leviticus 17-26: "You shall therefore keep my statutes and my ordinances, by doing which a man shall live" (Lev. 18:5). In this passage Moses is holding before Israel's eyes the example of the Canaanites whose expulsion from the land was a punishment for their sexual excesses. In this respect the "statutes" and "ordinances" of Yahweh were strict and inexorable, and their keeping guaranteed "life." Paul substitutes the phrase **the righteousness which is based on the law** for the "statutes" and "ordinances" in Leviticus 18. His purpose, however, is not to contrast two types of righteousness, but rather to compare the righteousness of faith with deeds by which one might supposedly achieve righteousness (cf. the same contrast in Gal. 3:12). By introducing his quotation with the words, **Moses writes,** Paul does not intend to make the Lawgiver the advocate of a righteousness based on law in the teeth of grace (the verses which follow clearly set Moses on the side of the righteousness by faith). And indeed, the "life" promised here is a far cry from the life which Paul always has in mind—it is mere protection against the death penalty.

Next follows Paul's "pesher" or line-by-line commentary on two conflated texts from Deuteronomy that contrast the performance or use of the law which Moses describes with the righteousness of faith. But by what right does Paul refer the word from Deuteronomy to the righteousness of faith? The subject of Deuteronomy is the commandment! The context of Paul's introductory clause in v 6 (**Do not say**), gives him the right: "Not because of your righteousness or the uprightness of your heart are you going in to possess their land, but

163

because of the wickedness of these nations . . ." (Deut. 9:5).
The "sermon" in Deuteronomy is addressed to the psychological situation to follow the taking of the land. Israel will have
subjugated peoples mightier than herself, and from which she
might infer her own good conduct ("it is because of my righteousness that the Lord has brought me in to possess this
land"). But in his "valedictory," Moses announces that Yahweh
had quite other motives which moved him to act. Israel's conduct was not effective, indeed, she remained a "stiff-necked"
people. To this point, at least, the Deuteronomist is on the side
of a righteousness which excludes performance.

The warning in Deuteronomy 9 is then merged with the
"proverb" in Deuteronomy 30 (cf. Ps. 139:8): The word of
Yahweh to Israel is final and all-sufficient; it does not require
any human effort to render it contemporary: "This commandment . . . is not too hard for you. . . . It is not in heaven, that
you should say, 'Who will go up for us to heaven, and bring it
to us . . . ?' Neither is it beyond the sea, that you should say,
'Who will go over the sea for us, and bring it to us . . . ?'" (vv
11-14). Paul has altered the second question to read: "'Who
will descend into the abyss?'" Even if the alteration results
from associating a Psalm-word with the text in Deuteronomy
("He commanded, and raised the stormy wind, which lifted up
the waves of the sea. They mounted up to heaven, they went
down to the depths," Ps. 106:25-26), it suits the "pesher" beau-
tifully. Once again, the notion of deeds or performance is
excluded. Once again, Moses ranges himself on the side of a
righteousness exclusive of human conduct.

Into his quotation of the proverb Paul sets two comments of
his own, the one attached to the question, "'Who will go up
for us to heaven?'" and the other to the question, "'Who will
go over the sea for us?'" To put the first, Paul writes, is the
same as to ask: "'Who will bring Christ down?'" To put the
second is the same as to ask: "'Who will bring Christ up from
the dead?'" If Paul's primary purpose with the conflated texts

is to support his contention concerning a righteousness *not* based on law, the net effect of his commentary is to identify the "commandment" with Christ himself. What thus was implicit in his comments on 9:32-33 has become explicit here.

Paul concludes his quotation with a final word from Deuteronomy 30:14, and again attaches a comment to it. The command, that is, Christ or **the word of faith which we preach** (note the progression!) is **near,** so that none need ascend or descend to it. It is in the heart, in the mouth, for God has brought it near. The word **near** is only a synonym for that term **revealed** in 1:17 (recall the lines in that old Latin hymn: "Given from on high to me, I cannot rise to Thee!"). There is one important omission in Paul's quotation. Deuteronomy 30:14 adds to the word of the nearness of Yahweh's commands the phrase, "so that you can do it." If the Deuteronomist is truly on Paul's side, then the omission is not an alteration of the sense of the text, but an "interpretation" consonant with the writer's theology.

Paul then gives the reason for the nearness of the word: **Because, if you confess with your lips that Jesus is Lord and believe in your heart that God raised him from the dead, you will be saved** (v 9). In 1 Corinthians 12:3, after reminding his readers of the equivocal nature of their gift of "tongues," Paul struggles to bring the phenomenon under a Christological control: "No one can say 'Jesus is Lord' except by the Holy Spirit." If in that passage the apostle does not intend to say that however lofty his readers' moment of rapture, it can never jeopardize their Christian confession, here he does not intend to say that the mere uttering of words has its result in salvation. For this reason he appends the word, **and believe in your heart that God raised him from the dead.** Confession *and* faith have salvation as their consequence. So near is the word, since the mouth yields one and the heart the other! The verse is a comment on v 8, and at the same time gives the content of that word: **Jesus is Lord . . . God raised him from the dead.** Verse

10 likewise indicates the nearness of the word, but whereas in v 9 the final clause reads simply **you will be saved,** the dual use of the untranslated preposition in v 10 suggests two results—justification and salvation. The two terms are not identical, but they appear here for the sake of the parallelism of "mouth" and "heart" in v 8 which is repeated in v 9.

Again, in v 11, Paul appeals to the promise in Isaiah 28:16. The "oracle," God himself, is Guarantor that the nearness, that the exclusion of performance, deeds, or conduct does not jeopardize results. It is the God of Scripture who is Guarantor, for he has laid this stone, set this command, revealed this Christ, established this word—so near!

10:12-13 One Lord for All

Verse 12 furnishes the commentary on v 11: If God is Guarantor that nearness does not jeopardize the Word, he is also Guarantor that the word is near to all. In Galatians 3:28, Paul writes that with the advent of faith there is neither Jew nor Greek, slave nor free, male nor female. The movement is thus from the God of the Gentiles "also" (3:29), to the One who is "Lord of all" (v 12), and lordship takes its definition from that bestowal of riches "upon all who call upon him." This is no usual definition of lordship. Lordship commonly denotes ownership, control, the right to satisfaction from the slave, but this lordship consists in giving, bestowing (cf. 2 Cor. 8:9!). A strange and curious thing!

If the word is near (v 8); near as confession and faith (v 9); near as heart and mouth (v 10); if that nearness does not jeopardize results (v 11); and if that word is near to all (v 12), then all who call on the Lord's name will be saved. Now Paul cites a portion of the great salvation oracle in Joel 2 (v 32), a chapter interpreted messianically in primitive Christianity (cf. Acts 2:17-21). In the midst of Judah's economic ruin, the fourth century prophet announces that God has heard his people's cry, and promises a riddance to the grasshopper plague, a pouring out of his Spirit and the deliverance of Judah and Jerusalem from all their enemies. And the condition for such deliverance is that "all who call upon the name of the Lord shall be delivered." The New Testament community referred that "name" to Jesus (cf. Acts 2:21ff.). From the passage in Joel may even have derived the first naming of Christians as those who "call on" or are "named by the Lord" (cf. e.g., Acts 9:14; 22:16, and Paul's numerous references to those who are "called" in the introductions to his epistles and elsewhere). For Paul, Joel's oracle was proof of the universal scope of the gospel. The seer may have been no more conscious of this than he was of Jesus of Nazareth, but he did recognize that the condition for Judah's deliverance lay not in membership in the people of Zion, but in a confession of Yahweh. For Paul, it remained only to say "there is no distinction between Jew and Greek."

The apostle has come full circle: From **The word is near you** (v 8), to **confess** and **believe, justified** and **saved** (vv 9-10), to **no one who believes in him will be put to shame** (v 11), to **the same Lord . . . bestows his riches upon all** (v 12), to the final phrase in v 13: **Every one who calls upon the name of the Lord will be saved.**

10:14-21 Israel Heard

There is a climax in vv 14ff.—each subsequent clause repeats the most important word in what precedes. There is also a retracing of steps: **How are men to call upon him** (cf. vv 13 and 12); **how are they to believe** (cf. vv 11, 10, and 9) and **how can men preach,** etc. (cf. v 8). The verses thus lead back to the nearness motif: The word *must* be near, for there is no calling on the name without believing, no believing without hearing, no hearing without preaching, no preaching without sending.

Paul concludes this portion of his argument with an "enthronement" Psalm from Second Isaiah, in which hope for the exiles' return is secured in the prophet's vision of a messenger's report: "How beautiful upon the mountains are the feet of him who brings good tidings, who publishes peace, who brings good tidings of good, who publishes salvation, who says to Zion, 'Your God reigns'" (Isa. 52:7). In their present context, the lines refer not to a cultic but to a historical deed which alters Israel's history. For Paul and for Second Isaiah "good news" consists in the identification of peace and salvation with God's royal rule. This identification explains Paul's substitution of the event of Jesus Christ for what the tradition which preceded him had called "the kingdom of God."

A century later, Second Isaiah's announcement was echoed by a prophet who saw God's will in the foreign policy of his king. When the methods of the youthful Josiah began to achieve their first success, Nahum in vision saw a runner on the mountain thoroughfare leading from the north to Jerusalem. From his posture and from his shout, one could guess the news—reunion of north with south. Second Isaiah's unequivocal identification of God's mercy with his righteousness may have rendered him Nahum's theological superior, but historical events, the succession of the neo-Babylonian empire upon the Assyrian rule and Israel's further misery rendered the word of both prophets a mere anticipation of a grander event they would never live to see. But it was an anticipation for all that, and what made it so was the prophets' vision of the invisible God behind that earthly, visible event, the God some day to act in Jesus Christ.

Paul next inventories Israel's history against the list in vv 14-15a. **They have not all heeded the gospel** in 10:16 echoes the phrase in v 14: **How are men to call upon him in whom they have not believed?** They could have called on him—the word was near! But however near that word of faith we preach (v 8), the content of which is **Jesus is Lord** whom **God raised . . . from the dead** (v 9)—defined here simply as the gospel—and however much Israel heard, "not all obeyed." The latter phrase qualifies everything stated from v 8 (or v 6) onward, and resumes the themes struck in vv 2-3.

In v 16 the Scripture quotation does not end, but rather begins the argument. In the opening lines of the "creed" in Isaiah's "Fourth Servant Song," the "nations" not merely repeat Yahweh's word that his power is revealed in the servant's weakness, but express their amazement that it should be so: "Who has believed what we have heard?" (Isa. 53:1). Paul sets the quotation in an entirely different context, so that the expression of awe or wonder on the part of those who still believe what they have heard is altered to a lament that none or almost none have believed it. "So," Paul concludes in v 17, if justification is by means of faith, faith is by means of hearing and hearing by the agency of the "word" or **preaching of Christ** (the genitive is both objective and subjective—it is Christ's "word" and the word about him).

Paul then asks: **Have they not heard?** The question is put so as to require a "but certainly!" and corresponds to the question in v 14: **How are they to believe in him of whom they have never heard?** In reply, Paul cites a Psalm in which the singer describes the sky as bursting forth in a chorus of praise to God; one day, one night after the other join in the song. By inference at least, Paul has "historicized" the great cosmic song of praise. No longer do the heavens, day, or night comprise the chorus, but Paul and his contemporaries, preachers of the gospel. Again, by inference, the apostle and his company are the subjects of Isaiah's "enthronement Psalm," and Nahum's prophecy; they are the "confessors" of the Fourth Servant Song.

More, it is no longer the Creator who is hymned, but the God revealed in Jesus. Only the scope of the hymn has remained intact—**their voice has gone out to all the earth, and their words to the ends of the world.** It was to accent the scope of the "telling" that Paul chose the Psalm—Israel had heard! But he still removed the hymn from its setting and shaped it to his message. Presumably, the old song was not without its historical occasions—a "good yield" for Jewish farmers and a "harvest home festival" reenacting the creation —but such occasions could only furnish the analogy to what the apostle had in mind. This sovereign use of the Old Testament roots in Paul's conviction that the act of creation or the deliverance from exile had its culmination in the event of Jesus Christ.

Again, this was not a conclusion Paul drew from Old Testament events, but from the event of Christ. In light of that event, from the perspective of that event, and quite apart from whatever "vision" the law and the prophets may have had, or however faithfully or accidentally Paul may have suited his word to their original, historical contexts, the "law and the prophets" waited for the Christ. What might have been overlooked till now with all Paul's references to what "is written" is clear: Scripture not merely furnishes commentary on the contemporary events, not merely adds the moral to the story— it describes the contemporary event.

Paul next asks whether or not Israel understood. The old Lawgiver is first to reply. The quotation in v 19 is taken from the "Song of Moses" in Deuteronomy 32, in which Moses' praise of God's activity is set in the context of admonition and instruction. The section of the song to which Paul refers is a "heavenly lawsuit," at the end of which God indicts his people and pronounces sentence: "I will stir them to jealousy with those who are no people; I will provoke them with a foolish nation." (Later, in v 20, Isaiah will answer Paul's question. Is the sequence of "law and prophets" which Paul follows in quotation an argument from "the lesser to the greater"?) Paul's answer to the question in v 19 is not direct; it must be deduced that Israel understood. The reason why is that Paul weaves into his answer two ideas, already hinted at in v 9, and taken up in Chapter 11: First, the initiative lies with God (**I will make you jealous . . . I will make you angry;** cf. the "election" of Isaac and Jacob in 9:6-13; the formula in 9:15-18; the "Handler-handled" theme in 9:20; and the Potter-theme in 9:21ff.); second, the Gentiles are elected so as to provoke Israel to jealousy and thus to faith.

In further oblique answer to his question, **Did Israel not understand?** Paul adds a verse from the community lament in Isaiah 65:1-2: "I was ready to be sought by those who did not ask for me; I was ready to be found by those who did not seek me" (v 1). The apostle prefaces the quotation in good Semitic style with the expression, **then Isaiah is so bold as to say,** and slightly alters the word order of the Septuagint (is Paul quoting from memory here?). In v 21, the answer to the question is squarely put, and again from the community lament in Isaiah 65: "I spread out my hands all the day to a rebellious people" (v 2). Israel was "disobedient" (cf. v 16: "But they have not all obeyed").

■ 11:1-36 In Israel's Future

11:1-6 The Remnant

Now *what of Israel's future?* The question and the answer in vv 1-2 appear to be phrased after the style of the community lament in Psalm 94, or the "sermon" in 1 Samuel 12. In the Psalm, the poet engages in indignant debate with the haughty and godless, announces their doom, but for his own people promises final deliverance. In the "preached history" of 1 Samuel 12 the prophet who views Israel's hankering after a king as a dire affair, promises that Samuel will teach God's people as before, that "the Lord will not forsake, cast away, reject."

Paul puts the verb in the past, and cites himself as proof: **I myself am an Israelite. . . .** (Note similar references in 2 Cor. 11:22 and Phil. 3:5.) If **not all,** yet Paul obeyed, and in himself symbolizes the "remnant" (cf. 10:16 and 9:27). He is

- one **from the Jews** (9:24);
- "belonging to Israel" (9:6);

- "adherent of the law" who shares the faith of Abraham (4:14);
- an "inward" Jew (2:29);
- "child of Abraham" (9:7);
- of Benjamin's tribe (11:1);
- **entrusted with the oracles of God** (3:2);
- with a **zeal for God** (10:2);
- to whom also belongs **the sonship, the glory, the covenants, the giving of the law, the worship, and the promises . . . the patriarchs and . . . the Christ** . . . of whom also is the God over all! (9:4-5).

Paul's reply in v 2 is emphatic enough—**God has *not* rejected his people!** But the reply carries an odd weight—it is in the nature of a promise: **whom he foreknew!** The only other instance in which Paul uses this term is in 8:29, and of those destined for glory. Is this perhaps a signal that Israel is destined for more than, something else than a "vessel of wrath"? Paul shores up his argument with a free recitation of the oracle to Elijah at Horeb, following the prophet's flight from Ahab. Unaccompanied by wind, earthquake, or fire, but quietly and intelligibly (in a "still small voice"), that is, in a manner hardly anticipated in the traditional liturgy, God appears to Elijah and asks: "What are you doing here?" The prophet answers in the complaint that he has been fanatically devoted to Yahweh (a devotion just demonstrated in the slaying of the Baal priests), but alone is left among his defenders. Following the command to anoint kings of Syria and Israel, and to appoint his own successor, Elijah is promised that Yahweh has seven thousand loyalists who have not done homage to Baal or kissed its image.

Why this curious reference? For one thing, the revelation at Horeb constituted that single event in primal history which prepared the way for a prophetic concept of revelation within the framework of ordinary human existence (**who was descended from David according to the flesh,** 1:3!). And, for another, that tradition identified the cave where Elijah heard the oracle with the cleft in the rock where Moses was granted a revelation of God as "merciful and gracious, slow to anger, and abounding in steadfast love and faithfulness, keeping steadfast love for thousands, forgiving iniquity and transgression and sin" (Exod. 34:6-7).

But is it possible that Paul recognized in the Horeb event something akin to what he himself had suffered through, and with reference to the same subject—Israel's survival? Once having identified himself with Isaiah's messenger or the Psalm's heavenly choir, would he have paled at sitting for Elijah's portrait, especially when identification of the Tishbite with Jesus' "forerunner" was not achieved till after the apostle's death? That term "oracle" (used only here in all the New Testament), and so blandly translated **reply** (v 4), may not merely reflect Paul's awareness of the context in which the utterance was originally given. The term may have been chosen with the conscious intent of marking the disclosure of a "mystery"—within or apart from the context of ordinary human experience—the mystery to which Paul refers in 11:26.

From the passage just cited, Paul will draw three conclusions:

1. Scripture not merely yields an analogy;
2. there is a "remnant"; and
3. this remnant is "by grace."

The theme in 9:11 is thus resumed: The "remnant" is Isaac, Jacob, but here for the first time "grace" and "election" or "choice" are paired.

If in v 5 the "election" is defined by "grace," in v 6 "grace" is defined by "election"—**no longer on the basis of works** (cf. again the Isaac-Ishmael, Jacob-Esau saga in 9:11-12). If it is **by grace,** and thus **no longer on the basis of works**—otherwise grace is not grace—then grace is somehow "purpose according to election," since "purpose" is **not because of works but because of his call** (9:11).

11:7-10 The Remainder

In v 7, Israel—the name of God's choice—and the **elect** are contrasted! The religious community, marked by its striving with God, did not achieve what it sought though the **elect obtained** it. Reference to the elect (the **remnant** in v 5; cf. 9:27), as well as use of the passive voice in the phrase, **but the rest were hardened,** renders problematic an interpretation of that failure to achieve as something contingent on human activity.

In the merger of the ancient deed with the present which characterizes all Paul's reading of the Old Testament, and which is so clearly reflected in Chapters 9-11, the apostle once more summons up the old text in support of his assertion that the Jews' unbelief has its explanation in the divine willing. He does so first of all in a conflation of texts from Isaiah and Deuteronomy 29. From the community complaint in First Isaiah, Paul takes the single phrase, "God gave them a spirit of deep sleep" (Isa. 29:10), and links it to the "covenant-formula" in Deuteronomy 29. There, Moses surveys Israel's adversities in the wilderness, in order to explain the conditions attaching to the covenant. The distresses and deliverances were sent by God to test his people, a purpose Israel did not understand at all, but which was left to Moses to disclose: "To this day the Lord has not given you a mind to understand, or eyes to see, or ears to hear" (v 9). Curiously enough, the word of Israel's reprobation in Isaiah 6:9-10, and which the Christian tradition referred to Jesus (cf. Mark 4:12 and parallels; John 12:40 and Acts 28:26-27), is missing in Paul's argument—evidence, no doubt, that the combinations of Old Testament passages in Romans were not new with him.

Paul then quotes a petition from the individual lament in Psalm 69, which enjoyed long history in the earliest Christian community and is clearly reflected in synoptic accounts of the Passion. Following his complaint, the psalmist hurls an imprecation at his enemies, not merely because they add to the suffering willed him by Yahweh ("they persecute him whom thou hast smitten, and him whom thou hast wounded, they afflict still more," v 26), but because he suffers innocently ("without cause," v 4)—indeed, for Yahweh's own sake ("for it is for thy sake that I have borne reproach . . . for zeal for thy house has consumed me," vv 8-9). Paul's purpose, however, is not to concentrate on the sufferer or the cause of his suffering, but rather to indicate that the psalmist's invective is still in process of being realized, and in Israel's unbelief: God has **let their eyes be darkened so that they cannot see.**

11:11-24 Israel for the Gentile

To the question, **have they stumbled so as to fall?** (cf. 9:33), Paul once more replies in that expletive which denies foul play to God. God set the stone, but the stumbling was Israel's own affair. Still, Israel's stumbling is not the last word: Salvation has come to the Gentiles so as to provoke Israel to jealousy and thus to faith! God's sovereignty over human activity, whether unbelief or faith, is at issue here, but it is a sovereignty of grace. Neither Jew nor Gentile is a tool for the other's benefit, for God will be gracious, and to all alike. In vv 11-12 Paul exclaims: Conceive the possibility, no, the eventuality—if Israel's unbelief has all this as consequence, what consequence will its **full inclusion** have! The subject of v 12, like that of v 2 and v 11, is "Israel," remnant or no.

In v 13, Paul breaks off his dialog with the Jew and turns to his Gentile audience: **Inasmuch then as I** (really) **am an apostle to the Gentiles, I magnify my ministry.** That "behold, we turn to the Gentiles" in Acts 13:46 was not a second best, a life-raft for a preaching gone shipwreck on the Jews. Paul had invested life and limb in it to provoke Israel to faith. In the original Greek the little phrase translated **in order to** (v 14: **in order to make my fellow Jews jealous**) reads, "if by any means," and expresses Paul's uncertainty with respect to the outcome of his apostleship. His request for the Romans' prayers in Chapter 15 is evidence enough of that, but the "vision" he is given in Chapter 11 allows of no uncertainty as to what *God* will do with Israel (cf. 10:19). The reference to Israel here is a tender one—"my flesh" (rsv: **my fellow Jews**). In 1 Corinthians 9:22, Paul speaks of his having made himself a Jew to the Jew, outside the law to those outside, and weak to the weak, indeed, all things to all, that he might by all means save some. The apostolate was a gift of grace, hence the norm of Paul's activity could only be dependence on Christ. But precisely because Christ was his norm, he was committed to the other, dead set on being "approved" (2 Cor. 10:18). So Paul was both free and bound. But, if God were not still the acting subject, there would be no "if by any means" (cf. 1:10). The apostolic office, the preaching to the Gentiles and as a consequence the labor for Israel, the trip to Rome, the offering of the olive branch in the collection for the Jerusalem saints, the reception of the offering—all this is in God's hands.

Paul leaves no doubt as to the author of Israel's present fate (v 15; cf. **God gave them a spirit of stupor,** v 8; **the rest were hardened,** v 7). The riches of the world and of the Gentiles may be the instrument of Israel's "stumbling," "transgression," and "failure" (vv 11-12), but the cause is God. He has not cast off, but has indeed rejected. Still, and since v 11 this is the primary thing, the process does not end with hardening (Chapter 9), does not end with a **not all obeyed** despite the nearness (Chapter 10). Israel's unbelief is not a tabled motion, not unfinished business, not a pendulous, hanging, unresolved thing. It has consequences—**the reconciliation of the world** (v 15). Paul first used the broadest possible term, **salvation;** next, he used "fullness" or **full inclusion** in v 12; now, he employs the term **reconciliation.** If Israel's rejection has as its consequence the reconciliation of the world, what will be its **acceptance** if not life from the dead? The **full inclusion** of v 12 is thus defined as to cause—**acceptance.** But whose **life from the dead** will Israel's acceptance mean?

From vv 16 through 24, Paul uses the metaphors of the leaven and the olive tree to indicate:

- the relation between believing and unbelieving Israel;
- the dependence of the Gentiles upon Israel;
- the necessity of acknowledging God as sovereign in Israel's unbelief and in Gentile coming to faith, thus of standing in awe; and
- Israel's future.

The first metaphor is abandoned for the second in vv 17ff.

Metaphor number one: If the first fruit is holy so is also the lump. If those in Israel who have come to faith as a first offering to God are holy, so is the remainder of that "crop" still held back. The relationship between **first fruits** and **lump, root** and **branches** is religiously or theologically established. There is a decree in Numbers 15:17-21 regarding an offering to the sanctuary or its priests, a "lifting" of the first yield in grain threshed out into "groats" or "crushed grain meal." There is a similar argument, though in an entirely different context, in 1 Corinthians 7:14: The unbelieving spouse and children of a mixed marriage are hallowed by the believing husband or wife. That same notion of corporate existence underlies Paul's argument here. It does not mean that the faith of one will do for all (cf. v 22: **provided you continue in his kindness**), but it does mean that there is no faith of the one without the unbelief of the other.

Metaphor number two: **And if the root is holy, so are the branches.** The reference is to Israel as such, Israel as **root,** source of Gentile existence by faith. The context in which these words are set describes a process entirely contrary to nature (cf. v 24): **Branches were broken off** (the passive voice again leaves no doubt that God is the acting subject), **and you, a wild olive shoot, were grafted in their place.** So the phrase, **and also**

to the Greek marks a truth or event at whose base lies the unnatural and unexpected, because of which anyone with an eye
to what normally prevails, cries either "foul play!" **(Then what
advantage has the Jew?** 3:1) or "there must be something in
us that furnished the efficient cause for this remarkable turn of
events!" **(Branches were broken off so that I might be grafted
in,** 11:19.)

To this anticipated response from the Gentiles Paul retorts:
Do not boast over the branches, then he gives the reason: **It is
not you that support the root, but the root that supports you.**
If Israel is the root, and the Gentile a "volunteer" dependent
on it, then the Gentile is dependent on Israel, root and branch
(and by virtue of the breaking off and *thus* leaving room for the
grafting)! Boasting is thus out of the question. To the possible
rejoinder that "the purpose or end result of this horticultural
curiosity was my grafting in; Israel was rejected so that I
might be elect!" Paul replies: Agreed, true! The leaves were
**broken off because of their unbelief, but you stand fast only
through faith!**

Paul then draws his conclusion by repeating the word in v 17:

- Since you do not bear the root (which is holy *together*
  with its leaves, broken off or remaining, v 16),
- since the branches were broken off due to unbelief,
- since nature or "disposition" has nothing to do with this
  activity,
- and since you stand through the instrumentality of faith,

do not be high minded, but fear! For Paul, "standing" or
"standing by faith" is never a position which once assumed can
never be altered, and for two reasons: So long as existence "in
Christ" is at the same time existence "in," though not "according to the flesh" (cf. Gal. 2:20), so long as life is marked by sin
which must always be fended off, the danger of succumbing
to that which would hinder the "one Body" or "new creation"
from its goal is always real. Further—and this is Paul's point

here—"standing" has nothing to do with the psychological in which repetition is always possible. It occurs within God's own good time. With Paul, both reasons are in the final analysis one and the same, since the sovereign God decrees Israel's **failure** and **riches for the Gentiles** (v 12). For this reason Paul introduces the element of uncertainty in his injunction to fear (cf. 1 Cor. 10:12: "Let any one who thinks that he stands take heed lest he fall"). Even for himself, the apostle holds out the possibility of being "disqualified" (1 Cor. 9:27).

In what follows, Paul makes explicit what till now has been implicit in the metaphors and the use of the passive voice: If God did not spare the natural leaves, neither will he spare the unnatural. Where God is at work, humankind does not have the upper hand, and only fear is appropriate. Origen wrote that in vv 17-21 Paul reversed the actual order—in reality, the shoot of the old tree is grafted into the wild—because he was ignorant of the horticulturist's art, as is any modern city dweller. At any rate, sanctification stems from the root, and the destiny of the Gentiles grafted in when they puff themselves up is the same as that of the branch broken off. Verse 22 continues the motif of uncertainty (**do not boast . . . do not become proud, but stand in awe,** vv 18 and 20), but strikes a new note. The metaphor begun in v 16 is interrupted, and the theme of "falling" in v 11 is resumed.

Paul pulls tight on the reins to bring his readers up short. God is the acting Subject; what has been done is his doing, and his activity is characterized in a twofold way: "Goodness and severity." As for the objects of this activity, the role of the one, at least, may be reversed: "You too will be cut off" (a theme also of v 21: **neither will he spare you**). The condition for the nonreversal of roles is "continuing in his kindness," defined in the negative by not boasting or becoming proud. If the "principle of faith" excludes boasting (3:27), then the nonreversal of roles must be conditional upon faith. But then, the notion of God as acting Subject who is able to reverse the roles, and the idea that the nonreversal of roles is conditional upon faith seem to contradict each other. If God is acting Subject, sovereign, how can there be a reversal or nonreversal of roles due to human behavior? Everything Paul has written till now appears to be challenged by v 22 and what follows.

Till now, Paul has rejected the following alternatives: I am responsible, and therefore God is not free since he is obliged to requite me; *or,* God is free, therefore I am not responsible. The apostle has been wrestling with these alternatives throughout the epistle; Chapters 9-11 only magnify that struggle against the background of his concern for Israel "according to the flesh." The only solution open to Paul is to assert

- that God is free *and* that we are responsible;
- that he will have mercy on or harden whom he will, *and* that Israel's cutting off (not the stumbling—that was an act of sheer mercy, to set Christ in Israel's path!) is the consequence of Israel's unbelief;
- that Gentile coming to faith is by election through Israel's reprobation *and* that failure to "continue" in the kindness of God will result in Israel's being cut off.

Indeed, that solution merely reflects the fact that in Jesus Christ Paul sees God's grace and at the same time humanity's sin. Without grace, humanity is either in the hands of blind fate, or is left totally to itself. Grace thus creates this "paradox" of divine sovereignty and human responsibility. From out of grace follows the decree respecting Israel and the Gentile: Israel rejected now in order that the Gentile might be elect. All that God did in the past was not in vain, and what he does in the present is not the expression of an angry deity—the Jew must forego the promises that the Gentile might come to faith. Grace must have the mastery! And grace will have its way in the ultimate, since the election of the Gentiles will issue in Israel's "grafting back" into its own olive tree (v 24).

Thus far, the salvation of Israel embraces a remnant; only a remnant believes, and grace comes by way of faith. But if faith is *also* gift, do we not finally fall into the hands of fate, however compassionate? Paul does not inquire of individuals— his vision is of peoples. He does not search beyond grace. God gives opportunity for faith, that is his grace, and for this reason faith is no mere "response," nor the efficient cause of grace. "Efficient cause" takes human initiative for granted. At the same time, Jews or Gentiles are responsible for their "falling," "trespass" and "failure," for taking offense at grace, or for "continuing" in the kindness of God.

Humans do not create grace, do not create faith—if they did so, it would be neither grace nor faith they created, but something else, and like all human production, plagued with uncertainty. And humans are responsible for rejecting or remaining in grace—if they were not, if they did not need to "fear," grace would not be grace but a human certainty, which is no certainty at all. It all comes round to the same thing—grace, thus no certainty apart from the divine sovereignty; grace, thus no certainty apart from human responsibility.

Paul continues his theme of the reversal of roles in v 23, but now in respect to Israel: **Even the others, if they do not persist in their unbelief, will be grafted in. . . .** In v 24, the manner of Israel's grafting in is described, and in antithetical correspondence to that of the Gentiles. **If you have been cut from what is by nature a wild olive tree, and grafted, contrary to nature** (cf. v 17—the calling of the Gentiles is unnatural), **into a cultivated olive tree, how much more will these natural branches be grafted back into their own olive tree?** How much more *what?* [57] Paul intends to say that if the grafting in of the Gentiles was "contrary" to nature, the Jews' grafting in again will be by contrast the more "natural." Verses 23-24 thus return to the motif of v 12—**if their trespass means riches for the world, and if their failure means riches for the Gentiles, how much more will their full inclusion mean!**—and of v 15: **What will** their acceptance mean but life from the dead? (Significantly enough, Judaism of the fourth century nourished the reverse expectation, namely, that in the last time, Christians would become Jews.)

11:25-32 The Mystery

There is no hint of a change in addressee, but a restriction of the word to Gentiles would be strange. The **brethren** are thus the Roman readers, Gentile or Jew. **I want you to understand this mystery.** Is the mystery analogous to the phenomenon of speaking in tongues? Paul regards such speaking as of no use to the church unless someone is present to interpret, but here he may be assuming the role of seer and of interpreter (cf. 1 Cor. 14:2-5). Paul's disclosure in 1 Corinthians 15:51 may furnish an analogy to our verse. Certainly, nowhere else is there reference to such a mystery as Paul is about to reveal. And the reason for its revelation is to root out the notion that this entire, "unnatural" event of the cutting off and grafting in falls within the sphere of human possibility (**lest you be wise in your own conceits**). Paul next gives the content of the mystery: a hardening has come upon part of Israel (cf. the term **some** in v 17, and again vv 1 and 2) **until the full number of the Gentiles come in** (cf. v 12). Again it is clear: Gentiles cannot boast or be "wise in their own conceits," for their "coming in" hangs on the hardening "come upon" Israel.

And so, Paul writes in v 26, **all Israel will be saved.** To what does that **all** refer? Is it the remnant, or is the remnant restricted only to **the present time** (v 5)? If every last Israelite shall be saved, does not God at last turn out to be the God of Jews only (3:29)? Or does that **full number** of the Gentiles (v 25) equal **all,** in which case all, every last man Jack, or every woman Jane will be saved? And if so, then what of grace, divine sovereignty, and human accountability?

Some scholars in the early history of the church interpreted the verse to mean "all spiritual Israel," that is, all Jews who come to Christian faith. Sixteenth and seventeenth century interpreters referred the prophecy to the time of Jerusalem's ruin, when some Jews are alleged to have converted to Christianity, or they read the verse as flattering Jews and urging Gentiles to work for their conversion. To such a notion, one old scholar querulously replied: "Why call this a mystery, since it took place publicly? What is mysterious about 'all spiritual Israel's' being saved?" [58] Others referred the verse to "all Israel according to the flesh." From here it was a simple step for a host of interpreters ancient and modern to conclude that Paul had in mind a universal salvation. Karl Barth's great commentary on Romans carried the same weight. Asserting that "the unity of the divine will is divided only that it may be revealed in overcoming the division," he asked:

> What if the existence of—vessels of wrath—which we all are in time!—should declare the divine endurance and forbearance, should be the veil of the longsuffering of God, behind which the vessels of mercy—which we all are in eternity!—are not lost, but merely hidden? [59]

The conclusion seems logical enough, for if Paul has in mind the universal salvation of Israel, shall the Gentile be saved only "in part"? Is the "moral" of the story of the Canaanite woman in Matthew 15 that the Gentile must be content with all Israel's being saved, since Israel was the instrument in the divine economy for the Gentiles' coming in? Ought not the Gentiles suffer "great sorrow and unceasing anguish" for *their* kinsmen by race, and yearn for the revelation of a mystery to equal Paul's? Though the Gentiles must be content with crumbs, will not God also answer them: "Be it done for you as you desire"? To infer universalism is to venture into the unknown. One had best follow Barth's own rule: Believe the love of God and at the same time bow to those descriptions of him as One who takes rejection seriously.

Referring our verse to "all Israel according to the flesh"

appears the only genuine alternative. The issue cannot be side-stepped. The verse must be interpreted to read that the entire fleshly Israel is gathered in, but without second-guessing God, without singling out persons or individuals. So the question of the **all** is never answered. Those who attempt an answer either exclude (by way of the **remnant**) or include, but one or the other device is a way of leaving things as they are. The "ministry" needs magnifying—there must be a "provoking" to faith, even though to do all is not within our power. But God will do what we could not, will do something new, something prefigured in Jesus' own career. The Father will hasten to his lost son. The God of Abraham, Isaac, and Jacob will not be swerved from his mercy. What Paul sees, the **mystery** he tells, remains a mystery for us, a thing still hidden—it is as if he has looked behind, back of grace to the "naked God," where no one else can go. And what he tells is finally no explanation, but only a question! Together with v 27, the final clause in v 26 yields the Scripture support, the phrase **as it is written** then marking the end of this major section.

If Paul did not find his **mystery** disclosed in the Old Testament, he at least found its corroboration there. The verses he cites in vv 26 and 27 are a merger of passages from First and Second Isaiah. The first three lines of the quotation are from that lament to which Paul had earlier referred in Chapter 3. After the prophet spurns the people's complaint and heaps up accusations against transgressors, he announces that God will intervene to judge his enemies and redeem a penitent Zion: "And he will come to Zion as Redeemer, to those in Jacob who turn from transgression" (Isa. 59:20-21, a text interpreted messianically also by the rabbis). The lament in Psalm 14, to which Paul had also linked Isaiah 59 in Chapter 3, concludes in a similar vein. After venting his wrath on evildoers, the singer concludes with a cry of hope for Israel's final deliverance: "O that deliverance for Israel would come out of Zion! When the

Lord restores the fortunes of his people, Jacob shall rejoice, Israel shall be glad" (Ps. 14:7).

Linking the one passage to the other with a phrase from the oracle, "and as for me, this is my covenant with them" (Isa. 59:21), Paul completes the quotation with a line from Isaiah 27, a prophecy of atonement for Jacob, uttered against Samaria's already occurred or awaited destruction. The prophet announces that the people of the north will share the coming salvation when the pillars marking the epiphany of heathen gods and the altars on which they stand are all thrown down: "By this the guilt of Jacob will be expiated, and this will be the full fruit of the removal of his sin" (Isa. 27:9). The line in turn echoes an oracle delivered to Jeremiah, in which the Lord announces a "new covenant," new by virtue of the fact that what he commands he will give; that the law will no longer be that of an alien will, but "written upon the heart"; that obedience will be altered from duty to desire—a covenant whose goal is the knowledge of God, a knowledge which serves his self-disclosure. It will be a covenant characterized by an unheard-of immediacy of fellowship, at the beginning, midpoint, and end of which is God. And the guarantee that this covenant, which extends beyond all historical limits to time beyond time, will never be supplanted or surpassed, is that God "will forgive their iniquity, and . . . remember their sin no more" (Jer. 31:31-34).

The merger of quotations leaves us with the same enigma as Paul's own disclosure of the **mystery** in 11:26. First and Second Isaiah indicate Jacob's "turning" as the condition for the deliverance: "He will come . . . as Redeemer, to those in Jacob who turn from transgression" (Isa. 59:20); "the guilt of Jacob will be expiated . . . when he makes all the stones of the altars like chalkstones crushed to pieces" (Isa. 27:9). For Jeremiah and the psalmist, standing between the two Isaiahs, neither the cry of hope nor the oracle hides a condition: "Jacob shall rejoice, Israel shall be glad" (Ps. 14:7); "I will make a new covenant with the house of Israel and the house of Judah" (Jer. 31:31). But one thing is certain to prophet and poet alike —God will intervene on Israel's behalf and without human aid! "He saw that there was no man, and wondered that there was no one to intervene; then his own arm brought him victory, and his righteousness upheld him" (Isa. 59:16).

In v 28 (Paul is preaching again!) what was to be inferred from v 17, or what was put in the mouth of the Gentile respondent in v 19, and thus was to be inferred from vv 11, 12, and 15 (perhaps even from vv 20 and 22), as well as from the temporal adverb **until** in v 25, is now crystal clear: **They,** that is, Zion, Jacob (cf. v 27), **are enemies of God** *for your sake.* On the other hand, **they are beloved for the sake of their fore-fathers.** If Ishmael, Esau, and Israel were "hated" in order for Isaac, Jacob, and the Gentiles "to be loved," then Ishmael, Esau, and Israel are the instrument, the occasion of God's love. Till now, Israel had not been described as **beloved;** till now, as possessing sonship, even glory, but not beloved. Israel, vessel of wrath but nonetheless beloved, and for the sake of the promise to the fathers. What Israel received from God, her "advantage" as well as her "vocation," for the purpose of which she received the "gifts and the call" (the little conjunction "and" could be translated "in order to"), and which constitute her **beloved,** will not be revoked. This vocation, for the fulfillment of which any and all covenants were given, still stands.

All of this applies to Israel "according to the flesh"! But if the **election** in v 28 refers to something more than Israel's serving as instrument of the divine love, so does the **call** in v 29 (vv 30-31 continue the same thought): Israel, elect for salvation. **Beloved** then embraces Israel as both the means and the object of the divine love.[60] And through it all God is cause, God who has "carefully locked all up" to unbelief that he might have mercy on all. Hence, the Gentile disobedient once, but the Jew disobedient now; the Gentile obedient now, but the Jew some day to be—and the one for the other, the means through which the other is what he is; the one nothing without the other, whether believing (no Gentile believer without the Jew!) or disbelieving (no disbelieving Jew apart from the Gentile!). And some day, the one to be the other, and the other the one! In vv 30-32 all of Romans 9-11 is summed up. And even though the scope of that **all** in v 26 eludes our grasp, this much of the mystery we have seen. Paul's language is far more guarded in Galatians 3:22, where he writes that "scripture consigned all things to sin, that what was promised to faith in Jesus Christ might be given to those who believe." Here, the language derives from that **mystery,** its revelation standing between Galatians 3 and Romans 11.

11:33-36 The Hymn

What Paul has seen forces him to break out in a hymn to God.[61] God's judgments are unsearchable and his ways inscrutable, but they are known. Paul imparts to the "mature" God's "secret wisdom," hidden from the world (1 Cor. 2:7), and the "mind" of God which some cannot grasp because their thought is restricted to the radius of the world is also known to him (cf. 1 Cor. 2:16, in which the same text from Isa. 40 appears as in our hymn). But this knowledge is by revelation (cf. 1 Cor. 2:9-10), not by intuition or "recollection," so that the **mystery** made known is not the same as the **depth of the riches and wisdom and knowledge of God.** What Paul has seen is the mystery of Israel's destiny, and it forces him to praise the God who still remains hidden despite all he has revealed.

Paul weaves two lines from Second Isaiah and Job into two verses of his hymn. The connection is not accidental. Both passages consist of rhetorical questions; in both the context is that of a disputation; in their structure and content both reflect the "wisdom" genre shaped into a form all its own. But the connection is striking, since this genre appears nowhere else in Second Isaiah: "Who has directed the Spirit of the Lord, or as his counselor has instructed him?" (Isa. 40:13).

The quotation from Job puts the question to which Paul's formula in v 36 gives the answer: "Who has ever initiated anything with God, since all originates with him, is created by him and has its destination in him?" Then follows the doxology: **To him be glory for ever. Amen.** The formula need not have been Paul's own—it admirably suits that Stoic notion that God is origin and goal of all that exists. But if not, he has lifted it from its original setting and pressed it in the service of his teaching: The God who has shown himself as Zion's "stumbling stone" and the Gentiles' "hope" in order that Zion may finally obtain mercy—he is origin, means, and goal!

In 1 Corinthians 8:6, the apostle appends an explicitly Christological statement to the ancient "pagan" formula: "And one Lord, Jesus Christ, through whom all things, and through whom we exist." The end result in both cases is the same—the historical appearance of Jesus does not exhaust the "mind" of God. Mercy, grace, and the Son (1 Cor. 8) were present before creation. Note the similarity of this context to that in which Abraham **gave glory to God** (4:20). In face of the promise, Abraham believed the God who gives life to the dead and calls into being things that are not; he hoped against hope; did not weaken in faith when he considered his own body "as good as dead"; did not doubt the promise but was strengthened in faith, giving glory to God. Abraham and Paul—birds of a feather.

THE SHAPE OF RIGHTEOUSNESS
12:1—15:13

■ 12:1-2   The Theme of Chapters 12-15

"What I on earth have done and taught
Guide all your life and teaching;
So shall the kingdom's work be wrought
And honored in your preaching.
But watch lest foes with base alloy
The heav'nly treasure should destroy;
This final word I leave you."

Now to what is vulgarly and erroneously called the "practical" portion of the Romans letter! Following the task of drawing the boundaries of a true confession, Paul turns now to the task of describing the *shape* which faith assumes. The difference between these tasks is not that the one does not deal with the other, but that the same question is differently put. What Corinth (or the Augsburg Confession, Article VI) put asunder, Paul (or Luther) never once divided—the believing and the doing, the sun and the shining!

The progression of thought in Chapter 12 is as follows:

- The theme for Chapters 12-15 is stated (vv 1-2);
- the principle is enunciated (v 3);
- the reason for the principle is stated (vv 4-5);
- the situation which needs facing up to is outlined, and the imperative is uttered in the concrete (vv 6-8, 9-19a);
- support is then taken from Scripture (vv 19b-20);
- a final imperative draws the conclusion (v 21).

189

That adverb in v 1 translated **therefore** does not introduce a practical admonition. It should read "Now then!" The phrase, **by the mercies of God** may denote an urgent request, but it can also mark the Agent, even the Originator. It not merely refers to ownership, but to source as well, just as the phrase, "father of mercies" in 2 Corinthians 1:3. Paul is pressing the entire Old Testament rite of sacrifice into symbolic service to Christianity: **Present your bodies as a living sacrifice!** Is he summoning the Romans "to become what they are"? This would set the discussion in the context of indicative and imperative, but somehow, that old distinction must be left behind. If what God gives is power *and* gift, then the relation between the two is not that of sound to echo. Havergal's "Thy life was given for me: What have I given for Thee?" is not part of Paul's hymnody—to insist on moral exercise in "response" to God's grace is to lessen the value of the justifying act. What then? Possibilities of the new existence are being held up before the readers' eyes! Here the terms "summons," "demand," "imperative" do not apply. Grace, mercies, and demand are not partners.

Paul has already responded to the query concerning moral laxity: **Our old self was crucified with him** (6:6). He is not about to turn around and heap up demands once he has written that glorious Chapter 6. What then of "beseech," of **appeal?** Is it enough to say that the divine sovereignty does not rule out responsibility? There is more—the appeal has the same character as the demand in v 2. It is opportunity, possibility!

What is presented is **your bodies,** that to which mortality clings but which cannot be equated with "flesh," the totality of one's earthly existence. (The reference to **mind** in v 2 is not for the purpose of adding what was lacking in the reference to **bodies** in v 1, but another way of referring to the whole person.) **Present your bodies as a living sacrifice, holy and acceptable to God.** If **holy** is not something which the "presenters" can attach to their sacrifice, but rather a quality which inheres

in what is God's (cf. 7:12 and 11:16), then the term **acceptable**
cannot be construed as the response of God to the living sacrifice. This presentation, Paul writes, is **your spiritual worship.**
   Then follows the word: **Do not be conformed to this world
but be transformed.** . . . (Note the seven **do not** constructions
in 12:2, 3, 14, 16, 19, and 21, all of which draw the limit to the
shape of faith.) The alternative to moral exercise is not sinless
perfection; the problem of sin remains a reality. The difference
between the terms translated "conform" and "transform," a
difference often obscured in translation, is that the first includes
a component close to our English "scheme," and denotes a
disguise (cf. 2 Cor. 11:13-15). "Conform" refers to a posture or
attitude which may be changed at will, whereas "form" at the
heart of "transformed" refers to what grows out of necessity
from an inward condition. "To be conformed," thus means to
suit oneself to the changeable, to what is transitory and passes
away (cf. 1 Cor. 7:31).
   Back of the reference to **this world** (in the Greek, "to this
age") lies an ancient despair over the possibility of redemption's
issuing from the conditions of this world, and the resulting conviction that deliverance comes only with the destruction of
this "present evil age" (Gal. 1:4), and the coming of a new age
prepared by God. According to Paul, the revelation in Christ
signaled the arrival of that new age, so that the two ages now
coexist, though one is constantly giving way to and will finally
be displaced by the other. (This conviction is expressed in
2 Cor. 5:17: "The old has passed away, behold, the new has
come.") But it is not only this which distinguishes Paul from
end-time expectations in Judaism. For the latter, the hallmark
of the new age was visibility—in the new world, God would
visibly manifest himself and his rule. For Paul, this idea was
shattered at the cross which signified the appearance of the
new age under the sign of its opposite, and thus entry into the
new was an entry "by faith."
   Scholars are wont to emphasize the wholly inward character

of the transformation, since the **mind** is object of the renewal. But the context (the appeal to **present your bodies** in v 1), together with the heaping up of terms (**by the renewal of your mind**) designates an activity of the entire person in all its aspects. Explanation for this curious usage lies in the fact that the word "mind" has no real counterpart in Hebrew. For the Greek, "mind" could denote an abstract, objective, and theoretical activity of a neutral character. For the Jew the mental process was never neutral but always immediately influenced the will and thus the total personality. The mere faculty of "mind" as popularly conceived was not sufficient to express what Paul had in view; it was necessary to indicate clearly that the renewal effected a radical transformation at the core of personality. Indeed, if the use of the term "transformation" in Mark 9:2-8 and parallels, in harmony with classical usage, has reference to physical appearance, and if it can in any way serve our understanding of the term here, then the aspects of such renewal are not confined merely to the believers' behavior. (Cf. the difficult passage in 2 Cor. 3:18, which uses the verb "transform" to denote a change which believers undergo while still in their earthly existence.)

What is the force of the phrase, **that you may prove?** Does it designate purpose or result? Interpretation must decide the grammarian's question—the transformation has its result in proving what is the will of God. The old KJV set "what is good and acceptable and perfect" in apposition to "the will of God," and what resulted seemed redundant. Accordingly, the RSV translates **what is good** as a second object of **prove.** In fact, in 2:18, knowing God's will, and "approving what is excellent," that is, discerning what is essential, appear to comprise two distinct though not separate activities. (Note the almost exact parallel in Phil. 1:10.) But redundant or not, vv 1 and 2 are logically parallel: The will of God, the divinely-intended result of being **transformed,** is the **good, acceptable,** and **perfect** as a presentation of the bodies as a **living sacrifice, holy and accept-**

able. . . . The word *acceptable,* to say nothing of *perfect* (synonym for "spiritual") yields the clue, and the little conjunction in the phrase, **what is good and acceptable and perfect** merely introduces the same thought viewed differently.

■ 12:3-21 Life in the Body
12:3-8 Spiritual Gifts

Again, Paul's addressee is **every one,** Jew or Gentile (cf. the use of **brethren** in v 1 and 11:25). The limit to the shape of faith drawn here is "not to think beyond what is necessary to think, but to think with a view to sobriety." In 11:20, the injunction was **do not become proud,** addressed to Gentiles regarding unbelieving Jews. Here, the injunction is in the setting of the community of faith, and is directed to both Jew and Gentile. From the RSV translation (**not to think of himself more highly than he ought to think,** etc.) we might infer that one ought to think highly of oneself, yet not too highly—in analogy with that popular, narcissistic interpretation of the command to love one's neighbor "as thyself." To "think highly," however, is to think contrary to what one ought to think, so that the contrast is between thinking **highly** (keeping one's nose in the air) and thinking **with sober judgment.** 1 Corinthians 4:6 yields the same sense: "I have applied all this to myself and Apollos for your benefit . . . that none of you may be puffed up in favor of one against the other."

The phrase, **each according to the measure of faith which God has assigned him,** more appropriately translated "as God gave each the measure of faith," does not refer to quantity or amount, so that where the measure is reached one is clear of responsibility (cf. the statement in John 3:34: "It is not by measure," that is, by quantity, "that he gives the Spirit"). The phrase, rather, sets the standard for behavior, and, it is a standard "of faith," that is, a standard which rejects the usual distinctions between persons. What is limited then is obviously not **sober judgment,** but an existence which results in pride, boasting, and thus in division. This standard or "limit" (2 Cor. 10:13) is the same for all—it does not vary with each individual but is rooted in the **mercies of God,** in the one Christ who did not "please himself" (15:3). But if this standard constitutes a limit, the fact that it is given by God is the guarantee that the believers will "walk" by this norm. Once again, the apostle's call is not to perform a moral exercise, but to heed the possibilities of the new life.

There is a finely-honed parallelism of members in vv 4-5: **For as in one body we have many members, and all the members do not have the same function, so we, though many, are one body in Christ, and individually members one of another.** The device is frequent in Paul, and nicely executed in Chapter 12. The verses give the reasons for the appeals in v 3. Now the setting is clear which demands such definition of faith's shape as appears in vv 1-5—the use of the spiritual gifts:

- In vv 1-2 the opportunity is offered—**present your bodies, be transformed,** and its consequence, **that you may prove what is the will of God;**
- v 3 then advances to a preliminary definition of that proving—do not think beyond what is necessary to think, but think with a view to sobriety;
- in v 4 follows the reason why such behavior is necessary— we are all one Body in Christ, and members of one another (cf. the remarks on 6:6 and 8:10).

The argument moves from the universal to the particular, but not till v 4 is it clear as to precisely what is meant by this presenting of bodies or in what setting it appears. Outside the Romans letter, the Body motif makes its first appearance in 1 Corinthians 6:15 ("do you not know that your bodies are members of Christ?"), but the context is quite different from that of Romans 12. It appears again in 1 Corinthians 10:16 but in reference to the Supper. (In 1 Cor. 10:17, the language is all but identical to that here, "we who are many are one body," but again the context differs.) It may be possible to interpret "profaning the body" in 1 Corinthians 11:27 of the one Body, just as here, but it is 1 Corinthians 12 which clearly and unequivocally sets the discussion of the Body within the context of the members' relation to each other. It is this chapter which most closely resembles our own.

Verse 4 telescopes the argument in 1 Corinthians 12:12a-b, 14-26, and v 5 sums up the argument in 1 Corinthians 12:12c-13, 27. The discussion in Romans 12, however, is the reverse of that in 1 Corinthians 12, in which Paul advances first to the treatment of varieties of gifts, then proceeds to describe the physical body as analogous to the Body of Christ. The arrangement in Romans 12 is thus more "logical," while the discussion in 1 Corinthians 12 suits either Paul's response to the Corinthians' inquiry (marked by that phrase, "now concerning spiritual gifts," 1 Cor. 12:1), or his desire to come immediately to grips with the crisis of fanaticism before proceeding to the analogy. Has Paul been informed of a particular problem or crisis besetting the Romans; say, the problem of discrimination in respect to gifts—the Corinthian problem? Speaking in tongues, which gets such thorough treatment in 1 Corinthians 12, is not mentioned at all here, so one could perhaps argue from silence and conclude that speaking in tongues was not a problem at Rome (such utterance may indeed have occurred there, cf. 8:15, 26).

Wherever Christians were gathered in the early church, two postures or stances were always represented—legalism and fanaticism or enthusiasm. No precise knowledge of the Roman situation was required to address oneself to these problems. If the "Jewish problem" was inevitably that of the law, the "Gentile problem" was that of fanaticism. Who knows, for example, but what the injunctions to Gentiles in Chapter 11 are tailored to fanatics, and who knows, for that matter, whether the discussion of the law in the chapters surrounding it (together with the accent on "the Jew first," the Jews' "advantage" and the sanctity of the law) were also pitched to them? Paul need not have been on the scene, but may have merely assumed that what plagued other churches plagued Rome as well—legalism and fanaticism, which are at bottom the same phenomenon.

The thought in Romans 12 and 1 Corinthians 12 is thus the same: Diversity in the Body of Christ, as in the physical organism, is a necessity (willed by God, cf. 1 Cor. 12:18), first, in order to prevent schism (cf. 1 Cor. 1:12: "I belong to Paul . . . to Apollos . . . to Cephas . . . to Christ"), and second, to cause each to care for the other. (The term **function** in the phrase in v 4, **and all the members do not have the same function,** does not separate the members of the Body *from* one another, but distinguishes them from *one* another, and later, *for* one another.)

So there are **gifts that differ** (v 6; cf. 1 Cor. 12:4-6). Paul thus destroys that "individualism" which is the twin of fanaticism by stating that each person has a gift from Christ,[62] and that each gift must be used for others (in 1 Cor. 12:7, "for the common good"). Paul emphasizes the *use*, not the appearance of these gifts, and once more proves himself pioneer. If using these gifts for the other gives meaning to that **measure of faith** (v 3), then whatever is good is a charisma and every Christian a charismatic. Then nothing is virtuous, holy, or sacred in itself, and applause is nothing to desire.

The grammatical structure of vv 6 and 7 indicates that the rank or importance of the gifts is not at issue here, though some of the gifts ("service," "exhortation," "contribution," "doing acts of mercy") may have been uppermost in Paul's mind, due to the collection trip (cf. comments on 15:23-29) and his experience with the "liberality" of the Macedonians and Achaeans (cf. 2 Cor. 8:2). None of the lists of gifts in Romans and 1 Corinthians is thus exhaustive.

If the inference to be drawn is that there is not a Christian who does not have a "gift," v 6a makes clear that it is a *gift* and not something initiated by the Christian—**according to the grace given to us.** This giving of gifts entails variety (the thought is identical to that in 1 Cor. 12:4ff.; cf. v 18)—the requirement that each must have the same gift would not be according to grace. (In 1 Cor. 12:10; 13:2, 8; 14:6 and 22, "prophecy" is an activity linked to the knowledge of mysteries, and for the benefit of believers; cf. 1 Cor. 13:2; 14:5 and 22. This activity, Paul enjoins, shall occur **in proportion to our faith.** In other words, what is hidden must still accord with what is revealed.)

Paul then aims at preserving the difference between the gifts by restricting each one to a specific purpose. In such fashion, the Body is built up. So there is a division of labor here—the hod carrier oughtn't play the mason, though this may apply only to **service, teaching,** and **exhortation,** not to "contributing," **giving aid,** and doing **acts of mercy.** The reason is that the latter designate gifts which by their very nature cannot be restricted. Paul's appeal to cheerful giving is therefore addressed to all (2 Cor. 9:7).

12:9-21 The Virtues

Paul now moves from the gifts in vv 6b-8a to the virtues in vv 9-21.[63] Romans 12:9 is a title-verse, vaguely reminiscent of Amos' lament and summons to repentance, set in the context of Israel's covenant renewal ritual: "Seek good, and not evil, that you may live. . . . Hate evil, and love good, and establish justice in the gate" (Amos 5:14-15). Paul's appeal to genuine love ("without hypocrisy"), followed by a summons to **hate what is evil,** suggests the opening lines in the hymn to love in 1 Corinthians 13: "Love is patient and kind . . . not jealous or boastful . . . not arrogant or rude . . . does not insist on its own way . . . is not irritable or resentful . . . does not rejoice

at wrong, but rejoices in the right" (1 Cor. 13:4-6). Philippians
2:3 furnishes a parallel and interpretation of v 16b: "In humil-
ity count others better than yourselves." The word translated
be aglow in v 11 literally means to "seethe," and is an echo of
1 Corinthians 14:1, "desire the spiritual gifts," or of 1 Corinthians 14:5, "now I want you all to speak in tongues, but even
more to prophesy."

Verses 10-13 with their injunctions grouped into pairs, the
last injunction echoing the first, give the specific contents of
the "good way" referred to in the title-verse. The admonition
to **serve the Lord** in v 11 seems to serve as focus for what precedes and follows. All that is done is done to the Lord, hence
the object of faith and the ethical goal are a unity, and this
unity is guaranteed by the fact that the doing of all these things
constitutes a "service," an action which it is not in the Christians' power to decide, as though there were something they
ought or could or should or must add as supplement, but which
is rather the natural consequence of their faith. When Paul
writes in a parallel to v 10 that the Thessalonians need none to
write to them of brotherly love, since they have been "taught"
by God, and in the next breath admonishes them to love "more
and more" (1 Thess. 4:9f.)—a "tension" constant in Paul, and the
occasion of so much confusion—what is reflected is not a dis-
parity between what God has done and what remains to be
done; not a summoning to an existence impossible to fulfill,
nor a concept of Christian life as visible progression toward a
goal, but rather a concept of the new existence as a dynamic
though hidden reality that renders the exhortation a promise
(cf. the remarks on 6:12).

There are end-time clues in v 12: **Rejoice in hope . . . be
patient in tribulation** (cf. 5:2-3, and the call to rejoice in face
of Christ's imminent return in Phil. 4:4-5). The admonition to
constancy in prayer—indicative of mood rather than of formal
exercise—has its parallel in the exhortation to "ceaseless"
prayer, or "in everything" to make one's requests known to

God in 1 Thessalonians 5:17 and Philippians 4:6. Does v 13
contain a summons to assist the Jerusalem poor? (Cf. 15:25ff.
On at least one occasion, Paul broke his own rule of waiving
apostolic right to financial support, cf. 1 Cor. 9:12-18, and was
a recipient of financial aid, cf. Phil. 4:14-18.)

The phrase, **bless those who persecute you** in v 14 echoes
Jesus' Sermon on the Plain in Luke 6:28: "Bless those who
curse you, pray for those who abuse you." Paul had characterized his own ministry as a blessing on revilers (1 Cor. 4:12).
Such parallels to our list of virtues which appear in Paul's
account of his life and work make clear that in this regard no
special grace attaches to apostleship. The appearance of this
"imperative" here, sandwiched in among those respecting
Christians' behavior toward each other, makes clear that the
"virtues" are not restricted.

Paul next writes in v 16, "have the same thing in mind toward one another" (the RSV: **live in harmony with one another**),
that is, eliminate all distinctions of class (cf. Phil. 2:5ff.). The
do not be haughty, etc. further defines the action enjoined (cf.
11:20 and the "class" distinction between Gentile and Jew).
Then follows the **never be conceited.** Here Paul may be quoting from an instruction segment in Proverbs, originally warning
against an intellectual flaw or character defect, but later altered to an attack on all human wisdom in its opposition to
the fear of God: "Be not wise in your own eyes; fear the Lord,
and turn away from evil" (Prov. 3:7). The verse in turn echoes
First Isaiah's "fourth woe." There, the prophet seems to de-
nounce as illusory and impious the "old wisdom" which set
such store by rational integrity, or he measures those who think
themselves wise against their own ideal: "Woe to (death waits
for, has already overtaken) those who are wise in their own
eyes, and shrewd in their own sight!" (Isa. 5:21). The motive
for Paul's injunction is vastly different from that of the sage
who promises bodily and psychic health to the one who fears

Yahweh alone ("it will be healing to your flesh and refreshment to your bones," Prov. 3:8), though he had already made clear his agreement with poet and prophet that the fear of God means keeping one's distance from evil (cf. Rom. 12:9).

In v 17, **repay no one evil for evil** (cf. the all but literal agreement with the admonition in 1 Thess. 5:15) seems to repeat Jesus' word in Matthew 5:39: "But I say to you, Do not resist one who is evil." This verse marks the change in object from the company of believers to persons in general (cf. the expansion of the term "good" or "noble" in Phil. 4:8), and is similar to the Greek translation of Proverbs 4:3: "And take thought for what is noble in the sight of the Lord and of men." The admonition is secular, international in character, not unlike instructions to officers of state in ancient Egypt. The virtues Paul describes in vv 18ff. have to do with all, indiscriminately.

The **if possible, so far as it depends upon you** in v 18, does not set a limit to peacemaking, as though the sentence read "to the extent you can find it in yourself to do so, live peaceably with all." There is a limit to what a person can *do,* but what a person *can* do is not limited. The same thought is stated here in reference to all as was stated earlier in reference to believers (**each according to the measure of faith which God has assigned him,** v 3). In v 19, the phrase **never avenge yourselves but leave it to the wrath** is an echo of Matthew 5. To what extent statements of Jesus may underlie the recitation of the virtues is difficult to determine, but the ideas certainly root in what Jesus had to say. The translation of v 19, **leave it to the wrath** is apt—according to Paul vindication or salvation is the sole prerogative of God: **Vengeance is mine, I will repay.**

Here again (cf. 10:19 and 11:11), Paul is harking back to the "heavenly lawsuit" in Deuteronomy 32, in which God attaches to his suit against Israel the promise to take vengeance on the tools of her punishment when he sees that her "power is gone" and neither "bond or free" remain (Deut. 32:35f.). Since for

Paul God's wrath was already hiddenly at work (cf. 1:18f.),
leaving it to the wrath did not reflect a shift from the "here and
now" to the "there and then." Though the apostle may have
altered his expectation of Christ's return from the imminent to
the long-delayed, he never abandoned his earliest conviction
that the revelation of wrath, however hidden now, would cul-
minate in a final, visible day of judgment (cf. 14:10-12).

I will repay, says the Lord. This is the first of two instances
in Romans in which a quotation is thus introduced. Why precisely here? Is there perhaps a saying of Jesus lurking back of
this word? In any event coupling the words, **for it is written,**
with the phrase, **says the Lord,** reflects a certain ambiguity in
Paul's attitude toward Scripture. The Old Testament is authori-
tative, divine (though Paul seldom refers to a Scripture word
expressly as "God's word," and then for the most part in connection with passages where God speaks in the first person;
cf. 9:15, 25), but it is also a summary of oracular utterances and
prophetic testimonies.

In v 20, Paul quotes from the second collection of Proverbs,
gathered by the "men of Hezekiah" (Prov. 25:1). Set in the
framework of concern for the harmful effects of antisocial
behavior on community life, the "sentence" in humanistic
fashion advises dealing with one's enemy by feeding him or
giving him drink, and in such fashion "heaping coals of fire on
his head" (Prov. 25:21f.). By bringing the enemy to remorse
with one's generosity—in a late Egyptian text, standing with
coals of fire on one's head is a rite of penitence—one has both
punished and reinstated him as friend. Characteristically, as
with all the wisdom sentences cited in this section, Paul omits
the sage's promise of reward (cf. Prov. 25:22b) though it may
have been the formal similarity of that promise with Paul's
word in v 19 which first called the quotation to mind. Finally,
v 21 resumes the thought of v 17 (**Repay no one evil for evil**).

First, the behavior described in vv 9-21 is "social" in character. *Second,* it is distinguished with respect to its objects—members of the community of faith (vv 9-16), and "outsiders" (vv 17-21). On the other hand, v 14 makes clear that there is not one set of virtues for one, and another for another group, with the result that though the *object* of one's action may be distinguished, the action itself cannot be. Genuine love or rejoicing with those who rejoice and weeping with those who weep may have anyone at all for its object. *Third,* two types of behavior are characterized, the one a service to the other, the other a refraining from distinctions or returning evil for evil. *Finally,* appeals of a less social character, clustered about the injunction to **serve the Lord** in v 11, comprise the wheel within the wheel of virtues. They describe the fundamental action, the shape of faith as before God. If 13:8-14 points in either direction, 12:14 and 12:17-21 do also and pave the way for a discussion of one's attitude toward the neighbor in Chapter 13.

The virtues are so common! There is no difference between Paul's catalog and that of other moralists, which suggests there is no perceptible difference between the morality of the Christian and that of any moral person. Christian existence is hidden: Being baptized into the Body as marked for death renders it so. The virtues thus possess no "uniquely Christian" character—the error of pietism. On the other hand, the virtues cannot be *identified* with those of the moral person—the error of rationalism or idealism. The uniqueness exists, but it is "in Christ," hidden. Paul's use of the Wisdom type to which all but one (Amos 5:14) of the passages cited in this section belong is not accidental. This type of literature most closely approximates the universal morality of Israel's contemporaries, early and late. It serves to indicate that there is no demonstrable difference between the life in and apart from faith. There is not a uniquely Christian ethic (to say nothing of an ethic distinguishable from faith), *but a uniquely Christian faith which takes specific shape!*

■ 13:1-14   The Other
13:1-7 The "Higher Powers"

The structure of thought in the first two sections of Chapter 13 is very similar to that of Chapter 12. In vv 1-7, the principle is enunciated (v 1a), the reason for the principle given (v 1b), the situation which needs addressing is outlined, and the appeal is repeated (vv 2-7). In vv 8-14, the principle is stated (v 8a), the reason given (v 8b), support is drawn from Scripture (v 9), and the conclusion stated (v 10).

Precious few portions of the New Testament have generated so much heat and so little light, or have inspired an application with such baleful results as Romans 13:1-7.

> Whoever attempts to review and analyze the interpretation of our text . . . strays into the tangle of a tropical jungle from which he can hardly get free . . . . neglect, stupidity and unbridled fantasy hang like a curse over the field and handiwork of the exegete. Speculation erects its towers on the tiniest space; scrupulosity wades through the deeps of boredom; again and again whims replace arguments, prejudices observation, and repetition thought.[64]

On the surface, this little paragraph in Romans 13 spells an awful contradiction of everything we know of Paul's attitude toward the world. At worst, it appears servile, cringing, an outright surrender of faith to things as they are. At best, it seems sly and opportunistic, a call to bide one's time, to wait in the wings till the world has gone to the devil. But in either case, whether faith dons or whether it shuns the habit of the world, things are left as they are.

If things here are what they seem, then elimination of these verses in the interest of some "analogy of Scripture" is the better course. Or perhaps we ought to draw their teeth by interpreting the **governing authorities** of angelic beings somehow acting through the political powers to bring all into subjection to Christ? "When in doubt, for the tradition"—better first to read the paragraph as if it were Paul's than to lunge at such desperate measures.

The language of the paragraph is "profane," bureaucratic. There is no lofty rhetoric here, no rhapsodizing, no reference to Jesus as prototype (whether or not there is an echo here of Mark 12:17 and parallels—"Render unto Caesar, etc."—is moot) —merely the clipped, terse jargon of Greek bureaucracy. So much for intimations of angels! At issue, rather, is a detail of Christian, everyday life without any grand, cosmic backdrop. Next, the exhortation does not deal with a doctrine of the "state," but with the relation between Christians and persons with political power. The **authorities** in v 1a are thus the **rulers, servants,** and **ministers** of vv 3, 4, and 6 (these terms lack any ecclesiastical reference!), and the **authority** (singular) in v 1b is merely the power possessed by the local official.

So there is no principle enunciated here, no high-flown notion of the "orders of creation," no "Christological" grounding of the state—just simple, homespun, garden-variety, practical wisdom. Further, if Paul were indeed enunciating a principle here, he would have stated it in the positive; he would have addressed himself to the problem of a government's acting unjustly, praising the evil and punishing the good. Finally, the command to love is conspicuous by its absence. Scholars for whom Paul is much too exalted a figure to deliver a piece of practical wisdom or prudence, and who seek to relieve him of the mundane by rhapsodizing on Romans 13:1-7 as deriving its meaning from the admonitions to love, ignore the splinter-character of the exhortations in Chapters 12-15, and their rough and ready attachment to the theme in 12:1.

Why such a word here? Why should Paul address himself to the problem of resistance to rulers? Was it anywhere a problem among Christians? Paul's addressees certainly had neither political power nor the prospect of ever gaining any. Nor could the apostle have conceived a time when Christians would have available to them the instruments which make for political change, when, say, they could hurl at a "German George" the challenge that all are created equal and endowed with certain "unalienable rights," that whenever any form of government is destructive of life, liberty, and the pursuit of happiness, "it is the right of the people to alter or to abolish it." But one might as well ask if any at Rome were proud (11:20), or thought beyond what it was necessary to think (12:3). A Roman Christian, any Christian for that matter, might at least in heart and mind spurn the old order still preserved; might in a mood of fanatical enthusiasm refuse open and critical participation in the affairs of a world God had still allowed to stand, might at least thirst for a bit of chaos, might chuckle over ruin—and in the reign of that butcher, Nero! To such, Paul replies with this word of "realistic opportunism"—ever and anon interpreted in the abstract by readers who never get beyond the phrase **be subject.** To such readers, Paul retorts that the Christian community is the enemy of political chaos. Why? For the sake of its task.

Let every person be subject to the governing authorities . . . and those that exist have been instituted by God (the term in the Greek means "to arrange, set in order"). True enough, more than the mere facticity of the state is being acknowledged here. Though the power of the state is not at all the equivalent of the revealed will of God—it is one thing to respect God's will in those who have power, and quite another to derive that power from God's will—Christians nevertheless encounter in it, as in other earthly things, an "ought," a divine requirement. But there is still an indirectness in all this talk of being subject. The relation between God and the **authorities** is not equal to that between Christ and his Body. The description of resistance to authority, not as resistance to God but to what he has appointed, is something less than giving definition to the shape of faith in a command to love. And when in v 3, Paul describes approval for doing the good as praise from the ruler and not from God (cf. 2:29), he further accents that indirectness, and may even have in mind that rulers, evil or good, cannot evoke terror in the one who does the good, or that their approval, their praise may be given reluctantly.

This person in authority, writes Paul, is **God's servant for your good,** "for your sake," and in one fell swoop government is torn from its pedestal and made the servant of God for the Christian. Despite all the talk of subordination and all the possible terror the **authority** can create, it exists and is instituted "for your sake," **for your good.** With that **for your good,** a further limit is drawn to the scope of authority—it is in its reference to the *good,* its intent on the good, that the authority is God's servant.

But if you do wrong, Paul adds, then the authority is a servant, an avenger for executing wrath on the one who does evil. So authority has a dual function: It is God's servant **for your good;** but it is also God's servant, an avenger, bringing wrath on the evildoer.

The admonition in v 5 harks back to v 1. Indeed, these two verses are the paragraph's center of gravity. But the thought **be subject . . . also for the sake of conscience,** is new—for conscience's sake, and that is, for freedom's sake, sober deeds arising from resolute responsibility need doing on the ruler's behalf. Paul here characterizes the Christian community as the gathering of those who are free, and who are not lamed by fear of the authorities. The "subjection" thus comports with conscience, with the new renewed self, since to be Christian does not mean to disavow the world as God's creation, to stand haughty and aloof from what is passing away. The world is already Christ's, insofar as those who are his enter it in service —"all things are put in subjection under him" (1 Cor. 15:27). The world is not yet Christ's, insofar as it remains fallen— Christ still waits (indeed, what separated him from the zealots of his day was that he could wait for God), and God is not yet "everything to every one" (1 Cor. 15:28). And between the two, between the "now already" and the "not yet" there stands, not a company of angels, but Christ's own Body which makes its way through weakness and humiliation in service to a fallen, threatened, godless world.

In v 6, Paul writes, "you pay your taxes because those whose business it is to handle such things are God's ministers." Then in v 7 follows the list of those to whom the Christian is obliged. If there should be a connection between these verses and the saying, "Render unto Caesar" in Mark 12:17 and parallels, one might well ask whether or not the phrase **respect to whom respect is due** in v 7 refers to what is due to God, since the term **respect** (in the original: "fear") is not normally used of what is paid an earthly ruler.

Between us and Romans 13 lie Constantine, the Holy Roman Empire, the Magna Charta, the Reformation on the left, the American, French, and Russian revolutions, whole continents throwing off colonialism for self-rule in a huge cluster of new and independent states, and each part of some vast chorus joined in by Christians: "We, the people. . . ." Never mind that Paul would not have countenanced the revolutionary movements which have brought us to this point. We must read this paragraph from the other side of the dock as well, since today *we* are, to a certain degree:

- those authorities, from God, instituted by God (v 1);
- God's "appointment" (v 2);
- the rulers, the terror (v 3);
- God's "servants" who bear the sword to execute his wrath (v 4);
- his ministers (v 6);
- to whom are due taxes, revenue, and honor, if not "fear" (v 7).

What lay outside the realm of possibility for Paul's earliest readers—the temptation to self-worship in the political sphere and thus to hallow the status quo, or to dissolve government when not pleased with it and thus to establish another status quo—is an old, tired reality for us, and sets us closer to Nero than to Paul's addressees. But to the extent that our faith is publicly and openly opposed by an infinite number of forces in our society, and the number of the lapsed growing by leaps and bounds, to that extent we are this side of the dock with the Roman Christians.

What then is the alternative to quarantine and decontamination? We cannot construct a principle from Paul's "occasional" injunction against contributing to the general chaos. But he does furnish us a referent—**do what is good!** What "good"? The term is general by design—Christians cannot be spared the use of their eyes or their understanding! Nor is the alternative to evil without a dying—the Jesus who said "render to Caesar" and "render to God" found himself hanging on a tree raised by king and priest. No matter if the authority should be evil, transgressing the limit as **servant,** as "minister," no matter if the authority should execute wrath on the good and approve the evil—do the good; there will still be no **terror!** And the good will be done!

13:8-10 Love of Neighbor

In vv 8b-10, Paul's reasoning yields the following structure: The appeal is given in v 8a—love! Then follows the major premise in v 8b—the lover of neighbor has fulfilled the law—and half the minor premise in v 9a and b: the law is summed up in love of neighbor (cf. the almost exact parallel in Gal. 5:14). The second half of the minor premise appears in v 10a—love does the neighbor no evil (cf. the portrait of love in the negative in 1 Cor. 13:4b-6: what love is not, it is not in relation to the other), and the conclusion is drawn in v 10b—love is the fulfillment of the law.

It is something of a leap from **governing authorities** to showing love to the neighbor, but to construe the **neighbor** in vv 8-10 as the **ruler** in vv 1-7, is to join what Paul put asunder. The world has had its fill of the victims of persons who have identified their possession of natural power with the law of God. God's will as encountered in the world and God's will as revealed may be the very same—*though an apostle is needed to show us that it is so!*—but it is revelation that makes them the very same (cf. the remarks on 2:13-16).

That at which the law aimed, but could not achieve by virtue of the weakness of the flesh, is now reached with Christ's coming. So, the first table of the law is met by faith (cf. 3:31: **Do we then overthrow the law by this faith? By no means! On the contrary, we uphold the law**), and the second is met by love. In v 9, Paul again cites the second table of the law, this time including the commandment—**You shall not kill**—which once pointed to a type of manslaughter leading to blood vengeance, but came later to mark an act of violence done from hatred or malice. The prohibition prepares for Paul's summary in v 10, taken from Leviticus 19. The section in the Holiness Code from which Paul draws his summary has to do with justice "at the gate" or people's court. Following the command against "hating your brother in your heart," that is, against handing down judgments prejudiced by an earlier disagreement, this section sums up all the prohibitions addressed to Israel in the best-known verse from Leviticus: "You shall love your neighbor as yourself" (Lev. 19:18; cited earlier by Paul in Gal. 5:14).

Paul's summary could scarcely have been truer to the original context, but however broadly Leviticus conceived the "neighbor" (Lev. 19:33-34 applies the term to "the stranger who sojourns with you"), that "pragmatic" criterion laid down in the ancient rule—"as thyself"—was not Paul's, despite the identity in wording. Between Paul and the author of Leviticus stood Jesus.

In 12:19-20, Scripture supported the contention that one must **leave it to the wrath.** Here it supports the contention that the lover has fulfilled the law—two sides of the same coin. The second table of the law is summed up in the injunction to love one's neighbor as oneself. But interpreting the command to read that "you shall love your neighbor as much as by nature you love yourself" is no truer to Paul. For the apostle, the "self" has changed, not through an imitation of Christ which allows the difference in persons to remain; not through an absorption into Christ which eliminates the difference, and in either case allows the conditions of this world to remain unchanged, but through a "putting on" of Christ (v 14), by which he becomes the Subject of an existence shaped to his suffering and death. Such a self, renewed, conformed to, living or dying **to the Lord** (14:8), and cannot **please** itself (15:1), furnishes Paul the criterion for love of neighbor.

This then is the shape which faith assumes, though that shape will be no different, outwardly, than compliance with an external command, but it will be a specific shape!

13:11-14 Putting on Christ

The thought in vv 11-14 is less an addition to what precedes than a furnishing of the context which gives urgency to the "command" to love. "Do this," writes Paul, "knowing the time" (rsv: **hour**). The possibility of loving one's neighbor is not a human possibility, but one set by God. Nor may it be elected or rejected on the assumption that one is able to create it. It has a limit, a time which renders its recurrence problematic. That **hour** [65] for waking has its limit set by a salvation **nearer . . . than when we believed** (in 1 Cor. 7:29, Paul described the "hour" as "shortened"). When **salvation** arrives, the possibility will have passed. The perspective is quite different from that assumed in Hebrews 6 and 12, in which the "time" is described as *faith's* possibility, and warning is given against letting it pass. Here the word is not a threat, but a rousing appeal to love in view of the coming glory.[66]

Paul, awaiting a great and final tribulation signalizing the end of time, did not counsel his readers to remain untroubled by distinguishing what did and did not "concern them," as the old Stoic cliche read, but rather to hurl themselves into engagement with the world. But the statement that the command to love is given urgency or has its limit drawn by salvation does not yet do justice to Paul. There is an urgency, there is a limit drawn, but it is not drawn by an object of fear. Paul's word to the Thessalonians that the "day" should not surprise them like a thief, and his admonition to "put on" faith, love, and hope since they had been destined for salvation reflects the same mood (1 Thess. 5:8-9). The "imperative" is thus totally, radically altered. It is one thing to say, "Wake up! Get your house in order, or suffer some horrible consequence," and quite another to say, "Wake up! Get your house in order; what you could not have conceived in your wildest dreams is about to occur!"

It is nowhere truer than here that the Pauline admonitions are not "true" imperatives. They have been twisted out of shape, transformed by the light of coming events. They are an answer to the summons: "Give us something to do, the suspense is killing us!" This is not an imperative "growing out of" the indicative but a call to activity till he comes. And if it should *appear* that such activity reduces love for neighbor to a mere "passing of time," so be it, but true love is never a matter of passing the time.

The reference to sleeping and waking in v 11 occasions the use of the terms **night** and **day** in v 12. In Paul's subsequent appeals, however, the sleep-wake, night-day motif is retained, but only as cipher for the opposition between good and evil—an old theme in Judaism. So the argument has shifted. How near is **salvation,** how near the limit to our possibility? **The night is far gone, the day is at hand,** nigh, at the very door—so near! "So," "therefore," "consequently," "then let us put off the works of darkness" (cf. the remarks on 6:3). In these verses, the combination of the "put off-put on" motif with the injunction to **make no provision for the flesh** is proof that Paul did not keep to neat distinctions respecting his "catechisms," but rather mixed them (cf. Col. 3:8, in which the command to "put off" is coupled with a catalog of vices). This usage earlier appeared in 2 Corinthians 6:7 ("weapons of righteousness"), and in 2 Corinthians 10:4 ("the weapons of our warfare"; cf. also Eph. 5:11, "take no part in the unfruitful works of darkness," or 6:11, "put on the whole armor of God," and vv 13-17).

Verse 14 functions less as a continuation of the cluster of admonitions than as a summing up. The structure, then, is as follows: Verse 12b admonishes to "put off"; v 12c to "put on"; v 13a to "conduct yourselves becomingly"; 13b "not in revelings, etc."; v 14a enjoins to "put on," and 14b to **make no provision for the flesh.** The negatives in v 13 then furnish the second member in the antithesis, as also the emphatic conjunction (rsv: **but**) in v 14. Note again the old climax device: **Put on the armor of light** (v 12c); **let us conduct ourselves becomingly** (v 13a); **put on the Lord Jesus Christ!** (v 14a). Paul is not calling his readers to adopt a posture in contrast to one they had previously assumed. The appeal is to Christians who have already put off and on. The grammarians have assumed only two alternatives in vv 12-14: Either one has or has not *already* put off, in which case a beginning must be made. But there is another alternative: The call to put on or off to persons who have already done so, but must do so again and again since their existence is not a static possession, and since the opportunities of their new existence are forever opening up anew. Here is another instance in which Pauline usage does not suit the grammar.

To "put on" Christ is Paul's metaphor drawn from the art of war and conjured up by a vision of evil drawn in battle array. It may be that Chapter 13, with its reference to resisting, to rulers who are a terror, to the authority which bears the sword (v 4), even to taxes, revenue, respect, and honor (v 7)—all those engines of state—suggested the use of the motif, though again the logical connections between the sections are loose indeed.

The warrior puts on his uniform and strides into battle, and this is as far as the metaphor leads us. Apt for describing the manner in which the Christian is "up and about" in anticipation of salvation, the metaphor does not exhaust the relation to Christ. To be sure, "to believe Christ is to put him on" (Gal. 3:27: "As many of you as were baptized into Christ have put on Christ"), but the more comprehensive term is "to be made one with him." Finally, vv 8-14 face forward to the problem of the relation between "weak" and "strong" in Chapter 14.

■ 14:1-15:13   Weak and Strong

14:1-9 The Eating of Meats and Observance of Days

The structure of Chapter 14, when compared with the basic elements in Chapters 12 and 13, shares something of their simplicity, though the description of the situation and the appeal in the concrete have the lion's share by far, interrupted by challenges (vv 4 and 10), and concluding with the beatitude and judgment in vv 22 and 23.

Now Paul turns from neighbor to believer. The problem roots in the relationship of the "weak" and "strong" within the fellowship. To a degree, Romans 14 recapitulates and reapplies the discussion of meats in 1 Corinthians 8 and 10. The principle (as in 12:3; 13:1 and 8) is first enunciated: **As for the man who is weak in faith, welcome him, but not for disputes,** that is, "not so as to occasion a fixing or evaluating of differences of opinion, by which one shapes his conduct." (The negative could have appeared earlier in the sentence, but Paul intends to state the case positively, then add his qualification, rather than build the qualification into the appeal by stating it in the negative.) Does the qualifier allow us to assume which side Paul himself is on—the "weak" are to be received, but not so as to cause a division which might ensue with their reception— or, does the qualifier apply equally to the "strong"?

In 1 Corinthians 10:23—11:1, Paul's sympathies clearly lie with the slogan, "all things are lawful," since the tradition which he cites so as to create order out of the Corinthian chaos is not a restriction but a declaration of freedom: "For the earth and its fullness are the Lord's" (1 Cor. 10:26). There Paul's argument read: "Buy where you please; eat what you please; accept whatever dinner invitation you choose, and eat whatever is set before you" (1 Cor. 10:25, 27). But his opposing to this adage the canon or norm of the other's need, the other's edification, the other's good and the other's conscience (1 Cor. 10:23, 24, 28-29), as well as his call to imitate him because he strives to "please all men in everything" (1 Cor. 10:33—11:1), is at least a nod in the direction of the "weak."

The term "weak" clearly derives from a peculiar eating habit. What principle underlies it Paul does not specify, but it is obvious that it is not for reasons of health. We need not search outside Judaism for an explanation to such behavior. The creation narrative of Genesis 1 contains a vegetarian rule which the ancient writer loosed from whatever event originally served as its life situation and which he made a law for all: "And to every beast of the earth, and to every bird of the air, and to everything that creeps on the earth, everything that has the breath of life, I have given every green plant for food" (Gen. 1:30). The verse reflects that "humanistic" strain in Jewish tradition by which the killing of living creatures to nourish other creatures was viewed as perverse. In his narrative of events following the flood, the "priestly" writer of Genesis is forced to admit the necessity of killing as part of present existence—what was true in the beginning is beyond the criterion of current experience—but he senses the tension between the Creator's intent and present necessity by describing God's word to Noah ("every moving thing that lives shall be food for you," Gen. 9:3) as a concession, not a command.

That God's blessing should somehow include the option of killing meant only that something absurd, contrary to sense

inhered in present existence. For the "weak" at Rome or anywhere else, a vegetarian diet might well have stood as symbol
that the Creator's original intention had come to its realization.
Paul shared neither such a concept nor preference for such
symbols, but the truth that the divine will had supremely
come to its own in Jesus was a truth he shared with the "weak,"
for which reason he left him to his symbol and called him
"brother."

The answer to our question raised with v 1 may be inferred
from v 3—the qualifier, **but not for disputes over opinions,**
touches both "strong" and "weak." Following the definition in
v 2, the appeal is repeated, but now enlarged by the definition:
**Let not him who eats despise him who abstains, and let not
him who abstains pass judgment on him who eats.** What is ab-
stained from or eaten is no doubt meat as such, not merely
meat sacrificed to idols (the question at issue in 1 Cor. 8 and
10), since the person referred to is a vegetarian. Choice of
the term **despise** for the one and **pass judgment** for the other
posture indicates that in the latter instance a religious-moral
principle is involved. But if the reference to the "weak" is at
base a reference to a conscience which operates according to
a norm athwart the freedom granted in Christ, then it is not
regular Jewish custom at issue here, since Jews were free to
eat meat, except from animals without a cloven hoof which
did not chew the cud (cf. Lev. 11:4ff.). "Weak" then defines an
ascetic position not required by "normative" Judaism. But
again, it is not necessary to locate such asceticism outside
Judaism (cf. e.g., the habit and diet of the Baptist, a prophet's
fare, in Mark 1:6; Matt. 3:4, or cf. 2 Kings 1:8; Zech. 13:4;
Judges 17:10, etc.).

In light of the mercurial activity of conscience, which by
definition derives its authority from outside itself, and in the
given instance can abandon a single, compelling norm for a
chorus of tutors, it is possible that the "weak" do not constitute
a party, but are "weak" only in respect to a given habit. But

since the vegetarian of v 2 is also an abstainer from meats (v 3), the number of scruples in vv 2, 3, and 5 is reduced from three to two, and their combination more easily attributed to a discrete body than to a random group. Use of the term, **pass judgment** in vv 3 and 4, just as in vv 10 and 13, is clearly distinct from its use in vv 5 and 13. (The rsv indicates the difference clearly enough; in vv 4, 10a, and 13a, the term is translated **pass judgment;** in vv 5 and 13b, **esteem** and **decide**). The reason why such scorning and passing judgment are inappropriate, Paul writes, is that God has "welcomed" the eater and the noneater. Again, it is the divine action that establishes the condition which requires such behavior as the requirement describes (cf. the "institution" by God in 13:1; the Scripture word in 13:9, and the reference to the **one body** in 12:5). The reasoning here is identical to that throughout Chapters 1-11 (cf. 8:31 and 33 on this verse and the following).

In v 4a, Paul hurls a challenge at the "weak"—a new note not heard in Chapters 12 and 13: **Who are you to pass judgment on the servant of another?** The problem of legalism, the concomitant sitting in judgment, and the resultant strife is of such moment to the apostle that he suddenly alters the person of his addressee from plural (v 1) to singular. He needs a single opponent—and returns to expressions used in 2:1, 17, and 9:20. As in 12:4-5, a metaphor is used (**the servant of another . . . it is before his own master that he stands or falls**), which then loses solely metaphorical significance and describes the situation as it actually exists: "Who are you to judge another's slave; to his own master he stands or falls, *and* he will be made to stand—the motif of *falling* in the metaphor is dropped; whether eating or not he will be made to stand—because the Lord is able to make him stand." ("Lord," rather than the rsv **Master,** which aims to preserve the metaphor intact, is the more appropriate, since the figure leans toward vv 6-9). Again, the divine activity furnishes the reason for the behavior required.

In v 5, Paul returns to definitions (cf. v 2), this time not with respect to diet, but to festal observance (the phrase, **one man esteems one day as better than another** corresponds to **the weak man eats only vegetables,** or **abstains** in vv 2 and 3, and the phrase, **another man esteems all days alike** corresponds to **the one believes he may eat anything** in vv 2 and 3). As in v 3a, the definition is followed by the appeal. This time, however, the appeal has to do with private conviction: **Let every one be fully convinced in his own mind.** It is apparent that problems of diet whether at Rome or elsewhere, had assumed an importance, far in excess of those touching gifts or government. Since God has "welcomed" both weak and strong, since both are his, the distinctions that exist are not a matter of common but of individual concern. If Paul actually has in mind a party or group, and not a universal phenomenon, he obviously does not view it on a par with the sect which prompted the Galatians' return to the "weak and beggarly elemental spirits" by sponsoring the observance of days, months, and years, and for which the apostle reserved his bitterest attacks.

The statement, **let every one be fully convinced in his own mind** is surprisingly ameliorative in view of Paul's concept of the Christian conscience as in principle free, in contrast to the notion that one is free only if conscience does not contradict. Indeed, if Paul had taken the "modern" view, he would have given legalism new entrée, for to commence, the ethical or moral question with the problem of my conscience guarantees me an autonomy, when in reality the norm of my behavior is never myself but always the other. (In 1 Cor. 10:28-30, Paul draws a clear contrast between a conscience which takes its norm from another's scruples, and an action which pays those scruples deference.) The error in pietism as well as in orthodoxy was the assumption that things which ought not furnish a basis for faith can on occasion do so. For Paul, such "indifferent" things remain indifferent, but never the disputes they occasion. In v 6, Paul makes clear that what is of individual concern, and thus does not furnish a basis for life in the Body, is not on that account only a matter of *private* concern. Now, that curious word in v 5 begins to make sense. It does not mean: "Let each, on the basis of his background, training, education, taste or appetite decide for himself," but rather, **let every one be fully convinced** *as before God,* whose servant he is. That matter of individual concern, that observance, eating or noneating is done to God's "advantage" *because* it is a "giving thanks." (In 1 Cor. 10:30, the eating is described as a partaking with thanks.)

In a resounding conclusion, vv 7ff. turn the contrasts in vv 2ff. into a unity—a device apparently peculiar to Paul. Verse 7 could simply be an old adage used by Paul which once asserted there is no such thing as existence in a vacuum. The statement is then given its specifically Christian interpretation in v 8: Neither life nor death, that intensely, incredibly "personal" affair, in human existence the most solitary and private event of all, is of oneself alone. Much may be individual, but nothing is *private*. Paul's purpose is not principally to give comfort, but to combat the notion that to be "fully convinced in one's own mind" means "there is no accounting for taste."

In v 9 Paul gives the reason for the situation described in vv 7-8. None of us lives or dies to our self—we live "to," we die "to"—precisely because Christ died and came to life (the verb "to live" here denotes the beginning point) with the result that he might be Lord of living and dead. Christ's death and rising are thus linked to our not living or dying alone as cause to effect. The underlying assumption is not merely that the existence of the self is by way of incorporation in the Body, but that this Body, brought into existence with the death and raising of Christ, is the Body of the Lord of living and dead! Here, then, Paul makes explicit what he often leaves to inference in those references to existence "in Christ," namely, that the One with whom we are united and who brings salvation is also the Lord before whom we stand or fall (v 4), to whose advantage we "esteem" the day, eat or do not eat (v 6); who owns us in life or in death (vv 7-8). This intention marks the difference between our verse and its closest parallel in 1 Thessalonians 5:9b-10 ("our Lord Jesus Christ . . . died for us so that whether we wake or sleep we might live with him") or in 2 Corinthians 5:15.

14:10-23 Occasions Are Not a Criterion

Passing Judgment (10-16)

Again, as in v 4, Paul hurls a challenge. The challenge trails a clause which makes a statement concerning the divine activity (**For to this end Christ died and lived again;** cf. v 3: **For God has welcomed him**). But it also precedes a clause which states what can or is about to occur: **We shall all stand before the judgment seat of God** (cf. v 4: **The Master is able to make him stand**). Note the oscillation between "God" and "Lord," or "Christ" and "God" in vv 3b-12. If by drawing a parallel in vv 3b and 4ff. between "God" and "Lord" Paul intends that we see some equality of function between the two, in vv 10 and 11 his intention appears to be to distinguish them. Or, though the term "Lord" in the quotation of v 11 was originally used of God, does Paul by the quotation intend the same "ambiguity" as in vv 3b-9, and leave us to draw the same inference? (In 2 Cor. 5:10, Paul writes that "we must all appear before the judgment seat of Christ"). There is no fully developed Christology in these verses, but the ambiguity in usage appears intentional, and at least indicates an equality of *function* between God and Christ.

Paul's challenge is hurled at both parties in the dispute— the vegetarian, that rectitudinous observer of festal rites (the verb **to pass judgment** is always reserved for him), and the daredevil who ventures to eat anything and regards every day alike (the verb **to despise** is always reserved for him. In v 4, Paul addressed himself to only one party to the dispute—the "weak," the vegetarian or abstainer who esteems one day better than another). What makes judging or despising inappropriate is not only that it assumes a spurious right to ownership **(Who are you to pass judgment on the servant of another?)** since, presumably, we may judge or despise what is ours, but also that it fails to realize that we must ourselves be judged: **For we shall all stand. . . .**

In support of his statement in v 10b, Paul combines four words from a line in Isaiah 49 with a half-line in Isaiah 45. Both passages have their historical context in the situation of the exiles for whom the question, "Who really is God?" was all-important in face of Babylon's world might. Both are segments of a dispute or judgment proceeding; both deal with an oracle or oath of Yahweh; in both the literary device of the dispute functions as promise, and in both the promise is future in character.

In the first dispute, Yahweh responds to Zion's complaint that he has forsaken her with the oath that all her sons shall be returned to the bereaved mother: "As I live, says the Lord, you shall put them all on as an ornament, you shall bind them as a bride . . ." (Isa. 49:18). Indeed, her children will be so many in number she will ask: "Behold, I was left alone; whence then have these come?" (v 21). In the second, God promises victory over the nations through his "servant" Cyrus, and swears that just as Cyrus, so also the nations who do not know him will confess his name.

If Second Isaiah was first to refuse to limit the divine promises to a discrete national entity, first to anticipate the establishment of a community upon the free confession of any and all who acknowledge that Yahweh alone is God—concepts absolutely decisive for the early Christian concept of the church as well as for Paul (1:17!)—it is what the prophet sees beyond even this great change that attracts the apostle to him here: An end beyond the end of the people of God as politically structured, an end when the goal of the divine history with mankind

is realized in the confession of any who have ever drawn
breath, free or no, persuaded or no, believer or no, that he
alone is God: "By myself I have sworn, from my mouth has
gone forth in righteousness a word that shall not return: 'To
me every knee shall bow, every tongue shall swear'" (Isa.
45:23) It will be another day as at Aachen, when Charle-
magne's fiefs crawled through the hole in his throne!

One event in human history has had the consequence of ren-
dering all subject, and all subject to One: **Christ died and lived
again.** This event shapes both present and future, and what is
about to take place before the judgment seat will occur because of it. The "end of the world" thus has a Christological
shape. God will not be God or Lord, knees will not bow or
tongues confess apart from the belief that Christ died and
lived again. The notion that the Christ-hymn in Philippians 2
has been "edited" by the apostle (cf. the remarks on 5:19) has
support in the fact that in Romans the lordship of Christ is not
the consequence of his exaltation but is rather the result of his
obedience "unto death." There is a new "authority" here, a new
"ruler," and to him all shall bow. That "all" or "every" in vv 10
and 11 means there is no area which could possibly fall outside
the sphere of the activity described.

Jesus' death and raising is thus not only an event which has
initiated a change for those who believe ("we are the Lord's,"
v 8). It is of universal, cosmic significance. In v 12, the ideas in
vv 10 and 11 are succinctly summed up: All shall give answer,
and all give answer to God. The context of the admonitions in
14:1-12 is that of warning, not of comfort. Do they on that account become law? The question is out of order. "Virtue" becomes concrete. Where legalism erred was in the assumption
that virtue was proof of faith. For this reason antinomians
spurned the concreteness. The "thou shalt not" is not for back-
sliders. Just as the "thou shalt," it is an engagement in the concrete, a setting of limits to the shape of faith.

Just as v 5b, v 13 contains the appeal following Paul's chal-

lenge and description of the situation. The conjunction ("now
then. . . .") resumes the subject of the appeal in v 3a: "Now
then," **let us no more pass judgment on one another, but rather
decide never to put a stumbling block or hindrance in the way
of the brother.** The stumbling block consists in the other's action when that action is initiated at the cost of conscience—a
"voice" never functioning according to an ideal norm, but
always affected by the concrete situation. But the resumption
does not simply repeat the appeal or the situation which needs
facing up to, nor does it replicate the context of warning. This
coin of not-despising and not-judging has another side, and
this side Paul is about to turn up now. Verse 13 is reminiscent
of 13:10 **(love does no wrong to a neighbor),** this time in reference to the "brother." The only stricture set to the shape of
faith in the matter of diet (and thus also in the matter of the
observance of days and feasts) is that no hurdle or trap be laid.
The other, God and the "brother" supply the content to the
"ought."

Just as in v 6a, so in v 14 Paul sets forth the concrete case:
**I know and am persuaded in the Lord Jesus that nothing is un-
clean in itself. . . .** (In those instances in which Paul uses the
name "Jesus" alone, he always refers to the historical person,
Jesus of Nazareth; cf. 4:24; 8:11 and 10:9. Joined to the title
"Lord," however, the reference is to the Jesus-tradition as
transmitted to Paul, marked by that phrase, "from the Lord" in
1 Cor. 11:23; cf. e.g., Mark 7:14ff., climaxing in the word that
Jesus "declared all foods clean"; cf. also Acts 10:15.) "To the
pure all things are pure" is hardly the inference to be drawn.
The discussion is of diet, and only in this context does Paul
leave the matter to the individual (cf. v 5b). Paul here identifies
himself with the "strong" (cf. again 1 Cor. 10:25-27), at least to
a point, but it is difficult not to view his use of the terms
"weak" and "strong" as ironic.

Here Paul makes relative what was held to be absolute, but
it can hardly be viewed as typical of Paul's attitude toward the

shape of faith, and for two reasons: First, Paul uncharacteristically appeals to the Jesus-tradition. Second, he recognizes that the ingestion of food, unlike the use of gifts or subjection to authority can only be an *occasion,* never the criterion of life together, since the occasion has in it the potential for becoming private, a matter of the self and its tastes. Paul knows enough to distinguish occasions from the criteria of life together. For this reason, the statement "but it is unclean for any one who thinks it unclean" is not the object of Paul's certainty. But when the occasion becomes a matter of the self and collision with another self occurs which results in injury, the criterion of life together is offended against: **You are no longer walking in love.**[67]

Christian behavior has its specific locale in the common life, and its norm in the other. To be neutral on the subject of food does not mean to be neutral on the subject of behavior. On the contrary, knowledge that "there is no God but one," that "an idol has no real existence," hence that in the matter of diet "all things are lawful" (corresponding to the persuasion in 14:14 that **nothing is unclean in itself**)—such formal knowledge which "puffs up" may be used to entrap, put the other in one's possession. Knowledge then is not fit to rule alone.[68] Paul declared that "every thought" needs taking captive (2 Cor. 10:5), that knowledge requires having its limits drawn by love. And now it is clear: A love which draws such limits is not a subjective feeling but an action for the other, a "walk."

The conditional clause in v 15 is directed to the "eater," to the "strong," since it is the strong who should recognize the distinction between occasions and the criteria of the common life. Indeed, *this is the strong one's boast!* The strong one should be able to surrender occasions when the "weak" is unable to distinguish occasions from criteria. Verse 15a thus corresponds to v 9, but v 15b begins a new complex which has no twin elsewhere, though the love motif is an echo of 13:8-10 and 12:9. Further, Paul's appeal to the "strong" logically follows from the conditional clause in v 15a, but it renders the antithesis there all the more biting: "Food" versus the **one for whom Christ died!** Paul then concludes: "Do not let your good be spoken of as evil" (the word translated **spoken of as evil** is used of outsiders; cf. 2:24 and 3:8).

Nothing to Make the Brother Stumble (17-23)

That **good** which must not be ill spoken of Paul now calls the **kingdom of God.** Verse 17 is the only instance in Romans in which this reference appears, and yet "kingdom" embraces the letter's central themes: righteousness, peace, joy in the Holy Spirit (v 17). Obviously, the kingdom was not elsewhere undefined—in the words and deeds of Jesus the kingdom took on specific contours—but it is still true that none before, and perhaps none after Paul so clearly and unequivocally gave that kingdom Christological shape. The movement from the tradition underlying the Synoptics to Paul is thus a movement toward substituting the person of Christ for the kingdom of God. For if the kingdom is righteousness, then it is a righteousness which has been revealed in the gospel **concerning his Son** (1:3, 9); if peace, then peace with God **through our Lord Jesus Christ** (5:1); if joy in the Holy Spirit, then in the Spirit **of Christ** (8:9). What could easily have been inferred till now, is made explicit: God's kingdom is his rule manifest in Jesus Christ.

By giving definition to the kingdom in v 17, Paul once more seeks to dissuade his readers from the folly of perverting occasions into criteria—**the kingdom of God does not mean food and drink, but righteousness and peace and joy**—and in v 18 Paul draws the consequence: **He who thus serves Christ is acceptable to God and approved by men.** The inferences to be drawn are twofold:

First, in the waiving of "rights," that is, in the abandoning of the occasion for claiming them, Christ is served. Indeed, the "brother" in vv 13 and 15 or the "one" in v 15 on whose behalf this activity occurs, is identified with Christ himself (the concept of the "Body" is never far away).

Second, whoever serves in this fashion pleases God and is approved before (not "by") men.

In v 19 the consequence is drawn in the form of an exhortation (just as in v 13): **Let us then pursue what makes for peace** ("serves peace" better suits the thought that peace has already been won, cf. 5:1; cf. also 1 Cor. 7:15 in which the preposition in the phrase, "God has called us to peace" may be construed "pregnantly," so as to make the sentence read: "God has called you into a peace in which he wishes you to live"). It is thus not peace itself which is to be pursued, but those things which manifest it. The same may be said of **upbuilding,** a term often used by Paul and which at first sight seems to hedge between a description of what is still to be achieved and what already exists. The apparent vacillation is due to the fact that the term belongs to Paul's language respecting the Body to which the concept of growth adheres. (Cf. e.g., 1 Cor. 3:9: "You are God's building," and 2 Cor. 5:1: "We have a building from God, a house not made with hands, eternal in the heavens.") Thus, even in passages which suggest **upbuilding** as a goal, the goal is conceived as something to be entered into by **walking in love** (v 15) or pleasing the neighbor **for his good** (15:2; cf. 1 Cor. 10:24).

What Paul left to inference was that **upbuilding** was nothing less than the Body's growth or maturation, and that this growth came from God through his gifts to the church. This is the conviction which furnishes the context for Paul's admonitions to "build one another up" (1 Thess. 5:11; cf. 1 Cor. 8:1, 10; 10:23; 14:4, 17 and Gal. 2:18, the only instance in which the term is used pejoratively).

In v 20, Paul addresses the strong, and hence resumes the argument begun in v 13. Why this painful repetition of the stumbling motif? True, the axiom, **everything is . . . clean,** turns up the positive side of the argument in v 14, and the clause following it makes clear that to do otherwise than as v 13 enjoins is wrong. But this could all have been inferred from what was already said. The repetition no doubt reflects the scope of the problem, real or imagined. That **work of God** which ought not be destroyed **for the sake of food** may be a cipher for the **one for whom Christ died** (v 15) and once again, the exchange of meat for what God has done is sheer folly. "Everything is clean" has all the earmarks of a slogan which Paul may have everywhere encountered, similar to the phrase, "all things are lawful" in 1 Corinthians 6:12 and 10:23. Paul agrees with the cliché (cf. v 14), and on the face of it, aligns himself with the strong.

But there is a condition, just as in v 14b, and this time addressed to the actor, not to the one acted upon: **Everything is indeed clean, but it is wrong for any one to make others fall by what he eats,** or better still, "the one who eats with offense has only the wrong for his share." In v 21 Paul continues the qualification: If it is wrong for the one who eats with offense, then it is good for such a person not to eat or drink or do anything else by which a brother stumbles. Because eating is a mere occasion, never a criterion—the boast of the strong is "everything is clean"—the strong must concede to the weak.

Paul is not demanding of the strong a lifelong abstention, but an abstention as occasion demands—not abstention but the "other" is the criterion! In such matters it is clearly the "other" who gives content to the ethical requirement: If stumbling ensues, do not eat; if not, eat away! The word could be construed as a relativizing of morals, if it were not that morality no longer has to do with adherence to an external standard, but with love for God and the neighbor. Once more, Paul is clear as to the difference between the causes and the occasions of love, and he is equally insistent on the necessity of love's taking concrete shape, whether or not that shape is understood as a proof of faith.

Paul's last appeal in Chapter 14 resumes the thought in v 5b, though it is again applied only to the strong: **The faith that you have, keep between yourself and God** (v 22). The **faith** referred to here is that of v 2, a persuasion, a confidence. Paul thus distinguishes the occasion that may become a matter for collision from the private persuasion which gives the occasion such a character. He allows the persuasion but refuses it the right to make of the occasion a norm or criterion for behavior, and thus a matter of conflict, by requiring that it be kept a matter between oneself and God. So there are instances in which what applies to one's relationship to God does not apply to one's relationship to others, and the faith described here is one of them. Paul then adds the beatitude: "Happy the man who does not judge himself for what he approves."

In v 23 Paul applies the thought of v 5b to the "weak." Since the strong is presumably described in v 2 as one who **believes he may eat anything,** the implication here is that whoever has scruples (or who hesitates for reasons of conscience; cf. 1 Cor. 10:25 and 27) about eating is "weak." **He who . . . doubts is condemned, if he eats**—the condition implies uncertainty: There is a question whether or not a person would ever be in such a position as is noted but if so, that person is condemned. It is one thing to say, "if the doubter eats he is condemned," and another to say, "if the eater doubts he is condemned." In the first instance, the condition of doubting awaits condemnation once the qualification has been fulfilled, and in the second the act of eating against one's scruples draws the condemnation. Paul obviously intends the second, but what does the word **condemned** mean? In 2:1 the terms "to pass judgment" and "to condemn" are used synonymously (on the other hand, in 1 Cor. 11:32 the two are clearly contrasted); in 8:3 sin is neither condemned nor destroyed, but divested of its rights; in 8:34 the one who condemns is the one who brings charge in 8:33, thus tantamount to the one who accuses. Further, if eating against one's scruples results in condemnation, then that

eating is equal to unbelief. Paul comes within a hair's breadth
of this idea, but his reason for citing such dire consequences is
not that acting against scruples is equal to unbelief, but that it
does not originate in faith, indeed, is sin. May something be
done "apart from faith" and faith still be present? The risk is
great; sin is not a thing of little importance, but it is difficult to
imagine the apostle has in mind an action which is unfor-
givable.

15:1-13 Bearing the Burdens of the Weak

Pleasing the Neighbor as Did Christ (1-6)

The structure of Chapter 15 is far simpler than that of
Chapter 14, and its two sections are symmetrical: The principle
and appeal are given in vv 1-2 and 7a; the conformity motif
is struck in vv 3a and 7b-9a; support from Scripture is drawn
in vv 3b (4) and 9b-12, and a prayer concludes the section in
vv 5-6 and 13.

The theme of Chapter 14 is continued here, but with a difference. Two new terms are introduced to describe the parties
concerned. Further, the matter of raising the occasion to the
level of an actual criterion for our common life is given its
proper name—**to please oneself.** Next the attitude to be assumed is described against the background of conformity to
Christ (vv 3 and 8), and finally the summons to **each** in v 2 indicates that what first applies to the strong in the last analysis
applies to all.

The **strong,** so far not singled out by any term, are here
called "able," and the **weak in faith** (14:1-2) "unable." The two
parties are such by virtue of what constitutes them strong or
weak—a persuasion (14:2 and 22) or the lack of it, a conviction
(14:5b) which one has or does not have before God. It is the
persuasion, then, which makes for strength or weakness, not
the action. How can irony be excluded here, for who then can

determine "weak" or "strong"? Next, the bearing of the "weaknesses" (rsv: **failings**) of those who are "unable" is described as
the obligation of the "able." This is a new note, easily inferred
from 14:13b, indeed from Paul's entire argument regarding the
weak person's liability to suffering. But the apostle finally
leaves nothing to inference. The "bearing" is an "ought" for the
strong; it is the shape which their **walking in love** must take.
That is the principle laid down.

And there is no neutral territory between "bearing" and
"pleasing oneself." Either one "bears" or "pleases oneself," and
pleasing oneself means that one

- despises (14:3, 10)
- sets a stumbling block (14:13)
- injures the brother, causes the ruin of the one for whom
  Christ died (14:15)
- lets the good be spoken of as evil (14:16)
- destroys the work of God, causes others to fall (14:20)
- causes the brother to stumble (14:21).

"Pleasing oneself" raises the private—that which should remain between oneself and God (14:22)—to the level of a criterion for life together, and results in distinctions. The term **to
please** serves as the word-crochet by which Paul will move
from the principle in v 1 to the appeal in v 2 to its reason in v 3.
The same injunction cannot be addressed to the weak—"we
who are weak ought to put up with the vagaries of the strong"
—because they are "unable," unable to distinguish the occasions from the criteria of our common life.

In v 2 as in 14:19, Paul speaks to the strong and includes himself among them (cf. the parallels in 1 Cor. 10:24 and 13:5: "Let
no one seek his own good, but the good of his neighbor . . .
love does not insist on its own way"). If in v 1 the alternative
to pleasing oneself is "bearing," here it is pleasing one's neighbor. These two activities are not at all identical. I am not summoned to abandon my own appetite conceived as a criterion

for my behavior, in order to embrace as a criterion the appetite of my neighbor. For this reason Paul adds the qualifier, **for his good, to edify him.** In v 1, "pleasing" is at the level of the subjective, "aesthetic"; here it is raised to the level of the "moral-religious," and may or may not result in personal satisfaction. On the contrary, it may cause frightful pain. "In fact," Paul writes in v 3, "throughout his entire life Christ did not please himself."

Till now, Paul has written of the believers' existence "with" or "in Christ," of their baptism into Christ's death, and of their burial with him (Chapter 6), or, he has spoken of their comprising with him one Body (Chapter 12), but here there is little to suggest that the believers' relation to each other is an "epiphany" of Christ. It seems rather that Christ's relation to the Father, his enduring of reproaches meant for God, serves as analogy for believers' behavior toward each other. But the analogy is curious, if analogy there be—as between the psalmist and God, so between believer and believer, between the weak and the strong. The analogy clearly breaks down. It can only refer to the bearing of something which belongs to another: **Let each of us please his neighbor . . . for Christ did not please himself; but, as it is written, "The reproaches of those who reproached thee fell on me."**

Nor does Paul call his readers to imitate Christ. The reference in v 3 is obviously to Jesus' historical existence ("throughout his entire life, etc.") and nowhere does Paul call for an imitation of it. This verse is one of those precious few in which the apostle refers to the historical Jesus beyond his death and resurrection (cf. 1:3). Actually, such a portrait of Jesus as is found in the Gospels may have been absent from his preaching. If Christ is not held up as model here, but rather as prototype, what is its relevance to the believers' existence?

The Old Testament text on which Paul draws gives the answer. In 11:9, the apostle's purpose with Psalm 69 was to show that the psalmist's prophecy was still in force. Here he identi-

fies the ancient sufferer with Christ and in effect gives the
explanation for the prophecy's persisting. More clearly than
anywhere else in the epistle, the Old Testament author and
Christ are here identified, indeed, for Paul, Christ himself is
the author of the "passion" psalm. (It would appear that the less
Paul narrates the historical details of Jesus' life, the more he
refers to the Old Testament, that for him the Old Testament
may have played the role which the Gospels later assumed.)
Thus, Christ's identification with his Father brings him suffering, and our conformity to Christ results in pleasing not ourselves but our neighbor. Or again, the psalmist did not seek
out the "reproaches of those who reproached thee," nor did
Christ become the Christ because he suffered (though indeed
he was exalted because he was obedient). He suffered because
he was the Christ, just as did the psalmist because he was a
believer. And, because we are his we cannot please ourselves.

Paul is able to conceive Christ as author of the psalm, not
only because the psalmist is a "type of the one who was to
come," because the Old Testament person, event or thing
points forward to its prototype, and somehow lives in it by way
of anticipation, but because it is the prototype which creates
the type; it is that by which the type "lives," without which
the type would have no significance, no meaning, no value.
**For whatever was written in former days was written for our
instruction** (v 4). It is one thing to say that I am included in the
history of a text's influence, to say that by virtue of my membership in the human community or in a community for which
that text is a peculiar treasure, I bring to its interpretation the
"memory" of the entire history of its understanding and use. It
is quite another to say that the ancient text was written with
me in mind. Again, the language here is to be explained from
the significance which Paul assigns to his starting point—the
revelation in Christ as God's supreme and final deed which
claims the past for itself, and while preserving its historical

integrity denies it any significance of its own (cf. the remarks on 4:23-24 and 16:26).

And the purpose for which all this was written is that **we might have hope;** that the fulfillment of the promise to Abraham (4:18); that the glory of God (5:2); the revelation of the sons and the sonship (8:19-20; 23-24)—that all these things that constituted the objects of the hope and longing of the "whole creation" should not take place without us; that Christ should not be Christ without us. If, because of our identification with Christ, Scripture had us in mind, then we have hope by virtue of our conformity to him.

Paul's reference to **steadfastness** and **encouragement** in v 4 serves as word-crochet for the prayer which concludes the first section of Chapter 15—all the elements of which are replicated in vv 7-13. As the content of the prayer makes clear, an imitation is not at issue here. Believers are not called upon to pattern themselves after a model—they are what they are by virtue of their being conformed. For to God belong the steadfastness and encouragement by which hope is possessed. It is he who enables us to "mind the same thing toward one another" (RSV: **live in harmony with one another).** Once again, that interpretation of Paul's demands as activities to be performed (imperative) on the basis of what God has done (indicative) is laid to rest. God will give what he commands, and for this reason the content of the command and the promise is the very same— the command makes specific the possibilities of the new existence; it sets limits to the shape of faith. (Cf. the identity of command and promise in 2 Cor. 13:11: "Live in peace, and the God of love and peace will be with you," and, according to one possible interpretation, in Phil. 2:5: "Have this mind among yourselves, which is yours in Christ Jesus".) That such outlining of possibilities should be needed, or should be done with harshness or irony, assumes that faith may be lost. And indeed it may, for believers still live "in the flesh."

Paul's prayer is that God will give this oneness of mind **in**

accord with Christ Jesus, again not by way of an exterior rule
laid down, but by way of conformity with him. Paul most
often uses the phrase, "to be of the same mind" to denote a
condition sprung from an activity in conformity to Christ or the
apostle. Here, the **harmony** results from not pleasing oneself,
just as Christ did not; in Philippians 2:2 it roots in having the
same love which was or "which you have" in Christ, and in
Philippians 3:13 from "forgetting what lies behind." In 1 Corinthians 1:10, the appeal to be "united in the same mind" presupposes the indivisibility of the Body into which all have been
baptized ("is Christ divided?" 1 Cor. 1:13). The purpose of this
"harmony" is that with one soul, one breath, one life you
may with a single mouth **glorify the God and Father of our
Lord Jesus Christ.** Colophon! The first and great commandment is love for God by faith in Jesus Christ, "with whom," "in
whom," "in accord with," in conformity to whom God is glorified. And the second is like unto it: Love for neighbor by which
God is also glorified—"man's chief end."

Welcoming One Another as Did Christ (7-13)

Verse 7 commences the second section of the chapter. It
does not introduce a novel thought, but resumes the note
struck in v 1, and just as vv 1-12, addresses itself to parties on
both sides of the aisle.

Many editors insert a comma after the pronoun so as to yield
this sense: "Welcome one another for the glory of God." This
seems to harmonize with v 6, but in light of vv 8-9 (**Christ became a servant . . . to show God's truthfulness**), Paul may be
describing *the activity of Christ* as having God's glory for its
goal. The conjunction "as" in v 7b, corresponds to the emphatic
"for," "indeed," "in fact" of v 3a, and once more introduces the
motif of conformity. But this time Paul tarries longer with the
motif, as well as with its scriptural support in vv 9b-12.

Verses 8-9a contain Paul's description of the manner in which

Christ's activity was prototypical: He became *(was made)* a servant (cf. 1:4 and 3:25) of the circumcision (cf. 1:3 and 9:4-5) for the sake of the truth of God, that is, for the sake of that by which God is shown to be what he is—this is the meaning of "truth"—Christ became a servant of the circumcision. Not even he was free of an anterior purpose or intention—the revelation of God as God. Christ, "for the sake of God's truth"! What was left to inference from the Psalm quotation in v 3 (Ps. 69:17: "Hide not thy face from thy servant") is now stated forthrightly. In his servanthood lay Christ's identification with God; for this reason he suffered the reproaches due to God. With that one little word, Paul has again set us within the context of what may have been the church's earliest Christology (cf. the remarks on 4:23-25). And the goal or destination of this "passion" was first the fulfillment of the promises to the fathers.

Here is the logic of v 8: God's truth was at stake; God must be revealed for what he is. For the sake of that truth, Christ was made a servant, in consequence of which the promises made to the fathers were kept. Thus, the truth of God is that he is a God who keeps his promises; first, that he is a God for the Jew. And, the truth about God is that he is "for"; whatever he may be in, of, and by himself is hidden, but what is known of him is that he is a God "for."

And the logic of v 9 is this: God's truth was at stake; God must be revealed for what he is. For the sake of that truth, Christ was made a servant, in consequence of which the Gentiles glorify God "over" his mercy. Thus, the truth of God is that he is a God who is merciful, that he is a God for the Gentile. Now the pronoun "you" in that phrase, "Christ has welcomed you" emerges with full clarity! By defining the "welcoming" as service to the truth of God as a God for us, Paul comes as close to asserting the unity of Christ with God as he ever will.

The phrase, **as it is written** signals the end of the section (it did not in v 3 but waited for its twin here in v 9a). The Scripture cluster in vv 9b-12 is gleaned from each of the major sections of the Jewish canon: The first quotation is from a royal complaint and thanksgiving, according to one tradition sung by David himself "on the day when the Lord delivered him from the hand of all his enemies, and from the hand of Saul." Composed, perhaps, on the occasion of a covenant renewal festival, the text is dominated by the narrative of God's intervention on behalf of the Davidic king, who does not promise the usual, more ancient animal sacrifice, but a thanksgiving of praise: "I will extol thee, O Lord, among the nations, and sing praises to thy name" (Ps. 18:49 = 2 Sam. 22:50). The second quotation is from the Septuagint version of the summons to praise which concludes the "heavenly lawsuit" in Deuteronomy 32, and the third from the smallest Psalm in the Psalter, once used as preface to a festal hymn (Ps. 117:1). The cluster concludes with a royal oracle from First Isaiah (Isa. 11:1, 10) announcing a new Davidic shoot.

The quotations are Judean in character (including the passage from Deuteronomy which assumes Jerusalem as center of worship), applicable to the ruler or congregation at Zion. In all, the "nations" are Gentile onlookers, summoned to praise on *Israel's* behalf, or are Jewish festal pilgrims gathered from near and far. The collapsing of political boundaries in one great fellowship is only apparent. Even the portrait of the "stump" or "branch" of Jesse in Isaiah 11 is restricted. The later supplement in Isaiah 11:10 reads that he shall stand as ensign for the people who ascend to Zion, but the seat of his administration of justice is in Jerusalem, and he has saving significance only for Israel. Paul's use of the Old Testament was never limited to the life situation of a given passage or to the original intention of its author, because Paul believed that the ancient text found its true meaning outside its own historical occasions in yet another and greater event.

But the apostle was not without appreciation for "original" contexts—a fact amply demonstrated to this point. His treatment of the Old Testament is neither that of a novice nor of a fanatic. And

- to the degree that this little cluster of passages treats of a future which none of its singers nor seers saw, a future in incredible contrast to their own miserable present;
- to the degree that it assumes a time when a revelation of the divine righteousness will give life to all, and
- to the degree that enigmatic "servant," "branch" or "root" comes finally to stand at the heart and core of the divine justice,

to *that* degree the similarity of horizons with that of Paul is enough to render the differences less striking.

The psalmist and Isaiah could not have seen what Paul saw, though the Septuagint translator of Deuteronomy 32, who allowed the nations more than a view from the balcony, and that anonymous editor of Isaiah 11, for whom the role of the "branch" led him to add the supplement in v 10, were much closer to Paul than their more illustrious predecessors. For Paul, however, Torah, Prophets, and Writings not merely promised mercy to the Gentiles, but as the passage at the apex of the cluster makes clear, they promised a mercy which fulfills the promise to the fathers: **The root of Jesse shall come . . . in him shall the Gentiles hope.**

In this cluster of quotations, the fulfillment of the promises to the patriarchs and the mercy shown to the Gentiles are not two acts joined by a conjunction, but one. There are not two separate arguments—one in v 8, the other in v 9—but one. In light of vv 9b-12, v 8 spells v 9, and v 9 spells v 8. In addition, this little florilegium contains not only the rationale for Paul's entire ministry (cf. 1:14), but also a description of his strategy:

- The confession of God among the Gentiles;
- the summons to Gentiles to join Israel in praise;

- the summons to all, indiscriminately, to praise the Lord, and finally,
- the identification of the ruler and hope of the Gentiles.

Just as in v 4 the **steadfastness** and **encouragement,** so here "hoping" serves as the word-crochet for the prayer in v 13, which again corresponds to the prayer in vv 5-6, and concludes the section.

The prayer in v 13, unlike that in vv 5-6, does not take up the theme of the section it concludes. The reason for this may be that the prayer not merely concludes the section from v 7 onward, but also the entire portion of the epistle beginning with 12:3. At any rate, the activity described, whether from vv 7ff. or from 12:3 to this point, is all a believing! The prayer has not introduced an alien thought—Paul does not differentiate believing from thinking with sober judgment (12:3), "welcoming one another" (15:7), and everything else between. It is *all* a believing, and if in vv 5-6 Paul as much as prayed God to give his readers faith when he asked that God grant them **to live in . . . harmony with one another, in accord with Christ Jesus,** here he prays that during the time of their believing God might give them **joy and peace.**

The "ought" of faith which can join hands with joy and peace is unlike any other—it is that "law of the Spirit of life" which "has set me free." Joy and peace are thus not a mood added to what would otherwise be an embarrassment but the true companions of faith, for which there is, finally, no "ought" but only a doing. (The formula here is kin to that in 14:17—since the righteousness of God is revealed in Jesus Christ, or since faith has Christ for its object, we have the merest hint at a trinitarian formula; cf. 15:16 which appears to edge closer to such a notion.)

THE REASON AND OCCASION
FOR THE EPISTLE
15:14-33

■ 15:14-17　　　　The Reason— Apostolic Authority

In this section, Paul includes at least four items:

1. The reason for writing the epistle (vv 14-17);
2. the explanation for the delayed visit to Rome (vv 18-22);
3. the occasion for writing, the matter of the collection (vv 23-29); and
4. the request for the Romans' prayers (vv 30-32).

The divisions are tentative: Paul's reason for writing and his explanation for the delayed visit intersect, and for the reason that in both responsibilities touching apostleship are involved.

Paul does not flatter his readers in v 14. What at first sight appears to be an exaggeration, in reality reflects Paul's conviction that what his readers are, they are by virtue of what they have been given (**full of goodness, . . . knowledge, and able to instruct one another**), and that the Giver hasn't been niggardly.

The interpretation of vv 15-16 depends on how the conjunction which opens v 15 is to be translated. The RSV renders it as: **But on some points. . . .** In this case, v 15 contrasts with v 14, and is in the nature of an excuse or apology. But if the conjunction is translated: "And now, seeing . . ." the contrast disappears, and v 15 furnishes not an excuse, but an explanation: "And now seeing that you are full of goodness . . . I write as I do because of the grace given me by God." The latter construction is preferred—Paul needs no apology. The contrast between the apostle's having and needing authority, so clear in 1 and 2 Corinthians and elsewhere, has been mistakenly transferred to the Romans epistle.

The language in v 16 is ceremonial. In terms drawn from ancient forms of worship, and which occur only rarely or no-where else in Paul's writings, he describes himself and his activity on behalf of the gospel. (**Minister** is used in Romans only here and in 13:6; **in the priestly service of** appears only here in all the New Testament; **offering** is used only here in the un-disputed Pauline letters; **acceptable** is used with this connota-tion only here and in 15:31, and the verb-form **sanctified** ap-pears in Romans only here.) Paul is a priest, inasmuch as it is the **offering** or faith of the Gentiles which he must inspect for acceptability and sanctity. The assertion is a bold one, since whatever pertains to Gentile faith comes under his jurisdiction (cf. vv 20-21). There is reason enough for Paul's writing to Rome, and boldly, without apology or excuse—he is apostle to the Gentiles! (Again, note the germ of a trinitarian formula in v 16: **A minister of Christ Jesus . . . in the priestly service of the gospel of God . . . the offering of the Gentiles . . . sanctified by the Holy Spirit;** cf. v. 30.)

Paul continues: **In Christ Jesus, then, I have reason to be proud. In Christ Jesus** is always the condition for the apostolic boasting (cf. 5:2, 3, 11, and 1 Cor. 1:31). The condition is then given definition in the phrase, **what Christ has wrought through me.** The work is God's but Paul is his minister or priest, the work is truly his as well. The apostle surveys the whole of his mission, the entirety of his turbulent life for the gospel's sake among the Gentiles, and has no regrets (cf. the speech to the Ephesian elders at Miletus in Acts 20:26-27).

■ 15:18-22   Explanation for the Delayed Visit to Rome

Again, Paul's intent is neither to appear demure, nor to im-ply that he may have something to boast of with which Christ had nothing to do. He disavowed whatever originated with himself (2 Cor. 3:5). His boast of having waived all rights to financial support (1 Cor. 9:15), or his boasting "as a fool" (cf. 2 Cor. 11:16–12:13) were only a boast in God who had compelled him to his service, a boast in weakness "for the sake of Christ." Paul's statement is to be construed in accord with the principle laid down in v 20 and elsewhere, that he must lay a foundation for others, lest he boast in others' work (1 Cor. 3:10 and 2 Cor. 10:15-16).

The means by which Christ has done his work through Paul are signaled in the two pairs, **word and deed, signs and wonders**, and in the phrase, **by the power of the Holy Spirit.** The reference is to the word of God, of reconciliation. (Elsewhere, Paul uses **word** without the article to denote the "word of God," or "the gospel," cf. 1 Thess. 2:13 and 1 Cor. 15:1.)

Deed takes its definition from the second pair: **By the power of signs and wonders,** in which the coupling **signs *and* wonders** is strategic. In the New Testament, the term "wonder" or "prodigy" never appears without its double (though the term "sign" may appear without "wonder"). The reason is not merely that the two together have hardened into a technical expression for awesome or supernatural events accompanying the preaching of the gospel. By this combination of terms, the divine origin of these events is qualified as visible only to faith.

Finally, **signs and wonders** take their further definition from the phrase, **by the power of the Holy Spirit,** which appears in apposition to the second pair. Elsewhere, Paul will refer to the marks of an apostle as consisting in "signs and wonders *and* mighty works" (2 Cor. 12:12), so that it is conceivable that the reference to the power of the Spirit is to be construed not only of the agency by which signs and wonders occur, but of those events as gifts added by the Spirit to the apostolic preaching (cf. 1 Cor. 2:4). In any event, Paul's intention is to indicate that what was wrought through him was not by word only, but by "demonstration" (cf. 1 Thess. 1:5, and 1 Cor. 4:20, in which the apostle opposes to the prattle of arrogant folk the kingdom of God "in power"). The result of all this activity is that Paul has fulfilled **the gospel of Christ** (in v 16, called **the gospel of God**— the Lamb has taken his place alongside the Ancient of Days!) **from Jerusalem and as far round as Illyricum.**

If the reference here is purely geographical, then we are obliged to twist and turn to adjust it to the silence of Acts or of Paul elsewhere, and at best to read that word "fulfill" (RSV: **fully preached**) to mean complete what was left of preaching in that segment of the circle of lands about the Mediterranean. But the reference may not be geographical at all. Elsewhere as here, Paul links the recitation of travels or travel plans to his "boasting" (cf. e.g., 2 Cor. 10:16 and Phil. 1:25-26). If we allow the boasting to interpret the odd geographical datum, the datum becomes a defense of Paul's obedience to the institution of the apostolate by the Lord, reflected e.g., in Matthew's Great Commission and in the prelude to Acts ("Go therefore and make disciples of all nations"; "you shall be my witnesses in Jerusalem and in all Judea and Samaria and to the end of the earth"). Set in the context of his boasting, of his insistence upon the authenticity of his apostleship, the formula **from Jerusalem and as far round as Illyricum** yields the reason for giving Paul what the "Eleven" enjoyed—the confidence and aid a true apostle deserves.

After citing his missionary principle in the negative, the apostle draws from the Old Testament one last time. Again, the quotation is from the greatest of them all, Second Isaiah, and yet again, from the oracle of Yahweh which frames the confession of the nations in the "Fourth Servant Song" (Isa. 52:15). God announces in oracle the success of his servant's activity, and thus the incredible incongruity of his deliverance. Though his humiliation and deep suffering were a horror to many, his exaltation will be so mighty a deed as to be perceived with amazement:

As many were astonished at him—his appearance was so marred, beyond human semblance, and his form beyond that of the sons of men—so shall he startle (amaze) many nations; kings shall shut their mouths because of him; for that which has not been told them (Paul adds "of him" from the Septuagint) they shall see, and that which they have not heard they shall understand (Isa. 52:14-15).

For Paul, the subject of the Song—a figure for whose portrait a host may have sat, a mean and disfigured man who, contrary to all religious tradition and conviction, experiences such affirmation and exaltation—was none other than the Jesus whom he preached. And though Isaiah may not have acknowledged the servant's exaltation as wider than Israel's limits, those limits were now extended through the preaching of the servant's apostle. So it is not merely Paul's activity **to the Gentiles** as such, but also the manner or mode of that activity, and the principle from which it derives which is by divine decree. Paul himself, then, Christ's **minister**, agent of the Christ's activity, is a fulfillment of the Old Testament word. And, it is this decree that explains Paul's delay. The thought expressed in v 22 repeats that of 1:13, but the reason for the delay has no longer been left to inference. In 1 Thessalonians 2:18, it was "Satan" who hindered Paul's arrival, but in Romans, the cause of the delay was God himself who commissioned Paul to preach where Christ was not "already named."

■ 15:23-29   The Occasion—
The Jerusalem Collection

The RSV erroneously begins a new thought in v 25. The verse, however, resumes the statement left dangling in v 23, and everything in between is to be taken as parenthetical. The verses should thus read: "*And now*—though I have no room to work in these regions, and have longed for a good many years to come to you when I journey to Spain, because I hope to see you while passing through, and to be sent on ahead there by

you, provided I first be filled by you—*and now*, I am going to
Jerusalem to serve the saints." (Cf. 1 Cor. 16:5: "I will visit
you when—inaccurately translated **after** by the RSV—I pass
through Macedonia, etc.")

Despite his desire to travel to Rome, the Jerusalem trip is at
the moment first with Paul. On that trip hangs the outcome of
his mission—the reception of the collection gathered in Macedonia and Achaia will spell the acceptance of his gospel (once
again!), his apostleship (once again!) and the equality of Jew
and Gentile (once again! cf. Acts 15). After attacks on his apostleship and gospel, following its initial acceptance by Peter and
the others, Paul awaits a final legitimation of his office and
work. And on that legitimation the fate of the Romans also depends—the epistle is, after all, "occasional," occasioned by the
Jerusalem trip.

As for the parenthesis, the change in Paul's affairs is signaled
by those "no longer" clauses. What he had begun in the Roman
"east" was now complete; the Jerusalem journey and having
fully preached (v 19) thus coincide. From the adverb **often** in
v 22, and the clause **for many years** in v 23 we may infer that
Paul had longed to come to Rome as often as he had been prevented. The phrase in v 24, "when I journey to Spain" indicates
Paul's intention to move westward—an intention never carried
out. Western Christianity might have assumed altogether
different shape if Paul had met with acceptance at Jerusalem,
had reached Rome unchained and proceeded from there to
Spain. But judging by the fate of Pauline thought in the east,
a wave of oblivion might have passed over him in any case.
Let Clement stand as symbol of what occurred at Rome—
"holding the form of (Paul's) religion, but denying the power
of it."

The *reason* for Paul's journey is not that Macedonia and
Achaia took up a collection. The reverse is true—Paul needed
an "olive branch," *hence* the collection (which also answered
to the "pillars'" original request, long before the emergence of

any hostile party, Gal. 2:9). Paul's pleading with the Corinthians to open their purses (cf. 1 Cor. 16:1-4; 2 Cor. 8-9), scarcely allows our assigning Achaia (of which Corinth was chief city) any initiative. Macedonia, Philippi, Thessalonica or Beroea, may have been "pleased" to contribute but Paul had to wring the collection out of Corinth (2 Cor. 9:1-5)!

The word in v 27, **they ought also to be of service to them** is again a Levitical term (cf. 15:16), and in the majority of instances in which Paul makes use of the term or its relatives, the reference is to financial aid (cf. 2 Cor. 9:12; Phil. 2:25, 30). But the use of such language even in reference to "filthy lucre" stems from Paul's understanding of the revelation of Christ as eliminating the distinction between sacred and profane, and of his assigning value to one or the other action according to its use. This verse is the only spot in Paul's epistles at which such an argument is used for the collection, but it may have often been used by Paul throughout his trip.

The meaning is not that the Jerusalem saints shared with the Gentiles something of a spiritual nature *beyond* the communication of the gospel through the apostolate. The collection-appeal is merely an extension of the argument concerning the right of preachers to financial support (cf. the parallels to our verse in 1 Cor. 9:11 and Gal. 6:6), the action of Christ ("though he was rich, yet for your sake he became poor," 2 Cor. 8:9), serving as prototype. This was a right which Paul himself did not claim, and his waiver signaled his compulsion as well as his freedom, concretized in service to the churches (cf. 1 Cor. 9:15-18). But a portion of the argument in 11:11ff. may also be in Paul's mind—the "root" is holy (11:16b); into it the Gentiles have been grafted, and made sharers of its fatness (11:17-18), supported by the root (11:18).

First then, to Jerusalem, then to Spain by way of Rome. And Paul will come "with Christ's full blessing." (This is the only passage in the New Testament where such a phrase appears.) The journey will not be attempted on his own initiative.

■ 15:30-33   Request for the
                      Romans' Prayers

Paul now moves from an explanation of his delay and the outline of his travel plans to the event on which the acknowledgment of his apostleship and preaching depend—the collection trip. **I appeal to you** (the verb is not used loosely, but is charged with the same intensity as in 12:1) **to strive together with me**—there is no doubt as to the investment Paul has made in his enterprise. Its outcome is in doubt, and the degree of the possibility of failure can be inferred from the intensity of the request: **I appeal . . . by our Lord . . . by the love of the Spirit . . . strive together with me . . . on my behalf!** (Cf. 2 Cor. 1:11 and 1 Thess. 5:25.)

Paul's prayer is twofold: First, that he be delivered from unbelievers in Judea, and second, that his service be acceptable to the saints (again the use of liturgical language). Why this anxiety, if the purpose of this journey is merely economic? The Achaeans nursed the suspicion that Paul was something less than conscientious in his care of funds, for which reason he informed the Corinthians he had set the project under the supervision of persons appointed by the churches so as to avoid criticism (2 Cor. 8:16-24). Rejection from believers could conceivably occur through mismanagement, but Paul had described the offering as "for the glory of the Lord and to show our good will" (2 Cor. 8:19), a unique designation for a mere "community chest." The intensity of the request, the anxiety expressed, coupled with requests made to the Corinthians (1 Cor. 16 and 2 Cor. 8-9) or with the extent of the trip itself, the meticulousness devoted to the gathering of funds, *and* Paul's uncharacteristic aloofness in the matter of the actual collecting (cf. 1 Cor. 16:3)—these all make clear that something more significant than the alleviation of economic distress is at stake. The course of events leading to the collection may have been as follows:

After his initial activity among the Gentiles, Paul set before the Jerusalem apostolate—of which Peter still sat as head (an inference drawn from Acts 15)—the gospel which he preached. This action took place in private. Those "reputed to be something" (Gal. 2:6, 9) consented to the ministry of Paul and Barnabas among the Gentiles, and the only condition which they set on Paul's activity was that he remember the poor. To all other conditions, he turned a deaf ear (Gal. 2:4-5a, 11-21). After Peter's disappearance from the scene, or perhaps emerging concurrently with Peter's headship (the event narrated in Gal. 2:11-21 suggests concurrence) another group, honestly or otherwise appealing to James ("false brethren") sought to impose new or additional conditions on Paul's activity.

(In Acts 15 and 21, the picture which Paul presents in Gal. 2 is considerably altered: Paul consents to additional decrees, and publishes them among his churches. Luke may thus have fused two separate events—the initial meeting with the Jerusalem apostolate, and the attempted imposition of the decrees. Paul further stipulates that he went up to Jerusalem by revelation; Luke writes that he was summoned. Paul writes that the encounter with the arch-apostles was private; Luke suggests that it was public. Nowhere does Paul suggest his appointment from Jerusalem to a mission among the Gentiles— on the contrary, he swears to his independence, cf. Gal. 1:15-24—but Luke suggests that his activity among the Gentiles was a Jerusalem decision. We must give priority to the word of the eyewitness, whatever the risk.)

From this group sprang that bitter opposition which together with hostility on the part of Gentile fanatics shaped Paul's life to the cross. But Paul was not content to let the matter rest there. He himself was a Jew, and though his Jewishness had resulted in persecuting the church of God (Gal. 1:13-14; 1 Cor. 15:8-9), he could not, any more than the God in whom he believed, cast off his people, his **kinsmen by race** (9:3; 11:1). If, indeed, life shaped to the cross belonged to his apostleship, if his weakness and hence his refusal to boast (cf. 15:18 and, e.g., 2 Cor. 11:16-33) were the proof of his apostleship; if his refusal to accept payment for services rendered (1 Cor. 9:1-8) symbolized the gospel as "free of charge"—in short, if the entirety of his apostolic life must be a conformity to Christ, then that life must signal the truth that there is no "partiality," no "distinction" with God, that he has indeed had mercy on all, "welcomed" all, Jew and Gentile.

The symbol lay ready to hand—remembrance of the poor as enjoined by the "pillars." So the collection was not merely Paul's olive branch, or his bid for the peace prize. It was the occasion for the legitimizing of his apostleship, and on its safe reception depended the recognition of his office and preaching. Paul did not anticipate the reception of his gift as a sure thing; he had known enough of disappointment. And, he could not know that its reception was by divine decree, unless we ignore the expressions in 1:10; the "hoping" in 15:24, to say nothing of the prayer itself. Indeed, "who hopes for what he sees?"

Paul's worst fears were realized. He was not delivered from the unbelieving, and if he ever learned that the gift had been welcomed and in this fashion his apostleship and gospel legitimized, we know nothing of it. The "stigmatization" of the apostle, his bearing on his body "the marks of Jesus" (Gal. 6:17), his "weakness"—a quality which his opponents viewed as something clinging to him merely from historical accident, but which he regarded as the mode in which the crucified and risen One must manifest himself, since earth still remains the sphere of his activity—this "imitation of Christ" to which he had been called, and called all to whom he preached, was something from which he would never get free. To the moment of his death, his life was shaped to the cross—from within and without. Let the chipped, peeling, and sweating plaster image of the apostle in the crypt of St. Peter's Basilica at Rome stand as symbol of the oblivion which passed over him the day of his death.

One tiny portion of Paul's prayer was answered—he arrived in Rome, though bound. Whether or not he was also **refreshed** we can only deduce from Acts 28:14ff., though according to Paul's lights one may be in chains and still be **with joy** (cf. e.g., Phil. 1:12-18). We know that Paul reached Jerusalem, was not rescued from unbelievers, was taken to Rome a prisoner, and that this letter is thus his last will and testament.

The epistle ends at v 33. Evidence for including Chapter 16 in the letter is so mixed and confused that we can say little more than that 15:33 is still addressed to Rome. One great nineteenth century scholar, Ferdinand Christian Baur, saw a deep division in early Christianity. He saw correctly, though he spelled out the division too neatly. Above all, he ignored the fact that it was Paul himself who struggled to heal the division. Small wonder, with peace between opposing parties uppermost in his mind, the achievement of peace in the acceptance of his collection as a fresh acknowledgment of his person and office after long and bitter years of conflict—small wonder he should conclude with a threefold blessing of peace (15:5-6, 13, 33)!

But Paul's prayer does more than reflect his mood or put the period. It gathers up the letter's opening, heart, and close. To the Romans Paul first wrote **grace to you and peace** (1:7). To the impossibility of a peace wrung from deeds in fulfillment of the law (2:10), he opposed a **peace with God through our Lord Jesus Christ** (5:1). It was a peace that should characterize the Christians' walk—that setting of the mind on "things of the Spirit" (8:6)—and their life with others (14:17). It was a peace to be pursued as possibility of the new existence (14:19)—and all of it God's peace, a peace whose source is God (cf. 1 Cor. 14:33; 2 Cor. 13:11; Phil. 4:9; 1 Thess. 5:23); not reserved for deity, but sprung from righteousness, justification, from the gift of Christ to whom faith is conformed.

We are still at war. The universal, law-free gospel has as tenuous, as fragile a hold on us as it had in the day of St. Paul.

CHAPTER 16

The greetings in vv 3-17 assume that Paul had a great number of friends in a congregation he had not yet visited. It is difficult, though of course not impossible, to conceive all these persons emigrating from the Orient to Rome. Further, the intention which Paul pursues in the body of his letter suggests that he is not greeting old friends but rather leading personalities of the community. The **church in their house** (16:5) corresponds better to another situation than to that at Rome. The reference is presumably to Prisca and Aquila together with their household, driven from Rome by the Claudian decree, who later went to Corinth and finally to Ephesus where they continued to live (the suggestion that in the meantime they returned to Rome is not convincing, though it may be true). The sharp warning against Judaizers in vv 17-20 does not appear to fit the situation at Rome, though wherever the church was established, the problems of legalism and enthusiasm were rife.

Stylistically, 15:33 has the character of a solemn conclusion to the epistle. So also does 16:20. Yet such doubling is uncommon with Paul. In addition, the doxology in 16:25-27 totally contradicts Paul's manner of concluding his epistles, and the text tradition regarding its original position is thoroughly confused. It appears at the end of Chapter 14, of Chapter 15, and at the end of Chapter 16.

In the last century a solution was offered to the problem of Chapter 16 which still appears to be the least unpalatable, namely, that Romans 16 contains the remnant of an Ephesian epistle of Paul. The solution reads: Romans ends with a recommendation for Phoebe in 16:1f., who travels on business by way of Ephesus to Rome. The epistle is handed to her, and the Ephesian congregation makes a copy of it. Paul had earlier written an epistle to Ephesus—so goes the hypothesis—not long after his departure from that city in which he had spent three years (A.D. 54-57). In that Ephesian letter appeared what we now read in Romans 16:3-24. The long list of greetings to old friends and acquaintances, the rescue owed Aquila and Prisca, but also the earnest warning against old enemies suits the Ephesian situation.

When, as early as the first century, Paul's epistles were collected in the Orient, the letter to the Romans as well as the Ephesian letter of our canon were taken from the archives at Ephesus. Romans was at the end of the collection, and whatever else remained of Paul was appended to it—the remnant of an Ephesian letter (Rom. 16:3-24), the doxology (Rom. 16:25-27), and individual leaves, scraps, remnants of lost, damaged or abbreviated pieces still preserved. The result, according to this theory, is that Romans 16 is a conglomerate, preserved by one of Paul's most important congregations—witness to the fact that the apostolic correspondence was richer than that come down to us in the New Testament. The debate over Chapter 16 will continue till doomsday though the contention that it comprises a fragment, or even an independent unit—shorter letters in the Graeco-Roman world contained greetings in practically the same proportions—has the better part of the argument.

■ 16:1-16   A Recommendation for Phoebe, and Greetings

The same reference to the church in "their" ("your") house in v 5 appears in 1 Corinthians 16:19 and Philemon 2. (As to the phrase, **the first convert in Asia for Christ,** note the remarks on 8:23.) If a commissioning by the risen Lord was constitutive

for the concept of an "apostle" (cf. the introductions in the four
major Pauline epistles, and in 1 Cor. 9:1), it is obvious from v 7
that the term had not yet been fixed to the point where it
carried only that connotation. In 2 Corinthians 8:23 and Philippians 2:25, Paul refers to anonymous brethren or to Epaphro-
ditus as "apostles" (rsv "messengers") of the churches. Conceivably, Andronicus and Junias (the ancient church regarded
them as man and wife) were just such persons, not merely
those held in esteem by the "apostles of Christ." These two as
well as Herodian in v 11 are called "kinsmen" (cf. 9:3), a portion of that "remnant chosen by grace" (11:5; cf. 9:27). Finally,
the summons to greet one another with a **holy kiss** in v 16 appears also in 1 Corinthians 16:20; 2 Corinthians 13:12 and 1
Thessalonians 5:26.

■ 16:17-20 Warnings and Benediction

If Chapter 16 is indeed a fragment of an Ephesian epistle,
Paul's reference to those who "serve their own belly" (whose
"god is the belly," Phil. 3:19), may be to persons known to
him for their unchastity. But the reference may be metaphorical, characterizing those for whom judgment and behavior are
matters of "taste" or disposition, thus for whom the self furnishes sole criterion for belief and action. Whether or not Paul
intends to include among them such as use the Torah to
serve their own ends, and are thus comparable to the audience
addressed in Chapter 2, in any event they breed dissension and
deceive the "harmless" with fair and flattering words (vv 17
and 19).

Twice, in the context of obedience, Paul calls his readers to
be "innocent" or **guileless** with respect to evil—here and in
Philippians 2:15. In midst of his discussion of speaking in
tongues, Paul calls the Corinthians to be "babes in evil," but
in thinking mature (1 Cor. 14:20).

Finally, if the prayer for the grace of the Lord appears at

the beginning of all the Pauline and Deutero-Pauline letters, it always appears at the close of the undisputed Pauline letters (cf. 1 Cor. 16:23; 2 Cor. 13:14; Gal. 6:18; Phil. 4:23; 1 Thess. 5:28 and Philemon 25; cf. 2 Thess. 3:18).

■ 16:21-27   Greetings from Paul's Companions and Doxology

In v 25, the term **mystery** is to be interpreted according to its broad and general use in the New Testament, that is, as God's ultimate revelation in Christ, once hidden but now made known (cf. 1 Cor. 2:7; 4:1, and the variant reading in 1 Cor. 2:1). What is striking in vv 25-26 is the description of the mystery as "kept in silence for long ages," and thus its contrast with the revelation. The use of the perfect participle in the Greek gives to that silent state a quality of permanence, of unalterability. The silence thus does not signal privation, absence, but plenitude, something into which a word may enter, but without putting an end to the silence. The **mystery** is the tool of the divine economy, agent of the divine design, but wedded to the silence it marks that design as something not altogether within our reach! The God who till now has "kept to himself" has not said everything he has to say. For if the word is God's, so is the silence, and the **preaching of Jesus Christ** has not destroyed it. God remains hidden, even for those to whom he makes himself known. So the boundary set here (by Paul?) is not between initiate and novice, as in some poor, hobbling pagan cult, but between Creator and creature. The mystery of God revealed in Jesus Christ remains a mystery—not from disdain, not in some rude selfishness, but because God can only be God.

Then follows the word that this mystery is **now** disclosed and made known through the prophetic writings. Why **now**, hundreds of years after it had all been written down? Curious phrase! Whoever the author of this doxology may be, for Paul the Old Testament was a book whose true meaning only Christ could disclose. For this reason he wrote of the Jew who "turns to the Lord" that "the veil is removed" (2 Cor. 3:16; cf. the remarks on 3:20). But it was not merely hardness of heart that rendered the Old Testament hidden. For the apostle, that hiddenness was quite apart from unbelief. It was part of the mystery, kept silent till the word should enter it, till the Christ should appear as its true interpreter, so that **now** it became clear that the law and prophets spoke of him **beforehand** (1:2; cf. the remarks on 4:23-24).

Here is the conviction underlying Paul's interpretation of the Old Testament, out of all harmony with popular, prophecy-fulfillment views which assume a recognizable line leading from the Old to the New Testament.

And after the **now** God still remains a mystery, his incognito here and there temporarily peeled back to allow a vision of the depth of his **riches and wisdom and knowledge** in Israel's last deliverance, or of that change "in the twinkling of an eye" (11:33; 1 Cor. 15:51-52); to allow an apostle to use his texts with a "charismatic" freedom and alter the entire perspective of a faith from crown to cross, in the train of that Lamb who was "worthy to open the scroll and break its seals" (Rev. 5:9).

Now to him . . . to the only wise God be glory (cf. Gal. 1:5; Phil. 4:20). And the glory, and the glory . . . !

NOTES

1. The construction "for . . . not," a portion of which is often omitted in translation, does not occur at every major division of the epistle, but its appearance does reflect a pattern: a) With one exception (6:14) it introduces an argument; b) it is most often trailed or preceded by another clause using the conjunction "for," "indeed," or the adversative "but"; c) frequently, a "whoever" is involved, denoted by the adjective "every" or "each," and d) finally, the copula most often appears. In the following instances: 6:14; 7:15, 19; 11:25; 13:4; 14:17 and 15:18, one or more of these four characteristics is absent.

2. O'Neill assigns the chapters to a later "commentator," imbued with the assumptions of Gnosticism; cf. J. C. O'Neill, *Paul's Letter to the Romans*, Harmondsworth: Penguin Books, 1975.

3. Rudolf Bultmann, *Der Stil der Paulinischen Predigt und die kynisch-stoische Diatribe*, Göttingen: Vandenhock und Ruprecht, 1910, pp. 107-108. Author's transl.

4. The great Swabian biblicist, Adolf Schlatter, contended that Luther translated our verse to read, "the righteousness of God is taught in the gospel," but here is what Luther says:

   In human teachings is revealed and taught a human righteousness, that is, who and how one is or may be made righteous before oneself and others. But in the gospel alone is revealed the righteousness of God, that is, who and how one is or may be made righteous before God—through faith alone, by which God's word is believed (*Luthers Vorlesung über den Römerbrief 1515/1516*, ed. Johannes Ficker, 4th edition, Leipzig: Dietrich'sche Verlagsbuchhandlung, 1930, II, 14, author's transl.).

   The doctrine which Schlatter lays at the door of a later orthodoxy and which reasoned syllogistically from an abstract concept of sin to the necessity of faith construed as mental assent, was not Luther's child.

5. *The Dead Sea Scriptures*, trans. Theodor H. Gaster, 3rd edition, New York: Anchor Books, 1976, p. 322.

Notes

6. For Luther as well, justification was Christ himself:

   So I rightly said that all our good, which is Christ, is outside us. . . .
   To believe in Christ is to put him on, to be made one with him . . .
   (WA LVI, 279, 22ff., and II, 535, 24, author's transl.).

7. Cf. Ernst Käsemann, "Gottes Gerechtigkeit bei Paulus," *ZTK*, 58.
   Jahrgang, 3, 1961, and Rudolf Bultmann, "ΔΙΚΑΙΟΣΤΝΗ ΘΕΟΤ,"
   JBL, LXXXIII, I, March 1964.

8. The idea is entirely different in the apocryphal Wisdom of Solomon,
   which like Romans rests on a specific apologetic tradition, but describes the Gentiles as unable to recognize the Creator behind the
   creature, cf. Wisdom 13:1ff.

9. The passives—**they became** (or were made) **futile in their thinking
   . . . their senseless minds were darkened**—may be construed in analogy with the phrase, **God gave them up** in vv 24, 26, and 28, that is,
   as euphemisms for the divine activity.

10. The repetition of slogans within a section belongs to Paul's style. Note
    his use of **law** in 2:12ff., and 7:7-8:2; of **righteousness** and **faith** in
    3:21-4:25, and of **righteousness** in 9:30-10:6. Ancient Greek writers
    could also linger with a word or concept without assigning it different
    meanings or allowing the repetitions to appear too closely together.

11. In Plato's *Symposium*, the intellectual pilgrimage of the *Republic* is
    altered to a journey from erotic, homosexual love to the apprehension
    of beauty in the absolute—a journey whose onset Socrates somehow
    manages to escape, though not for moral reasons.

12. The great Scottish thinker, David Hume, furnishes a commentary on
    Romans 1-2 in his *The Natural History of Religion*, but without Paul's
    solution.

13. Verses 17-20 contain the longest list of conditional clauses in Romans,
    and since the result clauses in vv 21-23 are interrupted by participles
    used as nouns, their reading is difficult. How explain this offense
    against literary propriety? The answer is clear enough, once the
    verses are read aloud—Paul's habit of preaching.

    At long last, someone again speaks Greek from out of a fresh, inner
    experience of life . . . . writes his epistles as substitute for his per-
    sonal activity. The style is Paul, none else than Paul. It is not pri-
    vate letter and yet not literature, a medium which cannot be copied
    though copied again and again (U. v. Wilamowitz, quoted in
    Feine-Behm, *Einleitung In Das Neue Testament*, 9te Auflage, Hei-
    delberg: Quelle & Meyer, 1950, p. 123, author's transl.).

14. Curiously enough, this merger of quotations can be found reproduced
    in its entirety in v 3, lines 3-10 of Psalm 14 in a few manuscripts of
    the Septuagint.

Notes

15. The verse from Proverbs, missing from almost all manuscripts of the Septuagint, warns the youth against criminals who try to win him with the promise of easy money, but whose thirst for death is never slaked—"they make haste to shed blood."

16. Is **by works** to be read in the same fashion as **by faith?** In 4:2, the statement that Abraham **has something to boast about** suggests the subsequent phrase **by works** is better translated "on account of works," "because of works." Note the phrase, **reckoned . . . as his due** in 4:4. In 9:11, certainly, the preposition "by" should be translated "because of." In 9:32, where **through faith** and **based on works** are contrasted, the causal is again the best reading. So the contrasts read: **Not because of works** and **because of his call** in 9:11; **by grace** and **on the basis of works** in 11:6; **God reckons righteousness** and **apart from works** in 4:6, and finally, **justified by faith** and **works of law** in 3:28.

17. The contrast in 6:22 is between **slaves** of sin or of God; in 7:6 between being **captive** to the law and **discharged from the law;** and finally, in 11:30, between being **disobedient to God** and having **received mercy.** The contrast is very often temporal, denoted by temporal adverbs and verb-tenses. In at least one instance, the contrast is purely logical, in 7:16-17. Here, the contrast is certainly temporal, but Paul's argument has proceeded to this point, so the adverb may be logical as well.

18. Walter Gutbrod, "Νόμος," *Theological Dictionary of the New Testament,* ed. Gerhard Kittel, trans. Geoffrey W. Bromiley, Grand Rapids: Wm. B. Eerdmans, 1967, IV, 1072.

19. Although the theme of 1 Cor. 1:26-29 is God's reversal of the conditions of this world by exalting what is low through the word of the cross, here too faith which receives salvation without recourse to one's position in the world excludes boasting. The composition of the Corinthian community itself attests to the impossibility of boasting, and thus to the freedom of the divine decree: "Not many of you were wise according to worldly standards, not many were powerful, not many were of noble birth. . . ."

20. The concept "by faith" occurs eleven times in Romans; twice in 1:17; in 3:28; twice in 4:16; in 5:1; 9:30, 32; 10:6, and twice in 14:23. With the possible exception of 1:17, in which the preposition may be taken as causal, the preposition is to be read as instrumental, equal to the instrumental dative of the noun without the preposition, just as in 3:28 and 11:20. Use of the noun in the dative in 4:19, 20 and 14:1 may be construed as local and thus translated "in faith."

21. *Catena In Sancti Pauli Epistolam Ad Romanos Ad Fidem Codd. Mss., Catenae Graecorum Patrum In Novum Testamentum,* ed. J. A. Cramer, Hildesheim: Georg Olms Verlagsbuchhandlung, 1967 Reprint, IV, 30, author's transl.

Notes

22. *Luthers Vorlesung über den Römerbrief 1515/1516,* II, 131, author's transl.

23. Karl Barth, *The Epistle to the Romans,* trans. E. C. Hoskyns, London: Oxford University Press, 1933, p. 176.

24. Rene Fülop-Miller, *Rasputin, The Holy Devil,* trans. F. S. Flint and D. F. Tait, New York: Viking Press, 1929, p. 242.

25. It is only theory that Paul's concept of baptism is influenced by the Hellenistic "mysteries" and their washings. The feminine noun "baptism" is absent in secular Greek and the Septuagint, while the masculine noun appears outside the New Testament only in Josephus, and in reference to John the Baptist. Pagan notions of baptism, from the viewpoint of its content, are so strongly influenced by the Christian tradition, that it is only as we fix on one or the other aspect of the act that any parallel with Hellenistic religion emerges. Further, it is not at all certain that the devotees of the Hellenistic mystery religions regarded themselves as magically participating in the dying and rising of their gods.

26. The Dead Sea sect and the New Testament community both practiced baptism. For this reason, the washings of the Qumran community are often viewed as analogous to Christian baptism. The underlying assumption is that of a direct connection between the sect and John the Baptist, alleged to have extended the influence of Qumran to Jesus. Such may be true in the given instance, but not as a general rule. There is little doubt that primitive Christian baptism is historically connected with the baptism of John, shaped by a vivid expectation of the impending day of doom. Nor can we deny that Qumran analogies reached the primitive community by way of the Baptist. Years ago, an American scholar wrote that because of John's use of baptism as an initiatory rite, the first Christians began to baptize into the name of Jesus, and suggested that as the little company headed by Peter and the Twelve halted at the scene of Jesus' baptism, it took on itself the same "baptism unto death" (Cf. Benjamin W. Bacon, *The Story of Jesus and the Beginnings of the Church,* New York: The Century Co., 1927, pp. 323-324). But there is a greater dissimilarity between the Baptist and Qumran than is usually assumed in the literature. It is further alleged that for Qumran as for the New Testament, baptism was an initiatory rite. But again, the most important document in respect of the alleged analogy—the "Manual of Discipline" or "Community Rule"—does not mention a rite of initiation. It states merely that after his year of probation, the novice could participate in the washings. Further, the Qumran washings are not described as effecting forgiveness or atonement—they rather make pure or dedicate—thus appear to derive from an intensification of the Old Testament levitical rules of purification. For this reason, Qumran required ritual purity as a condition for the reception of baptism (cf.

Notes

The Manual of Discipline, 3:6-11 and 5:13f., in *The Dead Sea Scriptures*, pp. 42-43, 48).

27. Cf. Eph. 2:5-6, in which the author does not retain the Pauline dynamic, but describes the believers as already "made alive," "raised" and "seated in the heavenly places" in Christ.

28. For grammarians it may be more natural to connect "his death" with what immediately precedes, but in the following clause ("we shall certainly be sharers of his resurrection"; RSV: **we shall certainly be united with him in a resurrection like his**), the term "sharers" is to be supplied, hardly "likeness." The less "natural" grammatical construction is to be preferred.

29. In Phil. 3:21 this body is called "the body of our humiliation," or "our lowly body," in contrast to the body which will have the same structure as that of Christ's glory; in 1 Cor. 15:44 it is called a "physical body" as opposed to the "spiritual body."

30. "As we have once obtained forgiveness of sins in Baptism, so forgiveness remains day by day as long as we live, that is, as long as we carry the old Adam about our necks," *The Large Catechism, The Book of Concord*, trans. Theodore G. Tappert, Philadelphia: Fortress Press, 1959, p. 446.

31. Description of the "teaching" as a piece of moral instruction which "followed with a wholehearted obedience, imparts to our lives a specific character and pattern," or reference to Paul's use of the term "to which you were delivered" as reflecting a "gross incongruity" due to an excess of zeal, results from staring too long at the "standard," and inattention to the dialectic in Paul's concept of sonship. Cf. F. W. Beare, "On the Interpretation of Romans vi. 17," *NTS*, V, 3, April 1959.

32. In Gal. 2:20, "life in the flesh" characterizes something quite different from existence under law, sin and death—earthly-natural life with its exigencies and obligations, a life which also Christians live. Here, obviously, it characterizes a being ruled by alien powers from which the baptized have been freed.

33. The definition of "written code" in 2 Cor. 3:6 applies here as well. It is the law of which the killing effect is predicated.

34. Matthew Pole, *Synopsis Criticorum Aliorumque Sacrae Scripturae,* Interpretum ac Commentatorum Adornata, Francofurti: Typis et Impensis Balthas. Christoph. Wustii, 1694, II, 140.

35. *Luthers Vorlesung über den Römerbrief 1515/1516,* II, 173.

36. Benjamin W. Bacon, *The Story of St. Paul,* New York: Houghton, Mifflin and Co., 1904, p. 42.

37. *The Dead Sea Scriptures,* pp. 161, 188.

Notes

38. *The Republic of Plato*, trans. F. M. Cornford, London: Oxford University Press, 1945, p. 304.

39. Paul's text is sometimes determined by the subsequent Old Testament quotation. Cf. the use of the term "call" in 9:24; "stone" in 9:32; "call on the Lord" in 10:12 and "avenge" in 12:19b. In each case, the use of the word is determined by its appearance in the Old Testament text which follows.

40. *Great Books of the Western World*, ed. Robert M. Hutchins, Chicago: Encyclopedia Britannica, Inc., 1955, p. 174.

41. The RSV: **I do not understand my own actions,** gets at only half of the dilemma. What *I* am doing I do not know!

42. Cf. WA 39, 1; 283, 1; 318, 16.

43. "The Hound of Heaven," *The Poems of Francis Thompson*, London: Oxford University Press, 1937, p. 94.

44. "The Everlasting Gospel," Supplementary Passages, *Blake, Complete Writings*, ed. Geoffrey Keynes, London: Oxford University Press, 1972, pp. 158-159.

45. *Epitome of Rev. Dr. Erick Pontoppidan's Explanation of Martin Luther's Small Catechism*, trans. Edmund Balfour, Chicago: John Anderson, 1904, p. 19: *The Book of Concord*, pp. 479-481.

46. The formula, "in the Spirit" may have derived from mysticism, with its accent on the heavenly sphere and inspiration, but for the apostle it is the Spirit who possesses the Christian, and the Christian who enjoys the Spirit in concretion. In opposition to those who interpreted Paul's concept of existence "in Christ" or "in the Spirit" as of a natural, physical transformation, or as in some sense analogous to existence in an atmosphere or ether, recent studies have tended to construe Paul's use of the preposition "in" adverbially. The Christians' union **with Christ is thus** conceived as a being drawn into the "history" begun with Christ. On this view, "in Christ" may be simply translated "Christian." But v 9 renders problematic this substitution of the adverbial for the spatial or local significance of the preposition. Whether or not the believer is described as in the Spirit or as the Spirit's dwelling (cf. also 1 Cor. 3:16), reference to "Spirit" or "flesh" is not merely to a norm but to a sphere, a locus of activity. Aversion to the notion of Spirit or flesh as an ether or current, and to which one is somehow mysteriously connected, is justified only to the degree the notion detracts from concreteness. The "life and peace" of v 6 and the hostility of v 7 are descriptive of *actual* life, whether hidden from observation or no. On the other hand, aversion to such a notion cannot be entertained to the degree the Pauline concept of existence as existence "in" is endangered, for it is Paul's conviction that an existence which is self-contained is a myth, so that it is not possible to speak of a life after the Spirit or the flesh according to

which "life" is the constant, bent now in one and now in the other direction. The substitution of existence conceived as a "solid" for an existence which is conceived as an ether or fluid is not a real alternative for Paul.

47. WATR 6, 148ff. author's transl.

48. *The Republic of Plato*, p. 347.

49. Other rhetorical devices appear here, e.g., the parallel, sharpened by the identity of opening or concluding words, or by the identity of both. Some words are identical in their next to last or final sound, and in an instance or two, each member of the parallel is divided into further parallels, and the number of repetitions is not limited to two.

50. C. S. Lewis, *The Screwtape Letters*, New York: Macmillan, 1961, pp. 44-45; cf. 2 Cor. 1:8-9; 4:8-12; 7:5; 12:7-10, etc. etc.!

51. Many see here nothing but an intermezzo, gotten up for reasons of the moment, and, like other temporally conditioned arguments when the need has passed, lacking in relevance. No argument from logic or syntax will convince, but the fact that the sequence of Paul's use of the Old Testament in Chapters 9-11 is strikingly similar to that in Chapters 1-8, indeed, that his use of the Old Testament in both sections forms a chiasma of sequence, is at least one argument in favor of the essential relation between them. For example, the sequence of quotations in 1:22—3:18 is an alternation of Writings and Prophets; the same alternation occurs in 11:26-35. The quotations in 3:18—4:3 are taken first from the Writings, then from the Torah; the same sequence occurs in 11:9-16. The sequence in 4:25—5:5 is that of Prophets and Writings, and is repeated in 10:11-18. The sequence of 5:5-19 is that of Torah and Prophets, and is repeated in 10:19-21, and the sequence of 6:21—13:9f. is that of Prophets and Torah, and recurs in 11:2-8. Since the two major divisions are unequal in length, the range of application of Old Testament texts in Chapters 9-11 is restricted, but lack of range is easily balanced by frequency of use. In addition, the correspondence in sequence is not limited simply to genre. For example, there is a correspondence of proportion in the use of individual and community laments in the quotations from the Psalter and Isaiah in 1:22—3:18 and 11:26-35; a similar correspondence in the use of the individual lament in 3:18—4:3 and 11:9-16, and in the use of the oracle in 6:21—13:10 and 11:2-8. A further comparison of Paul's arguments within these units of the two sections which form the chiasma tends to confirm our contention. For example, the quotations in 1:22—3:18, grouped about the argument of the revelation of God's wrath upon the Jew, are answered in the vision of Israel's salvation, about which the quotations in 11:26-35 are grouped. On the one hand, Israel disobedient, judged; on the other, Israel redeemed. The quotations in 3:18—4:3 serve the portrait of the faithful Abraham, to which the portrait of unbelieving Israel is con-

trasted in the section about which 11:9-16 are clustered. Of course, there are exceptions to support a contrary opinion, but the striking correspondence between Chapters 1-8 and 9-11 is sufficient to suggest that the exceptions prove the rule. Chapters 9-11 are essential to the whole.

52. WA, *Die Deutsche Bibel*, VII, 23, 26-24, 10, author's transl.

53. Immanuel Kant, *Religion Within the Limits of Reason Alone*, trans. T. M. Greene and H. H. Hudson, New York: Harper and Row, 1960, p. 111.

54. Frank Chamberlain Porter, "Christian Thinking about Christ," unpublished (n.d.), p. 8.

55. *Blake Complete Writings*, p. 214.

56. Quoted in Strack-Billerbeck, *Kommentar zum Neuen Testament aus Talmud und Midrasch*, München: C. H. Beck'sche Verlagsbuchhandlung, 1926, III, 185.

57. In *The New Oxford Annotated Bible*, the comment on this verse reads: "The restoration of Israel will be easier than the call of the Gentiles," p. 1374.

58. Wilhelm Estius in Pole, *Synopsis*, V, 254.

59. Barth, *The Epistle to the Romans*, p. 359; cf. also pp. 189 and 414.

60. The conjunctions with which vv 29 and 32 begin are causal: "As regards election they are beloved . . . *because* the gifts and the call of God are irrevocable," vv 28-30; "they have now been disobedient . . . *because* God has consigned all men to disobedience," vv 31-32; the phrase "their disobedience" in v 30, and the phrase "the mercy shown to you" in v 31 are to be construed as temporal—"just as you were once disobedient, but now have received mercy *in the time of* their disobedience, so also they have now been disobedient *at the time when* pity is shown to you"—or as instrumental—"through the time of their disobedience . . . through the pity shown to you"—but *not* as causal.

61. The hymn is replete with terms used only here in Romans; with words, the final letters of which are identical; with adjectives, the final letters of which are identical; with a heaping up of conjunctions, with parallelism and the identity of opening words in parallel—with all the devices dear to the heart of the Greek prose writer. There is even rhythm, though the reader will find little regularity to correspond with Greek prose. Experts have long despaired of scanning Paul's verse:

> He has too little of the artist or poet in him. He is much too hotly engaged to take pleasure in words apart from their content. And he is too little an imitator, but rather seizes only what directly serves his purpose (Bultmann, *Der Stil der Paulinischen Predigt und die kynisch-stoische Diatribe*, pp. 93-94).

Notes

62. In light of references to the **brethren** in v 1; to **every one among you** or **each** in v 3; to the **many** and the **members one of another** in v 5, the inference to be drawn from the phrase **having gifts that differ**, is that there is not a Christian who does not have a **gift**.

63. The movement from gifts in vv 6b-8a to virtues in vv 9-21 has a certain logic to it. There is even a rhetorical symmetry in the argument. Between these gifts and virtues are listed the less restricted gifts in v 8b. Vv 9-21 next yield two clusters of admonitions. The first cluster appears in vv 10-13, containing ten admonitions grouped in five pairs, and the second in vv 16-20, forming two antitheses (v 16 versus v 17; v 18 versus 19-20). Since the apostle can scarcely be described as meticulously adhering to the niceties and nuances of rhetoric—he had other fish to fry—the frequency of their occurrence, together with the imperative use of participles in this list of gifts and virtues suggests that Paul is dependent here on oral or written exemplars, originating, if not in Judaism, then in Jewish Christianity, and into which he may have inserted additional material.

64. Ernst Käsemann, "Römer 13, 1-7 in unserer Generation," *ZTK* 56. Jahrgang, 3, 1959, p. 316, author's transl.

65. Another apocalyptic term, used in Romans only here, and in all the Paulines used only here and in 1 Cor. 7 with this connotation.

66. With all their similarity, the difference between Paul and the Stoic is nowhere clearer than here. The Stoic could not conceive the cosmos as transitory, or himself as standing at the end of the world. Cosmos was indeed the purposeful, rational order of things, but it still called to withdrawal into the self for the purpose of getting oneself in hand, and thus of achieving superiority.

67. The force of the original is "according to love," that is, according to the norm laid down by Christ; the same thought is expressed in 1 Cor. 8:1, 11-13 and 10:32.

68. And "knowledge" was in the driver's seat at Corinth, a "wisdom" which had hatched the notion that heaven had already been reached, and the body mattered not at all; that "heaven can wait, this is paradise" with no pain or suffering between today and tomorrow. For Paul, "wisdom," knowledge by itself was as wretched a thing as no wisdom at all. Through knowledge the darkness could be summoned up (participation in pagan rites to nonexistent gods could evoke those awful powers which the nonexistent was calculated to serve, 1 Cor. 10:20-21). Plato wrote that "it will be the business of reason to rule on behalf of the entire soul," though his rules for breeding guardians in *The Republic* are matched only by sections of *Mein Kampf* for their brutality.

ABOUT THE AUTHOR

Roy A. Harrisville is a graduate of Concordia College and Luther Theological Seminary. He was ordained in 1949 and served parishes in Minneapolis and in Mason City, Iowa. In 1953 he received his Th.D. from Princeton Theological Seminary. Since 1958 he has been professor of New Testament at Luther-Northwestern Seminaries in St. Paul. He has done post-doctoral work at Tübingen and at other leading theological centers in Europe and America. A gifted speaker and teacher, he is in popular demand to lecture at churches and conferences. He has published numerous books and articles, and has translated significant theological works from German and French.